DEEP SONG

DEEP SONG

THE LIFE AND WORK OF FEDERICO GARCÍA LORCA

STEPHEN ROBERTS

REAKTION BOOKS

Published by
REAKTION BOOKS LTD
Unit 32, Waterside
44–48 Wharf Road
London N1 7UX, UK
www.reaktionbooks.co.uk

First published 2020
Copyright © Stephen Roberts 2020

Printed and bound in Great Britain
by TJ International, Padstow, Cornwall

A catalogue record for this book is available from the British Library

ISBN 978 1 78914 237 2

CONTENTS

Lorca in 1919.

Introduction

Federico García Lorca (1898–1936), Spain's most famous modern writer, has been transformed into a myth, a symbol, an icon, even a brand name and a trademark.

The process started well before his extrajudicial killing at the hands of Nationalist forces at the start of the Spanish Civil War (1936–9). In the 1920s he became known as a Gypsy poet, a tag that he mostly objected to (except when indulging in some myth-making of his own), mainly because he was not a Gypsy himself and did not wish his poetry to be typecast in any way. Second Spanish Republic, his work with a State-sponsored theatre troupe led him to be seen as a symbol of a reforming Republic that espoused culture and education rather than class struggle or revolution. His brilliance as a poet and playwright meant that he was perceived by many as representing the future of Spanish letters, although his liberal leanings, his close friendship with key figures on the Left and rumours about his sexuality meant that some on the far Right turned him into a living symbol of all that was for them most reprehensible about the Republic.

Lorca's murder intensified the myth-making process. His fellow poets who fought for the Republic during the Civil War, from Antonio Machado to Rafael Alberti and Miguel Hernández to Pablo Neruda, helped to transform him into a martyr, a victim not just of the Francoist uprising but of Fascism itself. Lorca's first biographer in English, Arturo Barea, writing from his post-Civil War exile in London, called him the poet of the Spanish people.[1] The attempts from the late 1940s onwards by mainly foreign researchers such as Gerald Brenan, Agustín Penón, Claude Couffon, Marcelle Auclair and Ian Gibson to clarify the causes and circumstances of his death ensured that Lorca remained an uncomfortable figure for the Franco regime and prepared the ground for a new generation of Spaniards, who, from the 1960s, would transform him into one of the main symbols of their struggle against the dictatorship.[2] Singersongwriters such as Joan Manuel Serrat and Lluís Llach set Lorca poems to music and thus started a tradition that has also involved foreign artists from Georges Moustaki to Donovan and Leonard Cohen to Angelo Branduardi. From the early 1970s his songs have also been sung by some of the greatest flamenco singers, including Enrique Morente and Camarón de la Isla, who wished to pay homage to this *payo* (non-Gypsy) who did so much to celebrate the often-marginalized Gypsy culture of southern Spain.

After Franco's death in 1975 and, above all, the Spanish Socialist Party's election victory in 1982, Lorca became the most prominent symbol of the political aspirations and cultural splendour of the Republican years that had been brought to an end by the Nationalist uprising. I still remember seeing a rather poor performance of Lorca's late play *Doña Rosita la soltera* (Doña Rosita the Spinster) – in a leading Madrid theatre not long before the attempted military *coup d'état* of February 1981 – that ended with a noisy standing ovation not for the play or the performers but for the author, whose name was chanted for at least fifteen minutes. More or less at this time, Lorca also started to become an icon of gay pride and identity. After almost half a century, during which his sexuality had either been silenced or had given rise to little more than salacious rumour, writers such as Paul Binding not only celebrated Lorca's sexuality but presented it as one of the keys to his artistic output, helping to establish Lorca's relevance in a new world of pluralism and identity politics.[3]

Since then, Lorca's iconic significance has continued to grow apace. The fact that his body still lies in an undiscovered mass grave has meant that his name has been at the heart of the often acrimonious debates surrounding the Law of Historical Memory that was passed by the Spanish parliament in December 2007 and which spoke of the right of the families of victims of Francoist violence to recover their loved ones' remains and to do so with the help and support of the State – a right that has often been more honoured in the breach than in the observance. The archaeological searches for his body in both 2009 and 2014–16 threw aspects of that law into sharp relief, not least because the Lorca family is resolutely opposed to any such search, preferring the area where the body is most probably located to be made into a park of remembrance, while the descendants of some of the other men who were killed and buried alongside Lorca wish to have their ancestors' remains found and returned to them.[4] Lorca's name is central to national discussions on how to remember Spain's traumatic past: the fact that most visitors to the killing fields between the villages of Víznar and Alfacar, just 8 kilometres (5 mi.) from the centre of Granada, appear to be more interested in the figure of Lorca than in the thousands of other victims still buried there led the mayor of Víznar to erect a monolith in 2002 that features just three recriminatory words, 'Lorca eran todos' (They were all Lorca). Granada continues to have a problematic relationship with its most famous son, who attracts visitors to the city from the world over and yet whose death speaks of painful wounds that have still not fully healed.

The polyvalent Lorca myth is immensely powerful and has helped to establish Lorca as the most famous Spanish writer, both within and beyond Spain's frontiers, and to get his poetry and plays translated, read and performed, a process that has been helped along by the painstaking work of his most insightful and industrious biographers, including Leslie Stainton and, pre-eminently, Ian Gibson.[5] Yet that myth can at times serve to obscure the work and also the man, whose life is sometimes told, explicitly or implicitly, in mythical, teleological terms as it is seen unfolding inexorably towards its dark and tragic end.[6] Lorca did not, of course, live his life as a victim, nor even as a myth or a legend. The life as it was lived was not as smooth, rounded or limned as that of a symbol or an icon but rather as chaotic, unpredictable and open-ended as any other human life. Lorca was a complex, joyous, exciting and protean human being whose contradictions and ambiguities give the lie to the simplicities that are to be found at the core of many of the myths. He was the son of a wealthy rural landowner who would become a champion of the poor and the oppressed. An urban sophisticate whose country roots were obvious to all. An iconoclast who retained a profound respect for tradition. A critic of the Church who possessed a deeply Catholic sensibility. An avant-garde artist who found much of his inspiration in the Spanish lyrical tradition and in popular songs, music and puppetry. A gay man who championed homosexuality and yet bitterly attacked certain forms of gay identity. A friend to the Liberal-Socialist President of the Republic Manuel Azaña and the Socialist Minister Fernando de los Ríos, but also to the founder of the Fascist Falange José Antonio Primo de Rivera.

This biography looks at the man and his work in the context of the places and the times in which he lived. Lorca was the product both of the countryside – the wide river plain known as the Vega that lies north of Granada where he spent the first eleven years of his life – and of the city of Granada, which would be his home until the age of 21 and remain his main family home until his death in August 1936. His worldview and sensibility would also be formed by his long stays in Madrid and New York and by his shorter visits to Catalonia, Cuba and Argentina. He experienced all these places at key moments in their evolution: the economic boom that transformed the Vega and Granada in the early twentieth century; the political instability that affected Madrid over the same years and would bring about both a dictatorship (that of General Primo de Rivera between 1923 and 1930) and Spain's Second and, until now, last Republic (1931–9); the Catalonia of the 1920s and '30s that proclaimed its own cultural identity and fought for greater autonomy; the New York of the Wall Street Crash; and Cuba and Argentina at a time of cultural expansiveness when local writers, after decades of turning their backs on the colonial metropolis, were starting to recognize Spain as a political and cultural equal.

Lorca's work, both his poetry and his drama, was created in response to these places. Lorca was the poet of the Vega de Granada and of Granada itself, of Madrid and New York. He was the poet who borrowed many of his forms, ideas and even language from the peasants of the Vega, the Moors and Gypsies of Granada, the Black people of New York and Cuba, and fused them with the avant-garde forms, ideas and language that he encountered above all while in Madrid and during his trips to Catalonia and New York. And he was the dramatist who was capable of revolutionizing Spanish theatre not only through his incorporation of Andalusian dance and song and the devices of popular Andalusian puppet theatre, but by placing the dramas and sexuality of Andalusian peasants and town-dwellers, especially women, at centre stage.

Lorca was the product of these places and also of his times. And those times were of an almost unparalleled cultural brilliance, when Spain was at the very forefront of the European avant-garde, with Pablo Picasso, Juan Gris, Joan Miró, María Blanchard and Salvador Dalí in painting, Julio González in sculpture, Manuel de Falla in music, Miguel de Unamuno, José Ortega y Gasset and María Zambrano in philosophy, Ramón del Valle-Inclán, Ramón Gómez de la Serna, Benjamín Jarnés and Rosa Chacel in drama and the novel, Luis Buñuel in film-making, and Rafael Alberti, Luis Cernuda, Jorge Guillén and Vicente Aleixandre in poetry. With his innovative verse and drama, his dialogue with other art forms including drawing, painting, music and puppetry, his immersion in the Spanish and Andalusian Arabic lyrical traditions, in the popular music, dance and poetry of his home region and in the latest poetry, drama and thought from the rest of Europe and beyond, Federico García Lorca would turn out to be the brightest star in a brilliant constellation. This book offers a celebration of an extraordinary cultural moment, an extraordinary writer and an extraordinary body of poetic and dramatic work. In this vital and literary sense too, 'Lorca eran todos.'

Lorca in 1917.

one

La Vega: His Own Private Arden, 1898–1909

About 1 kilometre along the road from Valderrubio to Fuente Vaqueros, in the wide river plain to the north of Granada known as La Vega, a farm track cuts off right and follows the course of the River Cubillas. Half a kilometre down this track there are a few, now overgrown, steps over the narrow irrigation ditch and down to the riverside at a place called Fuente La Teja. The teenage Federico García Lorca would sit for hours at this spot, with the river flowing swiftly in front of him and tall reeds and groves of poplar trees stretching away on the other bank. Behind him, across the rich, flat fields of wheat, potatoes, beans, garlic, onions, hemp and sugar beet, lay the village of Asquerosa, as Valderrubio was then known, where the family spent the summer months and holidays.

In his second oldest extant poem, written on 23 October 1917, at almost the exact mid-point of his short life, the nineteen-year-old Federico sits in the autumn fields at dusk and trains his gaze both outwards and inwards. Around him, he sees the fertile landscape of the Vega, with its thick copses, its sown fields crisscrossed with paths and ancient irrigation ditches, and the more distant olive groves on the higher land to the north. The coming night and the volume containing *A Midsummer Night's Dream* that he has brought with him gradually fill the landscape with shadows, thoughts and desires. Shakespeare's 'devilish sprite' has poured its poison into his soul:

¡Casualidad temible es el amor!
Nos dormimos y un hada
Hace que al despertarnos adoremos

Al primero que pasa.
¡Qué tragedia tan honda!, ¿y Dios qué piensa?
¿Se le han roto las alas?
¿O acaso inventa otro aparato extraño
Para llenarlo de alma?[1]

What fearful chance is love!
We fall asleep and a fairy
Makes us on waking adore
The first person we see.
What a profound tragedy. And what does God think?
Have His wings been broken?
Or perhaps He is dreaming up another strange invention
To fill with soul?

Why should we hang our heart in another's breast? What has God to say about that, and what might He say about Death, who walks the paths through this darkening landscape? As night falls, the poet makes his way home across the fields. Just as he reaches the fork in the path, he makes out a caricature of the Sphinx guffawing in the distance, almost definitely the strangely shaped mass of the Sierra Elvira peaks riding high above the plain and silhouetted against the looming mountain of the Peñón Colorado in the Sierra de Huétor some 20 kilometres (12 mi.) due east.

Lorca's anguished adolescent poem on love and death never allows this landscape to transform fully into a *paysage d'âme* (landscape of the soul). Throughout his early work, and indeed throughout his whole life, it would always also remain a real landscape, the landscape of his heart, his own private Arden. Much of the land that surrounded him in this poem, set between the villages of Asquerosa and Fuente Vaqueros, belonged to his father, who by the early 1900s had become one of the most important landowners in the Vega. He had come into a good deal of money on the death of his first wife and had used it to buy extra land on which he mainly planted sugar beet, an increasingly lucrative crop in turn-of-the-century Spain, which had lost Cuba and its sugar fields in the 1898 war with the United States. Federico García had remarried in 1897; his new wife, Vicenta Lorca, had arrived in Fuente Vaqueros just a few years earlier in order to teach at the local primary school.[2] The couple soon prospered, with Don Federico ambitiously investing and reinvesting his wealth, sometimes to the detriment of his local rivals, the Roldán and the

Alba families, with whom the Garcías had long intermarried. In 1909, for example, he and his brothers would allow the Roldán family and other investors to build a sugar beet factory in their fields, but they retained ownership of the land, meaning that the Roldáns' plans for expansion always depended upon the good will of the Garcías. And then, in 1931, Federico won a court case over the alleged pollution of this land, with the result that work at the Roldáns' factory was halted while the nearby factory he part-owned thrived. Such disputes over land, which can be found throughout Lorca's work, would play an important role in the poet's violent death.

Lorca was born on 5 June 1898 in Fuente Vaqueros. In 1907 the family moved to a more spacious house up the road in Asquerosa. Then, in 1909, Don Federico fulfilled the dream of any nouveau riche landowner by moving his family to the provincial capital, just 18 kilometres (11 mi.) or so away. From that time onwards, the house in Asquerosa would become a centre of operations for the father, who combined his landowning duties in the countryside with other pursuits, including money-lending, in Granada, and it would also serve as a holiday and summer home for the rest of the family, which by now included three further children: Francisco (b. 1902), Concha (b. 1903) and Isabel (b. 1910). For Lorca, therefore, the Vega would forever be associated both with his earliest childhood and with a later escape from city life. As he started to write in earnest in 1916,

Lorca's home in Fuente Vaqueros.

when he had already spent seven years in Granada, his written account of the Vega would always be mediated through his experiences in the city.

The main account of Lorca's childhood years in Fuente Vaqueros is a collection of six short prose vignettes that he wrote in March and April 1917 and that were published, long after his death, under the title of *Mi pueblo* (My Village). The nineteen-year-old Lorca looks back at his birthplace during the first nine years of his life with both a nostalgic and a critical eye, pointing out in the Prologue that 'its streets, its people, its customs, its poetry and its evil will be like the scaffolding where my childhood ideas will nest, fused in the crucible of puberty.'[3]

For most of *My Village*, it is nostalgia that predominates. Lorca, a poet of all five senses, first characterizes Fuente Vaqueros in terms of its smells. The morning mists bring with them the faint odour of fennel and wild celery. In summer the prevailing smell is of dry straw and, in winter, of burning straw and stagnant water. Fuente Vaqueros, he tells us, derives its open and joyful personality from the fact that it is built on and around water: the river and the irrigation ditches that give life to the surrounding countryside, the fountain in the central square that brought the village into existence and gave it its name, and the wells sunk into the patios of many of the houses. Some of Lorca's most vivid childhood memories are of that square, just a few metres from his house, where the young domestic maids would lay out clothes to dry in the sun or would gather at the fountain with their pitchers at dusk, wearing brilliant colours and flowers and telling stories of passionate or unrequited love.

It is clear that the young Federico felt happy and safe in this environment. He paints a moving picture of family life and of the rhythm of each day. After the sounds of the shepherds collecting the sheep and cows being milked had entered his waking dreams, he would become half-aware of the fleeting presence of his mother checking on her children and then of his father giving each of them a gentle, affectionate kiss before going off to work, trying his best not to wake them as he did so:

> I felt all this half-asleep through that stupor one feels in the mornings, and I would often laugh when I saw my father's face looking at me with love. His mouth would quiver and his eyes were so alive. Back then I would laugh when I saw his gesture. Now I think I would cry. That gesture was one of concern for us, his children of his soul. That quiver in his mouth was a prayer for our happiness.[4]

At 9 a.m. Federico's mother would wake the children up, open the balcony window to the sounds of the birds and the church bell calling the faithful to morning Mass, and lead them in prayer as they got ready for the day. Then, after giving them a glass of still-warm milk, she would send them off to the school where she herself had worked until she married.

The portrait of Federico García and Vicenta Lorca that we are given in *My Village*, and indeed in Lorca's later writings and in the memoirs of his brother Francisco and sister Isabel, is consistently warm and tender. The children never doubt the love of their parents and they celebrate the closeness of the whole family. Vicenta is a constant presence and source of security, while Federico is attentive to his children's every need, to the degree, Isabel tells us, that he would fuss over their slightest cold.[5] The parents also shared their love of music and literature with their children, with Federico playing the guitar and Vicenta reading to them aloud. But music and literature reached them in many different forms. They were surrounded by music both in the home and in the village, from the more classical songs sung by the extended family (often to the accompaniment of the guitar or the piano), to the more popular songs, including *cante jondo*, sung by the maids and workers, to the lullabies they heard when they went to bed each night, and the children's songs and verses that accompanied the games they played with their friends. Their paternal grandmother loved to read her favourite novels to them, especially the ones by Victor Hugo that would play an important role in Lorca's own early writings.[6] And the children would also create their own theatre, building altars and delivering sermons in the style of the local priest or copying the itinerant *titiritero* (puppeteer) and putting on plays in makeshift puppet theatres.

Listening to and telling stories was a favourite pastime. Lorca had a wide array of relations scattered around Fuente Vaqueros and the surrounding villages: aunts and great-aunts, uncles and cousins who all had tales to tell. He was particularly fond of his cousin Aurelia, whom he makes the central character of the play he was working on when he was killed, *Los sueños de mi prima Aurelia* (The Dreams of My Cousin Aurelia). Aurelia and her older female relatives live out the plots of the novels they read as if the characters were part of the family, and spend the rest of their time discussing the relative merits of Aurelia's various suitors. Lorca includes himself in the only extant act of this play as the character Niño, a lively and naughty child who wants to borrow Aurelia's necklace and threatens to curse her if she says no. He admires her waist, breasts and curly hair and

Vicenta Lorca, the poet's mother.

wonders why he doesn't have such things himself, while she admires the moles that light up his face like tiny moons made of tender moss.[7] The child, who decides that he should be able to marry the adult Aurelia, just as the baby Jesus married the tall and buxom St Catherine,[8] reveals himself to be very much at home in this imaginative and literary world of female relations, enjoying their stories and ultimately making them his own.

Lorca listened too to the shepherds and servants who worked for his parents, his favourite being the Compadre Pastor, an ageing farmworker who was Federico senior's closest advisor. He remembers often sneaking into the kitchen at night, where the farm workers would sit around the fire, smoking and telling stories. He would curl up on the Compadre's lap and listen to his tales of saints and lost souls, and of fights against wolves in the Alpujarra mountains. When he finally fell asleep, one of the Compadre's sons would carry him to Vicenta, who would then put him to bed.[9]

Lorca had a close relationship with people of all social classes, although he never forgot that he was the son of the local boss.[10] According to what he and his siblings say, the fact that he was the first born of Federico García Rodríguez, a well-loved figure in the village, gave rise to a sense of respect rather than of resentment among the locals. Lorca relates that he would take sugar and grains of coffee to his poor friends at school, earning their devotion and loyalty. They would also come to his home and play among the farm implements and drying fruit in the large loft. When they played a game in which most of them pretended to make up a flock of sheep whose owner sells them on to a buyer and then buys them back, Lorca would always play the role of the owner. Despite this awareness of social

Federico García,
the poet's father.

Lorca (front row, centre, wearing a hat) and classmates at school in Fuente Vaqueros, c. 1901–2.

difference, though, Lorca felt close to his companions and part of this community – at least until the family moved to Granada. Isabel García Lorca, who only ever experienced the Vega on holidays, recounts that all four siblings lived a double life that was divided between the city and the countryside, and that they often hid their city habits from their village friends.[11] This situation was all the more dramatic for Lorca, who, at nineteen, was very aware of the fact that 'today I have changed from being a peasant boy into a rich kid from the city'.[12] He regretted the fact that his old school friends treated him with deference now, not even daring to touch him with their dirty, gnarled hands, and he felt like an exile from 'that peace and that angelic state'.[13]

Not that everything was peaceful and angelic in the Fuente Vaqueros of his childhood. It was through his friends at school that Lorca became aware of the extreme poverty that surrounded him. The red cape that he wore to school in winter was the envy of the other children, while the sugar and coffee beans that he took them and the fruit that they ate when they played their games in the loft at his home were more than just luxuries for them. Lorca's parents seem to have been charitable, providing his school friends with castaway clothes and also taking good care of their maids and workers when they fell ill. Vicenta would occasionally send Lorca with alms to the house of a very poor couple who had numerous children, including a girl Lorca called his 'little fair-haired friend'. It was here, and especially in the figure of his little friend's mother, that he first encountered what he called true, wretched poverty. This woman, who from a very young age had been giving birth to child after child, many of whom had died in childbirth or shortly after, was so thin and exhausted that she was unable to breastfeed her babies. After describing such poor village homes as 'nests of suffering and shamefulness' where so many women died from giving life, the nineteen-year-old Lorca gives voice to a sense of indignation and anger that deepens further when he comes across his little friend, now grown up and with two children of her own. She has the same empty look in her eyes that the child Lorca had seen in the girl's mother.[14]

'How often, just how often have I seen the funeral of a mother with her child between her legs, both having died of wretched poverty and lack of assistance.'[15] Here, and indeed throughout *My Village*, death stalks the childhood paradise of Fuente Vaqueros. No wonder that Lorca would, years later, say that 'death (a perennial concern in Andalusia) is breathing on the other side of the door.'[16] It kills mothers and children, and it kills the Compadre Pastor, whom Lorca also sees laid out in his coffin. It also provokes one of Lorca's earliest crises, when, after a discussion about Adam and Eve with his little fair-haired friend, he starts imagining what death must be like and curses God for allowing it to exist in the first place. Only further thought and his mother's intercession help him once again to accept the idea that God is in fact good.[17]

But it was not just death that troubled the young Lorca. *My Village* contains a few casual references to the mysteries of the flesh, although it is in another short vignette entitled 'Mi primer amor' (My First Love), written more or less at the same time, that he deals most explicitly with this matter. The story told here is of the deep attachment between the child Lorca and a young woman whose photograph is kept locked up in a trunk. The family seems not to want to talk about her, although an aunt tells him that she had died young of a broken heart. Lorca feels a profound devotion to this unfortunate woman, and embraces and kisses her photograph in bed. But he then starts to change, to awaken to the mysteries of life, to feel new things, to see men and women as sinners, to become aware of his sex . . . and, amid all his new sorrow and desire, he forgets about his first love. She has been witness to his loss of innocence, to the transformation of his love from that of a child into that of an adolescent.

The story, however, includes a more mysterious and troubling passage that perhaps suggests that this transformation, and the sorrow and desire it brought with it, was influenced in part by a third party: 'A human form with black eyes and shaking hands deflowered my virginal purity and told me the plot of life and ripped from me the illusions and innocence of childhood . . .'[18] Is this the 'evil' that Lorca referred to when introducing *Mi pueblo*? Or is the evil that of poverty, of injustice, of death? There is no doubt, as we shall soon see, that Lorca's earliest writings, those he wrote about the Vega in his late teens and early twenties, often present death and sex as intimate bedfellows.

────────

Lorca always felt proud of his native village and of his family's place within it, telling its inhabitants in September 1931 that the Garcías and the Lorcas had made an important contribution to its culture: his mother had been a schoolteacher there and had read aloud to generations of its inhabitants, while the Garcías of the past had served the village through its Town Hall and other institutions, and one ancestor had even written many of the songs that the village still loved to sing.[19] But Lorca himself had not in fact lived in Fuente Vaqueros since 1907, when the family had moved 4 kilometres (2.5 mi.) up the road to Asquerosa. And he spent relatively little time in this new village too, as he was sent to a boarding school in Almería for a year in September 1908. His time at the school was cut short in spring 1909 due to ill health but, just a few months later, the family made the great move to Granada. For Lorca, therefore, Asquerosa was principally the place where the family would spend its summer holidays, which lasted from a few days after Corpus Christi until the end of the harvest season in August. Isabel García Lorca adds that it was the place where the four children relaxed, each in his or her own way, with all of them coming together at siesta time, when they would sing songs and play word games before resting.[20]

Francisco García Lorca points out that Asquerosa is built on dry, unirrigated land and that it is, as a result, a less joyful place than Fuente Vaqueros.[21] Isabel is more precise, explaining that Asquerosa is actually a village of contrasts, with the land immediately to the north being dry and producing only capers and that to the southeast abutting the River Cubillas and the last large irrigation channel in the Vega being much more fertile.[22] There is no doubt that their brother preferred this watered and forested land that lay between Asquerosa and his birth village of Fuente Vaqueros, and it is here, in this in-between land, that the vast majority of his earliest prose and poetry is set.

An almost straight line can be drawn on the map from Asquerosa in the northwest through Fuente Vaqueros and Granada to the Sierra Nevada in the southeast. From the upstairs windows of his house in Asquerosa, Lorca could see the snow-capped peaks of the far-off Sierra Nevada seemingly hovering over the woods beyond the River Cubillas. Influenced perhaps by the stories told by the Compadre Pastor, he appears to associate the Sierra with danger and the threat or even attraction of death.[23] But the Sierra Nevada also represents the exciting and exotic world of the Moors, in contrast to the low hills that lie to the north of Asquerosa, which Lorca presents as the gateway to Christian Castile.[24] Lorca's early poetic universe is bounded by these southern mountains and northern hills but is firmly centred on the fields, watercourses, woods and paths that lie in the Vega on both sides of the River Cubillas.

It is this shape-shifting landscape, whose appearance was constantly changing due to the regular harvesting of the poplar groves and the river's periodical change of course, that would provide Lorca's first poetry with its powerful sense of place. He depicts this landscape at different times of the year. In the poem 'Lux', written on 1 November 1918, he sees the

Lorca with his sisters and cousin Enrique by the River Cubillas, summer 1923.

autumn light of the Vega in liquid terms: as a mist that envelops the fields, as water that drenches the soul, as a rain of gold and blood. It is both a sensual light that highlights the continuing fertility of nature and a spiritual light that is full of hopes and longings. 'Lux', with its occasional references to gardens and mythological figures, seems at certain moments to veer towards the Symbolist fantasies of the Nicaraguan poet Rubén Darío, a huge influence on each and every poet writing in Spanish in the first years of the twentieth century, but the poem soon returns to the Vega, contrasting the vibrating, sexual light of summer and the cold, white, sickly, smoky light of winter with that of autumn, which is 'la luz que piensa, / la humilde, la escondida, / como las madres buenas. / Dulce como una leche / ordeñada a una estrella' (the light that thinks, / the humble, hidden light, / like good mothers. / Sweet like milk / milked from a star).[25] While autumn, though melancholic and full of yearning, is still alive with fruit, winter is harsh and barren. In one of the very few early poems dedicated to that season, 'Melodía de invierno' (Winter Melody), written on 23 January 1918, the Vega is seen to be exhaling a divine light through its mists, but it is also steeped in a frozen silence. The scene seems to give rise to a feeling of serenity and even lethargy in the poet but also presents him with the sight of a woman in rags with a skeletal child in tow, another early reference to the poverty that haunts the villages and fields.[26]

In contrast, the many poems dealing with spring and summer (the seasons when Lorca spent most time in Asquerosa) overflow with colour, sensuality and sexuality. April brings with it a serene air sweet with the perfume of the bean fields and full of the songs of the trees, the river and the peasants,[27] and also fills the fields with flowers, which Lorca associates with parts of the female body, the roses being 'Sexos de mujer potente, / fecunda, brava, feroz' (Pudenda of potent, / fertile, wild, ferocious woman).[28] May brings skies of an intense blue and turns the river into a 'Miel de grises, de morados, de amarillos' (Honey of greys, purples, yellows); it also fills the poet with both indolence and vague yearnings, which sometimes become so acute and painful that he feels that spring has mutated into autumn.[29]

In his summer poems, Lorca often characterizes the Vega as a body, with its rivers and other waterways bringing sap, blood and semen to the fields.[30] The whole landscape then explodes into life, colour and music, as he reveals in the chromatic symphony of sights and sounds that makes up 'Mediodía' (Midday):

Sol potente, quietudes inquietantes de fuego.
Remolinos de luces y cantar de cigarras.
Raros tonos de fa en trompetas enormes.
Gran espasmo de oro sobre un manto de grana.[31]

Powerful sun, disquieting quiet made of fire.
Eddies of lights and the cicadas' song.
Strange keys of F played on enormous trumpets.
Great golden spasm on a gown of scarlet.

Summertime, and especially summer afternoons and evenings, is the moment when the flesh is all-triumphant, the 'Maravillosa hora del beso en la boca' (Marvellous moment of the kiss on the mouth).[32] The whole of nature is coupling, pregnant or giving birth. July in particular is the month of potency that creates fire, wine and bread in the fields and sees men and women delivering their 'espasmo carnal' (carnal spasm) to the skies above.[33] Nowhere does Lorca better capture this life-giving and life-enhancing moment than in the poem 'En verano la vega amarilla del trigo' (In Summer the Vega, Yellow with Corn), written on 12 July 1918. Writing under the influence of the expansive verse of Victor Hugo, Lorca turns high summer in the Vega into a pagan Mass in which the yellow corn is magically transformed into the bread that sustains its inhabitants. The Mass itself is described using Catholic terminology, but the process that is being depicted is sensual and cosmic in nature. The altar is the now snowless Sierra Nevada, the officiating priest is the sun, the wine is the bloody sunset, and the missal is the sky afire with red clouds. The sun-priest matures and kills the corn so that it can hand over the gift of its living grain in what seems to be an act of natural transubstantiation. At this precise moment, the whole landscape becomes both a fertile body and a natural chalice:

Oh vega de Granada bajo el sol de verano!
Que antes fue lago inmenso y ahora es fecunda.
Gloria a tus cabelleras de trigales marchitos.
Gloria a tus hijos rudos que nos hacen el pan
Con rayas de esmeralda y ráfagas de gris.
Patena florecida bajo el peso del cielo,
Pupila de la tierra hacia el azul sin fin.[34]

Oh Vega de Granada beneath the summer sun!
Once an immense lake and now so fecund.
Glory be to your hair made of withered wheat fields.
Glory to your rough and simple children who make our bread
With emerald stripes and grey flashes.
Paten that has flowered under the weight of the heavens,
Pupil of the land turned towards the endless blue.

————————

This, the Vega de Granada, is the landscape of Lorca's soul, his Arden, the vision of paradise that will accompany him throughout his short life.

And yet it can be a dark and disturbing landscape too. The river is capable of taking life as well as of giving it, as can be seen in the poem 'La muerte de Ofelia' (The Death of Ophelia), where Ophelia's body floats on what looks very much like the River Cubillas, surrounded by the same trees and the same rustic sounds that had featured in Lorca's poem on *A Midsummer Night's Dream*.[35] The paths that cross the landscape can be veins that provide the fields with blood or trails that allow Lorca to seek after vague stars, but they can also lead the poet astray or confront him, as they fork, with impossible decisions and choices.[36] And the forest is a place of the greatest beauty, an 'acorde profundo de azul profundidad' (a profound chord of blue depths), yet at the same time, as we are told in the poem 'El bosque' (The Forest), a place of tragedy and sorrow.[37]

The extensive woods of the Vega represent a site of immense ambiguity in Lorca's early writings. On the one hand, they can offer the poet somewhere he can withdraw, especially at dusk, in order to search for himself and for a way of expressing his most intimate feelings. In one poem, entitled 'Los crepúsculos revelan' (Sunsets Reveal), he exhorts his readers to go to the forest at nightfall, as the shadows they will find there actually reveal 'el alma de las cosas' (the soul of things).[38] In 'Crepúsculo' (Sunset), meanwhile, the same setting allows the poet to express his existential and sexual angst, as he tries to purge himself of the feelings and desires that torture his adolescent body and soul:

Mi espíritu solloza
En los árboles yertos,
Fósiles de unas danzas

The Vega de Granada, with Sierra Elvira in the background.

De ramas y de ecos
Que abrumados se inclinan
En su penumbra quietos.
Y llora doloroso
Porque adivina en ellos
Guardianes de la senda,
De la muerte maestros.
¡Ay, dejadme que llore
Abrazado a sus cuerpos!,
Sintiendo la amargura
De sus marchitos huesos,
Enlazado a sus troncos,
Cubriéndolos de besos.
Que me dejen el alma
Exenta de deseos . . .[39]

My spirit sobs
In the stiff and lifeless trees,
Fossils of the dances
Of branches and echoes

That, overwhelmed and still,
Stoop and bend in their own half-light.
And it cries in pain
Because it sees in them
The keepers of the pathways,
The masters of death.
Ah, let me embrace
Their bodies and cry!,
Feeling the bitterness
Of their withered bones,
With my arms around their trunks,
Covering them with kisses.
May they render my soul
Free from desires . . .

On the other hand, the forest is also a place that Lorca associates with fear and even with evil. This evil is sometimes conventional and literary, as in the poem 'La noche' (Night), which is full of diabolic and perverted scenes worthy of Lorca's beloved masters, the Spanish painter Francisco de Goya and the French poet Charles Baudelaire,[40] but, at others, it is more personal and disturbing. The most terrifying expression of the awareness of the presence of evil can be found in the short story entitled 'Cuento de viejo' (An Old Man's Tale), written on 2 February 1918. This story takes the form of a warning addressed directly to the young girls who walk through the 'dark Forest'. At its heart, it serves to underline the traditional importance of purity and chastity, but the tone is much more urgent and more precise than one might expect from a fable or a morality tale. What this story conveys is not a simple allusion to the ancestral fear of the forest but a reference to a much more immediate and more specific danger:

> You girls who walk through the dark Forest, can't you hear how the wild dogs of passion are barking? Stop walking and turn back; if not, a dark and rough smell will wither you as if you were lilies. What lies in front of you is the ardent peasant's vile slap and scream of lust.

The story goes on to exhort the young girls to pray, to cover their ears in order not to hear the man's voice, to flee his breast made of burning coals. If they do end up in his arms, they will fall into the darkest, deepest well and become servants of man's basest passion, perhaps even prostitutes in a brothel. They must at all costs keep away from 'the Forest of disappointment and disillusion . . . the accursed Forest'.[41]

Is it possible that Lorca is referring here to a real danger, the danger of sexual initiation and abuse faced possibly by both girls and boys and associated forever in his mind with the woods of the Vega? When, eleven years later, he searches for his childhood self in the devastating poem 'Infancia y muerte' (Childhood and Death), which he wrote in 1929 during his stay in New York, he finally finds his little body eaten by rats at the bottom of a well. A dead man has chased him and plunged his hands into the well, and the poem concludes with the words:

Pero mi infancia era una rata que huía por un jardín oscurísimo,
una rata satisfecha mojada por el agua simple,
y que llevaba un anda de oro entre los dientes diminutos.[42]

But my childhood was a rat that fled through a pitch-black garden,
a satisfied rat that had been wetted by simple water,
and was carrying a golden box between its tiny teeth.

We shall never know for sure what may have happened in those childhood woods, but Lorca himself seems to imply on occasions that his experiences there had a profound and lasting effect on him. In one poem, he presents himself in the guise of a young boy with evil eyes who, 'from [his] black and centuries-old forest', listens to the innocent voices of the good boys who play nearby, hoping and longing that their laughter and kisses can help to clean and restore his soul.[43] Whether the sense of guilt and self-loathing expressed in such poems had its roots in a specific event – or more generally in his adolescent struggle with his complex feelings and desires – will forever remain a mystery, but what poems such as these do make clear is that there was, from the start, a dark side to Lorca's own private Arden.

Lorca with his parents, sister Concha and brother Francisco, Granada, 1912.

two

Granada: A Paradise Closed to Many, 1909–19

Granada in 1909 was a thriving provincial capital with some 80,000 inhabitants. Its new prosperity was fuelled to a large degree by the sugar beet industry that had taken off in the Vega back in the 1860s and had created many local fortunes, including that of Federico García and his family. The new middle-class families, many of them from the villages of the Vega themselves, took up residence in a city that had remodelled itself in order to accommodate their modern, bourgeois needs and tastes.

The two hills to the northeast of the city, on which the ancient quarter of the Albaicín and the palace of the Alhambra are found, had changed relatively little since medieval times and continued to attract Romantic tourists in search of vestiges of Moorish culture or glimpses of the still-thriving Gypsy culture. Much of the medieval centre just beneath the two hills, though, had changed almost beyond recognition. Between 1854 and 1884, the River Darro – which separates the Albaicín and Alhambra hills and carries on more or less in a straight line for another 600 metres (1,970 ft) or so before veering sharply to the southeast and joining the River Genil – was covered over from the Plaza Santa Ana to the Puente de Castañeda to create the Calle Reyes Católicos and the Calle Acera del Darro, two important arteries that met at the square known as Puerta Real, the very heart of bourgeois Granada. Then, the Gran Vía de Colón, a thoroughfare that replaced medieval houses and streets at the base of the Albaicín hill, was inaugurated in 1892 and created an access route from the Vega in the northwest to the Calle Reyes Católicos in the centre. A new, modern Granada was thus born on either side of the cathedral and rubbed shoulders with the ancient palaces and convents in this still deeply aristocratic, clerical and conservative city.

Lorca's father Federico García knew exactly what he was doing when he rented a three-storey house in the Calle Acera del Darro in the summer of 1909 and started to conduct some of his business from the terrace of a café in nearby Puerta Real. As many of his rich neighbours from the Vega had done for decades previously, and many more, including his relatives and rivals in the Roldán family, would do over the following years, he was announcing his arrival on the Granada scene and also creating the conditions for his young family to thrive. Some literary evidence might suggest that the eleven-year-old Lorca initially found the move to be somewhat traumatic. When he came in 1935 to write the play *Doña Rosita la soltera* (Doña Rosita the Spinster), he set the final act in 1910 and in a house in Granada that feels large and empty, where the only flowers are to be found in flowerpots or the greenhouse. Several early poems, such as 'Interior', written in February 1918, also capture the melancholic silence Lorca seems to associate with the salons of Granadan townhouses.[1]

But it appears that Lorca soon adapted to life in the big city. The family brought one of the children's favourite aunts and several maids from the Vega to live with them: their father's sister Tía Isabel played the guitar beautifully and sang *habaneras*, while the maid Dolores was like a second mother who spoke the colourful language of the Vega and taught the children all sorts of superstitions.[2] They also received constant visits from relatives and workers from Fuente Vaqueros and Asquerosa. It seems therefore that the young Lorca soon enjoyed what became a very lively house, with its patio and small garden, as well as the busy streets on its doorstep. He also started school along with his brother Francisco, who in his memoirs provides a vivid evocation of their time together both at school and at the university. Francisco informs us that their liberal-leaning father deliberately chose not to send his sons to a religious school and so the boys were enrolled in the public Instituto, which they attended in the mornings, and the private Sagrado Corazón de Jesús College, which was run by one of Vicenta's cousins and, despite its name, devoted little or no time to religious instruction.[3] Both schools were found close to the cathedral just off the Calle de San Jerónimo, so the boys would cross the bustling Plaza Bib-Rambla and cathedral quarter on their way there and back each morning and afternoon. Lorca would study in these schools until he completed his baccalaureate (*bachillerato*)

in May 1915. He then started his degree in September of that year, in the university building almost next door to his schools.

Lorca was not a particularly good student at school or, later, at university – mainly, Francisco and others say, owing to a lack of application and interest. He was also known to bunk off school quite regularly and to make his way up to the top of the Albaicín or the Alhambra hill, from where he could just about make out Fuente Vaqueros in the far distance.[4] Lorca's mother, a former teacher herself, would implore her son to do his homework, but his father appears to have been less worried about the poor marks he brought home from school. It is possible that both parents were more indulgent with him, at least during the early years in Granada, because of the illnesses that befell the family. After the birth of Isabel in 1910, Vicenta Lorca fell ill and had to spend some time bring treated in Malaga, and a year or two later, Lorca himself suffered from typhus – almost dying of the disease, according to Francisco.[5]

Francisco draws attention to the fun that was had at school, and Lorca himself makes reference to the schoolboys' naughty tricks in *Doña Rosita the Spinster*, where some of his teachers appear under their real names and report how they have jugs of water thrown over them or pins and cat droppings placed on their chair – the antics, they say, of spoiled children who never get punished by their rich parents.[6] But Francisco insists on several occasions that Federico did not enjoy his studies or the school itself. He was something of a clumsy boy who even found it difficult to train his hand to write properly and therefore did badly at calligraphy.[7] According to a former classmate of Lorca's whom Ian Gibson interviewed in 1978, he was also mistreated by many of the boys and even shunned by one of the teachers because he was perceived as being effeminate. The boys took to calling him 'Federica' and would often refuse to play with him.[8]

Lorca took refuge in music instead. Federico senior, who had himself been brought up in a musical family, insisted that his three eldest children learn the piano. At first, Lorca was taught by the cathedral organist, but he soon started to have lessons with local composer Antonio Segura Mesa (1842–1916), who became the first of a series of older mentors who would guide the young Lorca in his adolescent and young adult years. Segura Mesa quickly realized that Lorca was a highly talented pianist and started to prepare him for further study in Paris.[9]

The year 1916, when Lorca turned eighteen, was an important one in his life. There was some upheaval at home, with the family moving to a flat in the Gran Vía before settling down in the Acera del Casino,

Lorca with his younger sister Isabel, Granada, 1914.

opposite their original house in the Acera del Darro. Lorca's arts degree, which he had started at the university in autumn 1915, was not going particularly well. Francisco reports that his brother put time into his literary and artistic subjects but failed those he found more demanding, such as historical grammar and anything that involved ancient or foreign languages.[10] And then, on 26 May, his beloved piano teacher Segura Mesa died. Lorca himself would later claim that this event changed his life forever: without his teacher's support, his parents refused to allow him to go to Paris and become a professional pianist. As a result, he adds, referring to himself in the third person, 'García Lorca channelled his (dramatically) pathetic creative urges into poetry.'[11]

As with many of Lorca's self-pronouncements, there is both truth and falsehood in what he says here. His earliest writings do indeed date from October 1916, that is, not long after Segura Mesa's death, although they take the form of short prose pieces that capture his impressions of different cities during the study trip he made to Castile and Galicia that month.[12] Then, in January 1917, he started to write more substantial and personal prose pieces, with his first extant poem dating from late June of that year. Between the start of 1917 and his departure for Madrid in spring 1919, Lorca would write a huge amount of prose and poetry. This was therefore very much the period of his apprenticeship as a writer.

———————

Lorca's early writings have a literary as well as a personal urgency about them. He is both learning his trade as a writer and exploring concerns and themes of a highly intimate nature. They show that he was a voracious reader – of novels, theology and philosophy, as well as of plays and poetry. There are constant explicit and implicit references to the classics, from the Greek tragedians to Shakespeare and from the *Song of Songs* to St John of the Cross and St Teresa, but also a clear emphasis on the European poets of the previous sixty or seventy years. Favourite among these are the French poets Victor Hugo (1802–1885), Charles Baudelaire (1821–1867) and Paul Verlaine (1844–1896) but above all the Spanish and Latin American Romantic and Symbolist poets José Zorrilla (1817–1893), Gustavo Adolfo Bécquer (1836–1870), Rubén Darío (1867–1916), Antonio Machado (1875–1939) and Juan Ramón Jiménez (1881–1958).

There are times when Lorca seems to be using his early prose and above all his poetry to try out different voices and styles, all of them borrowed. His obvious fascination with the latest poetic vogue, the Hispanic form of Symbolism known as *modernismo*, leads him to set some of his poems at liminal times of day, especially dusk, and occasionally also in abandoned gardens with fountains and the odd glimpse of fauns and satyrs. At these times, he fuses Darío's sensual and sometimes openly sexual response to the world with the vague longings and intense melancholy of Juan Ramón Jiménez's verse, all the time recognizing the central influence of Paul Verlaine on both these poets:

El alma sufre su más allá
En momentos de la tarde callada.
Pierrot empolva su arrugada cara
Con el polen que la Muerte dejara.
Doliente engañifa rosada.

Ven nuestros ojos los hilos fatales.
¡Ay! ¿Quién solloza?
¿Son las almas divinas otoñales?

¡Ay! ¿Quién solloza?
¿Son amargos espectros inmortales?
¡Ay! ¿Quién solloza?
¿Acaso el Verlaine de las Saturnales
Sus liras roza
En infinito rumor de rosales?[13]

The soul suffers its world beyond
At moments of silent evening.
Pierrot dusts his wrinkled face
With the pollen that Death has left behind.
A sorrowful trick of pink.

Our eyes see the fatal threads.
Ah! Who is sobbing?
Is it the divine souls of autumn?
Ah! Who is sobbing?
Are they bitter immortal spectres?
Ah! Who is sobbing?
Perhaps the Verlaine of Saturnalia
Strums his lyres
With the infinite murmur of rose bushes?

In poems such as these, Lorca, again following the example of Juan Ramón Jiménez, shows how his soul travels through the world and inhabits the gardens, the stars, the twilight itself; as he puts it in one poem: 'Y yo soy Todo ahora / Pues Todo lo comprendo. / Soy estrella y montaña / Y rosa de rosal' (And I am Everything now / Since I take Everything in. / I am star and mountain / And rose from the rose bush).[14] As we saw earlier, though, the landscape that the poet's soul comes to occupy in the vast majority of the early poems is actually a real one, that is, the fields and woods of the Vega. Lorca's poetry can as a result be reminiscent at times of that of Antonio Machado, who gave expression in *Campos de Castilla* (Fields of Castile, 1912) to an essentially mystical relationship with the landscape of his adopted homeland of Soria in the north of Spain, a land that he says comes to inhabit his soul. Lorca's Machadian mix of objective description and Platonic longings can be found in poems such as 'Tarde de abril' (April Evening), which ends with the words:

Mi alma se derrama por la vega inmensa.
Mi alma entre la duda gris crepuscular
Se extiende vibrante
Sin alas ni forma
Sobre los perfumes gratos del habar.[15]

My soul pours itself over the immense Vega.
My soul amidst the grey doubt of twilight
Spreads vibrantly
Without wings and formless
Over the pleasant odours of the bean fields.

It is through his dialogue with writers such as these that Lorca searches for his own voice as a poet, although that search takes the form of a dialogue with other art forms too. When Lorca gave up the idea of becoming a professional pianist, he certainly did not give up playing the piano, and he would become well known later in life as much for his recitals as for his poetry readings. He also imported his love of music into his poetry and prose, both by making explicit references to his favourite composers – from Handel, Mozart, Beethoven and Berlioz through to Chopin and Debussy – and by incorporating musical effects into his verse, some of them borrowed from Renaissance madrigals and others from children's songs or the popular and religious songs of the Vega.[16] He also appeared to perceive music in the world around him, from a specific key that sounds forth from the landscape, often that of F, to the more general melody of winter or the operatic aria that is spring.[17] He even entitles one of his more existential poems 'Dúo de violonchelo y fagot' (Duet of Cello and Bassoon) and reveals how music, whether it is a single chord or Beethoven's *Appassionata*, helps to score or illuminate his thoughts and moods:

Pero el corazón no se desata.
Existe la mujer y el tono menor.
Aún vive Equidna con su negro horror.
Suena el andante de la Apasionata.
. . .
Nada nos salvará. Llega la Muerte.
La Sombra mata al Hechizo.
¿La quietud del convento? No. No.
Formidable acorde gris plomizo.[18]

Lorca at the piano, Granada, 1919.

But the heart does not break loose.
Woman exists, and the minor key.
Echidna still lives, with her black horror.
The andante of the *Appassionata* sounds forth.
. . .
Nothing will save us. Death arrives.
The Shadow kills the Magic Spell.
The stillness of the monastery? No. No.
Formidable chord of leaden grey.

As in this last line, Lorca often fuses music with colour, exploring and extending the synaesthetic effects that he had found in the work of the *modernista* poets. His Vega poems are in fact as painterly as they are musical and are full of the strong outlines and bold colours of Spanish Impressionists such as Santiago Rusiñol (1861–1931), who had visited the region in 1898 and produced a well-known series of paintings of gardens and landscapes in Granada and nearby Víznar. When reading a poem such as 'Tardes estivales' (Summer Evenings), it is difficult not to find oneself adrift in the sensual world of Rubén Darío, one that is rooted in the Vega and appears at the same time to have been animated by the rich colours of Rusiñol and the haunting music of Debussy:

Tardes estivales. Sol en las honduras.
Los pueblos como faros de nieve sobre un mar.
Nubes de gris y rojo como pechos de aves.
Vibraciones ardientes sobre cielos suaves.
Aguas estancadas . . . Inmenso dormitar . . .
Tardes estivales. Soledad dorada.
Caminos silenciosos, cintas de claridad.
Alamedas verdosas en fondos pasionales.
Acordes de oro vivo parecen los trigales.
Inquietante quietud. Raro tono de fa.[19]

Summer evenings. Sun in the depths.
The villages like lighthouses made of snow on a sea.
Clouds of grey and red like birds' breasts.
Blazing vibrations on soft skies.
Stagnant waters . . . Immense drowsiness . . .
Summer evenings. Golden solitude.

Silent paths, ribbons of light.
Greenish poplar groves against passionate backgrounds.
The corn fields seem to be chords of bright gold.
Disquieting quiet. Strange key of F.

Despite the occasional clumsiness or over-emphasis, there is an original voice starting to emerge in these poems, one that extends the effects found in the work of his poetic masters and piles image on image, impression on impression, sensation on sensation. Its main sentiments are Romantic and Symbolist in nature, and its idiom is that of *modernismo*, although it can also adopt a yet more modern accent at times and create striking metaphors, announcing the ones that would become Lorca's stock-in-trade as a mature poet. In 'Ribera' (Riverside), for example, he collapses several sights, images and sense impressions together when he asks of the black poplar trees:

¿Qué pensáis del sendero
Donde tantos peregrinos
Os vieron herir al cielo
Envueltos en luz de sangre?[20]

What do you think of the path
Where so many pilgrims
Saw you, wrapped in blood light,
Injure the sky?

But Lorca's young voice is not just an aesthetic one devoted to the depiction of natural beauty or to the creation of new artistic beauties, it is a voice that has something urgent and deeply personal to say. If we can take literally what he writes at the end of one of his very earliest pieces – the prose poem entitled 'La sonata de la nostalgia' (The Sonata of Nostalgia), written on 5 January 1917 – then the previous September (that is, the time when he was still coming to terms with the death of Segura Mesa and had not yet started to write in earnest) had also seen the end of his first love affair.[21] There is no doubt that unhappy love is a common theme of Lorca's early writings, especially after the summer of 1917 – when, according to Ian Gibson, Lorca started to agonize over his undeclared feelings for a young Granadan woman, María Luisa Egea González.[22] But whatever may have happened in September 1916, or perhaps, more generally, the awakening of sexuality itself, had already given rise to a profound crisis in Lorca that received its earliest expression in the prose pieces that he wrote from January 1917 onwards.

The nature of this crisis is best summed up in the title of a series of 22 essays that Lorca wrote between April and October 1917: *Místicas (de la carne y el espíritu)* (Mystical Writings (On the Flesh and the Spirit)).[23] These essays, which are part literary autobiography and part exploration of Lorca's many and varied readings, provide an insight into the mind of a gifted teenager as he tussles with questions relating to sex, sin, religion, social expectations and death. They show how he tries desperately to come to terms with the attractions of the flesh while dealing with the restrictions and prohibitions imposed by both the Church and society in general. We see him on occasions trying to abjure the flesh altogether, more often than not by attempting to return to the innocence of childhood,[24] but, in many of his writings, he shows himself to be unable and unwilling to deny his sexual impulses. He directs most of these towards a love object that is gendered female, although there are some writings where he seems to suggest that a woman's love might just possibly be inaccessible to him.[25] There are also a very few moments when the love object is clearly gendered male, as in the poem 'Visión' (Vision), written on 3 April 1918, which tells of how a strange man dressed in red passed by on a silver bull and gave the poet a huge poppy that flowered in his soul: was he, the poet asks, a star, a rose, a moon, a sex, flesh, a smell – or perhaps my other self?[26]

He also addresses same-sex love in a prose poem entitled 'El poema de la carne. Nostalgia olorosa y ensoñadora' (The Poem of the Flesh: Nostalgia made of Fragrance and Dreams), where he has Plato tell Sappho that

> I am he who adores and loves the ephebes . . . Their breasts may be flat but they give off a wonderful smell . . . Their hair may be short but they have both light and the aroma of oranges in their mouths . . .[27]

This prose poem offers a passionate celebration of carnal love: flesh, the poet says, represents the trinity of life, love and world, and the spirit and all mysticism are built on and out of it.[28] Elsewhere, though, the poet continues to fret over the relationship between the flesh and the spirit: he often turns for inspiration and guidance to the Spanish mystical poets of the sixteenth century or adopts a more pagan perspective that emphasizes the cycles of Mother Nature, who is seen as the transformer of bodies into souls and of souls into bodies that long for the infinite.[29] For much of the time, all of these different sexual and philosophical options are not given a cold, abstract form but are actually embodied in the landscape of the Vega itself, especially in the multiple paths along which the poet travels like a pilgrim in search either of a woman's kisses or of the vague stars and the illumination that comes with the morning light.[30]

There are also moments in these early works when the poet tries to understand the root cause of this enduring disassociation or conflict between flesh and spirit. The title of the final essay in the *Mística* series declares its interest in 'the brake that society applies to the nature of our bodies and our souls',[31] and the combined evidence of Lorca's early prose and poetry would seem to suggest that he places much of the blame for this 'brake' firmly at the door of the Catholic Church. There can be no doubting the attraction that the young Lorca feels towards a specifically Catholic religious sensibility, especially when it manifests itself in popular rites and customs, such as the Easter processions in Granada or the widespread devotion to the Virgin Mary, St Mary Magdalene or St Francis,[32] but he is deeply critical of the Church itself, an organization which, in his eyes, has transformed religion into a series of rules and conventions that are designed both to repress the flesh and to rein in the mystical flights of the spirit.[33] In *Mystical Writings* and poems like 'Salmo de noche' (Night Psalm), he hits out against the 'Pharisees' and the 'priests who are so only in name' and have turned St Francis and even Jesus himself into objects of mockery.[34] In this context, Lorca expresses a profound admiration and love for the original Jesus, whom he refers to as the marvel of love, the great knight errant, the bridge over death, the pilgrim of gentleness – and he even imagines that a return to the ideals of the primitive church might also resolve the suffering caused in him and in humanity as a whole by the dislocation of flesh and spirit.[35]

Lorca's state of mind and his self-image on the eve of adulthood are perhaps best summed up in two poetic short stories that he wrote in September 1917 and March 1918: 'Fray Antonio (Poema raro)' (Friar Antonio (Strange Poem)) and 'Pierrot. Poema íntimo' (Pierrot: Intimate Poem).[36] Although 'Fray Antonio' is narrated in the third person and 'Pierrot' in the first, they both act as a sort of fictional autobiography in which Lorca projects his own experiences onto those of a tortured young man and a character from *commedia dell'arte*. Friar Antonio is presented to us as a spiritual pilgrim who as a boy appears from nowhere in the Vega and is then seen as a young adult living in a house with a garden and a piano (both of which are described in rich *modernista* detail). In the central section entitled 'El camino' (The Path), Antonio walks through the Vega in search of self-knowledge. He travels, literally and metaphorically, along different paths, sometimes seeking after spiritual consolation and the true Christ, sometimes musing on the contrasting and often openly sexual charms of the three women with whom he is in love. In the following section, he is seen expressing all his self-doubt and melancholy, his ecstasy and his despair, through his beloved piano, an instrument, we are told, whose soul only awakens when it comes into contact with a heart that truly feels and suffers. Then, in the final extant section, Antonio attends the wake and funeral of his university friend Carlos, an experience that exposes him to the horror of putrefaction and the terror of death.

We appear to have in this story a clear portrait of the artist as a young man: a hypersensitive and tormented soul who is torn between the attractions of the flesh and those of the spirit, and who uses the piano in order to give expression to his innermost self. He is also a young man who prefers to live apart from the rest of the world and even sees himself as superior to his fellow men and women, who are presented as beings incapable of deep feelings and independent thought. Indeed, Antonio's reactions at Carlos's funeral are those of an angry adolescent who despises what he feels to be the insincere expressions of grief of his fellow mourners and the indifference of the officiating priests. And yet, at least according to the evidence provided by 'Pierrot', Lorca's Romantic self-image as tortured artist surrounded by an imbecilic and hypocritical society is counterbalanced by his awareness that he too is caught in society's trap just like everyone else, the only difference being that he is fully conscious of the fact. Pierrot is a lovelorn poet and pianist who is mocked by a materialistic society that despises those who feel too deeply. So he learns to be ashamed of his feelings, to sing of other things, at least in public, and to cover his face when he goes out into the street with the powder of indifference, imbecility and spite. He becomes an eternal mask, transforming himself into Pierrot at times and, at others, into Harlequin or Columbine. In this way, he keeps his real self hidden from others and perhaps, despite his private cultivation of poetry and music, even from himself. His is a mask that can never be removed – a motif and a theme that will resurface time and again in Lorca's work over the following two decades.

———

Lorca with his brother and sisters, Granada, *c.* 1917–18.

Despite the self-concern and often extreme introspection that are found in much of his early work, and his personal difficulties at school and at university, the teenage Lorca did in fact reach out to certain kindred spirits in Granada and joined a group of budding young writers and intellectuals that met most nights in the Café Alameda, situated in the Plaza del Campillo, just a few steps from his home in the Acera del Casino. The group became known as 'El Rinconcillo' because it originally congregated in a 'little corner' of the café next to the stage that was used for musical recitals. Here, from the age of seventeen, Lorca rubbed shoulders with the young artistic and literary élite of Granada, and there is little doubt that, from 1917 onwards, he would try out the early drafts of some of his poems and prose pieces on his supportive yet demanding companions. The group was devoted not just to serious discussion, though, but to fun, satire and parody, and, according to Francisco García Lorca's account, his brother's more extrovert side, which his family had enjoyed for years, started to flourish more publicly in the company of these subversive sons of the Granada rich. He also took a leading part in some of its more daring adventures, such as the invention of a fictional local poet called Isidoro Capdepón Fernández, whose work was devoted to singing the praises of Granada and her manifold exotic beauties. Francisco reports that the secret of Capdepón's success was that Lorca and others ensured that the poems they penned in his name were written in a correct, if for them stuffily academic and exaggeratedly picturesque, style.[37]

Lorca's parody of the self-exoticizing local poetry of Granada is just a playful expression of his complex and contradictory relationship with his adopted city. We have seen that by 1917 and 1918 he had come to the conclusion that his own self was split between an insincere exterior and a passionate if misunderstood interior, and it is clear that he applied the same Romantic paradigm to Granada as a whole. He often attacks what he claims to be the conventionality and hypocrisy of the local bourgeoisie and would later claim, in 1928, that their Granada, which was made up of 'copper and talcum powder', was simply dead:[38] the covering over of the River Darro and the creation of the Gran Vía – the urban projects that had become the bourgeoisie's badge of identity – were proof of their complete lack of sensitivity towards nature and towards the rich cultural and architectural heritage of the city.[39] At the same time, Lorca was fully aware of the Romantic image of Granada that had been created in the nineteenth century by foreign writers such as Washington Irving and Théophile Gautier, and he sometimes, as in 'Pierrot', excoriates the mostly foreign tourists who arrive in the city ready to consume the local culture and buy up as many of its 'exotic' artefacts as possible.[40] But it is not the Romantic view of Granada itself that really bothers Lorca: indeed, his earliest writings on Granada, and especially on the Albaicín quarter, are full of the local colour and legends beloved of his Romantic forebears, and he would also later celebrate the fact that the Alameda de los Tristes that follows the River Darro between the Albaicín and Alhambra hills was the true 'vértice' (apex) of the whole of European Romanticism.[41]

No: what angers Lorca is how the local bourgeoisie has ended up buying into a simplistic version of the foreigners' view of Granada.[42] The sort of poetry that the fictional Isidoro Capdepón Fernández cultivates is only a slightly over-embellished form of the picturesque and clichéd literary and artistic fare whose ultimate function, as well as to attract outsiders, is to reinforce the bourgeoisie's superficial sense of local identity.

Lorca's deeply Romantic response to this quandary was to seek out and champion the 'authentic' Granada, the one, he claimed, that was unknowable to tourists and a majority of locals alike.[43] He would do this over the years in several different ways. First, he would stress the complex geography of Granada, which is suspended between the heights of the Sierra Nevada and the flat plain of the Vega. He calls attention to the proximity of the Vega, which, he tells us, starts in the very outskirts of the city and is clearly visible from the Albaicín and Alhambra hills.[44] In the poem 'El Dauro y el Genil', he explores the different character of Granada's two rivers, both of which are born in the Sierra, as a way of establishing the geographical complexity of the city and of shedding light on its intimate personality. The River Darro (or Dauro, as he calls it, using an older form of the name) makes its way down between the two hills and nourishes the gardens of Granada before flowing into the River Genil near the centre of the city. The Genil then takes the waters of both rivers to the Vega, where it irrigates the fertile fields that feed the city.[45]

But the two rivers have a cultural, as well as a geographical, significance for Lorca. Each represents one of the two major cultures that in his eyes had helped to create modern Granada. The Darro is the river of the Moors, the people who once ruled the city; it is therefore a river that is old and tired and whose haunting song is in a minor key. The Genil, meanwhile, is a Christian river that has forgotten its warrior past and now sings always in a major key as it transmutes the Darro's sadness into joy and fills the Vega with vitality. The true soul of Granada, the poem suggests, is made out of the meeting of the melancholic and imaginative current of the Darro and the hard-working vigour of the Genil, whose waters allow a strong race of peasants to live and thrive. There is obviously no room in Lorca's personal Granada mythology for the bourgeoisie, who, moreover, are sometimes characterized as being both snobbish towards the people of the Vega and resistant to the idea that the Moors left any lasting trace in the city apart from a few of its buildings. In reaction to such cultural prejudice, Lorca makes a point of celebrating the Moorish and also the Jewish contributions to Granada,[46] going so far as to say in his last ever interview (where he also said that the Granada bourgeoisie was the worst in Spain) that their expulsion represented a tragedy and a disaster for the city.[47] Perhaps it is due to his awareness of such cultural prejudice too that Lorca sometimes claims that the Moorish and the Christian sides of the Granadan character do not in reality flow together like the Rivers Darro and Genil but rather live in deadly tension and conflict within the soul of each of the city's inhabitants.[48]

Beyond the geographical and historical-cultural search for the hidden soul of Granada, Lorca also paid attention to its everyday life. In the early essay 'Sonidos' (Sounds), he talks of the different sounds of the city at different times of the day and explores the song of the rivers and of the church bells[49] – an idea that he would expand years later in his talk 'Cómo canta una ciudad de noviembre a noviembre' (How a City Sings from November to November), delivered in Buenos Aires in October 1933, where he conveyed his feeling for Granada not only by evoking a soundscape made up of bells and the songs of each season but by conjuring up the smells of its streets and of its famous pastries.[50] But the text in which he most explicitly seeks out the secrets of Granada dates from October 1926 and carries the significant title – borrowed from seventeenth-century poet Pedro Soto de Rojas – 'Granada. Paraíso cerrado para muchos' (Granada: A Paradise Closed to Many).[51] Lorca starts with the bald affirmation that Granada loves everything that is tiny (*lo diminuto*) and goes on to explain this fact by making reference yet again to the city's topography. Granada, he says, is surrounded by its sierras and firmly anchored in the hollow between and beneath its two ancient hills. Unlike cities that are built by the sea or on large rivers, it cannot leave home and travel but is rather stuck in its hollow, its only natural port being that of the sky above. As a result, the city turns in on itself. Its people jealously guard their intimacy and are also more sedentary than adventurous, preferring to watch nature from the windows of their homes than to go out and explore it for themselves. This final statement sounds a little like the viewpoint of an outsider from the Vega, but Lorca does not in fact mean it as a criticism. Rather, he is making what we might now call the psychogeographical claim that the very location of Granada has led its inhabitants not only to prefer their homes to the outdoors but to look for ways of bringing the great outdoors into their homes, a drive that explains, for Lorca, their love of all that is tiny, from the small statues that adorn the fountains in their gardens to the small sculptures of the Virgin found in their streets to the arabesques they have copied from the Alhambra.

And yet, although he does not say so explicitly in this talk, it seems that Lorca's emphasis on the relationship between Granada's topography and her love of the tiny has another dimension too, one that has to do with perspective and will play an important role in his own imagination and work. When he says that Granada's only port is the sky, he is most likely thinking of the view looking sharply upwards from the River Darro towards the heights of the Alhambra hill above – a perspective that allows him to extend the boundaries of the city and to include the moon and the stars as part of his own personal Granadan universe. In Sounds, meanwhile, he locates himself in the palace of the Alhambra itself, from where he gazes across and down at the Albaicín quarter, with its patios and ancient galleries where nuns take their exercise. From high on the hill, the view of the Albaicín is mysterious and fascinating, he says, and further enriched by the multiple sounds that carry across the valley.[52] The *cármenes* (villas) with their gardens and the convents with their cloisters appear to be tiny worlds, almost miniature theatre sets, which are full of life and human drama. Lorca's job as poet – and playwright – will be to watch and listen from afar, as it is here, in these interior spaces and in these gardens that are closed to many, that the true personality of Granada is to be found.[53]

———

Before Lorca reached adulthood, before he started to turn fully from his tortured inner world outwards towards the world of others, he published his first book, *Impresiones y paisajes* (Impressions and Landscapes, 1918). This book would be the fruit – perhaps the only fruit – of the early years he spent studying (and often not studying) for his arts degree at university, and is the result of a series of cultural excursions that Lorca undertook with some of his fellow students under the tutelage of their professor of literature and fine art, Martín Domínguez Berrueta (1869–1920). Berrueta, who would become the second of Lorca's older mentors, believed that a rounded education involved much more than erudition and book learning. His pedagogical views had been forged by figures such as Francisco Giner de los Ríos (1839–1915), who, under the influence of the German philosopher Karl Christian Friedrich Krause (1781–1832), had in 1876 set up the lay college known as the Institución Libre de Enseñanza (ILE; Free Teaching Institution), which functioned in Madrid independently of the influence of both the conservative State

Cover of the first edition of *Impresiones y paisajes* (1918).

and the Catholic Church. Following Krausist ideas about the importance of establishing a harmonious relationship between and among the different human faculties, the ILE emphasized the need to cultivate both the mind and the body and instituted the practice of *excursionismo*, which for those in Madrid mainly involved walking tours in the nearby Guadarrama mountains. But those tours also had a cultural function, as they allowed teachers and students alike to get to know the villages of Spain and thereby to come into contact, as they saw it, with the *Volksgeist*, or spirit of the people, a concept beloved of Krause and his philosophical forebears Herder and Hegel. The ideas of Giner de los Ríos and the other Krausists soon spread throughout Spain thanks to the schoolteachers and university professors who took up posts in the provinces, including, at Granada University, Berrueta himself and the man who would become the third of Lorca's older mentors, Fernando de los Ríos.

Between June 1916 – just a few days after the death of Antonio Segura Mesa – and September 1917, Lorca went on five of Berrueta's trips. Some of these were short affairs, such as the very first one, which took Lorca and his companions to neighbouring Baeza and a meeting with Antonio Machado. But the trip in October 1916 took them much further afield – to Madrid, Ávila, Salamanca, Santiago de Compostela and other cities in Castile and Galicia – and the longest one of all, which saw them returning to Castile and spending weeks in cities such as Burgos, lasted from mid-July until early September 1917. For Berrueta and his students, these trips were a chance to study the local art and architecture and also to meet important writers, such as Miguel de Unamuno in Salamanca, and even to be interviewed by the regional newspapers. For Lorca, they were also an opportunity both to hone his writing skills and to get to know the customs and mores of other regions of Spain.

As its title implies, *Impressions and Landscapes* is in fact quite a mixed bag of mainly poetic prose pieces. Some, such as the sequence that deals with the Monastery of Silos near Burgos, are true travelogues that narrate the journey (in this case by both car and stagecoach) to a specific destination and offer a detailed description of what was found there – the landscape, the cell in the monastery where Lorca slept, the architecture, the sculptures, and the Gregorian chant during Mass.[54] Others, such as those belonging to the sections entitled 'Jardines' (Gardens) and 'Temas' (Themes) that bring the volume to an end, are more in the nature of prose poems that are less tied to specific places and evoke instead the emotions or sensations that Lorca associates with a particular type of landscape or time of day. But all of them, whether they deal with a named site or not, are highly impressionistic and lyrical in nature. Lorca prepares us for this fact in the Prologue, where he explains that the scenes that appear in the volume have been transformed through contact with the 'spiritual fire' of his imagination: he has poured his soul onto the objects he describes and has thereby discovered the poetry that exists in them, however ugly or even repugnant they may seem at first sight.[55] Little surprise, therefore, that this volume is so reminiscent of the unpublished poetry and prose that he was writing in Granada and the Vega at the same time: we find the same *modernista* sensibility, the same references to poets and composers, and the same use of both musical and painterly effects to describe the landscapes and those who live in them.[56]

One of the clearest influences on *Impressions and Landscapes* is José Martínez Ruiz, known as Azorín, perhaps the greatest *modernista* prose stylist Spain ever produced. But it has something else in common with Azorín's work too, especially with his own literary travelogues such as *La ruta de Don Quijote* (The Route of Don Quixote, 1905) and *Castilla* (Castile, 1912). Like Azorín and other writers of the *finisecular* (turn of the century) generation such as Unamuno, Lorca travelled with a purpose, which was to seek out the spirit of the different regions of Spain. Also at this time, he shared the older generation's particular predilection for Castile, which, in the aftermath of the disastrous 1898 war with the United States, was felt to be the decadent heart of a decadent nation. His depiction of Ávila, Zamora and Palencia as 'dead cities' in the section entitled 'Meditación' strikes a very Azorinian and Unamunian (as well as Rodenbachian) note, but so does his determination to populate these cities and their landscapes with the great figures of Castile's past, above all the mystics St John of the Cross and St Teresa, whose sensually spiritual poetry had thrown out a powerful challenge to the obscurantist and inquisitorial spirit of their age and might just also offer clues as to how the decadent Spain of the early twentieth century could be regenerated and modernized.[57] Lorca, who in October 1917 penned a violent diatribe against the rabid patriotism that was both causing the destruction of whole nations in the Great War and fatally distorting the outlook of his fellow Spaniards,[58] adopts in *Impressions and Landscapes* a liberal cultural nationalism that is in tune with that of the Krausist educationalists and of the Krausist-inspired intellectuals of Azorín's generation. His travels through Castile and Galicia made it clear to Lorca that Spain was made up of a series of diverse and vibrant regional cultures: his specific mission in the coming years would be to give expression to the soul of his native Andalusia and, within it, to the spirit of Granada and the Vega.

Lorca worked on *Impressions and Landscapes* over late 1917 and early 1918 and finally published it in April of this latter year. The edition, financed by his father, did not sell well, and Lorca soon stopped referring to it. It also caused a great deal of upset both for Lorca himself and for those around him. The members of the Rinconcillo had taken against Martín Domínguez Berrueta, questioning both his knowledge of art and the sway he held over Lorca. Clearly influenced by his opinionated friends, Lorca changed some of the contents of the work in order to remove the traces of Berrueta's ideas and then dedicated the volume to Antonio Segura Mesa, his late piano teacher, with just a small mention of Berrueta and his travelling companions added at the end of the text almost as an afterthought. Berrueta was mortally offended and broke all ties with his favourite disciple. This would not be the only time that Lorca would be swayed by the opinions of powerful friends or betray one of his guides and mentors.

By this time, Granada was starting to feel a bit small for Lorca anyway. He had strong literary ambitions that were obviously supported by his parents. Francisco García Lorca also points out that, while his brother was deeply devoted to his family, he did not cope well with the special and often deferential treatment he received as his influential father's eldest child or with the demands placed on him by the extended family, and that he was therefore the first of the siblings to crave independence.[59] Just as his father had made the great leap from the Vega to Granada back in 1909, Lorca by 1919 was ready to take a leap of his own, one that would land him in the nation's capital. But, just as his father never severed his ties with the Vega, so Lorca would always keep Granada and its surrounding countryside close to his heart.

three

Madrid: Cockroaches, *Cante Jondo* and Puppets, 1919–23

Madrid in 1919 was a politically unstable and culturally vibrant city of some 750,000 inhabitants. Although Spain had remained neutral during the Great War and had even seen certain sectors of its economy boom at the start of the conflict, an economic crisis soon set in, leading to a General Strike in 1917 and to lasting social and political unrest that placed an ultimately terminal strain on the corrupt parliamentary system. The violence on the streets never reached the same level of intensity as in Barcelona, which degenerated into a state of near civil war between workers and factory owners from the late 1910s onwards, but Madrid suffered its fair share of civil strife, brutal repression and also Anarchist activism, with Eduardo Dato's violent death in March 1921 meaning that three serving prime ministers had been assassinated in Spain since 1897.

Lorca, and the other sons of the provincial rich who became his friends in Madrid, seemed to care little about such events or about politics in general, even remaining quite indifferent to General Miguel Primo de Rivera's *coup d'état* of September 1923 that would usher in over seven years of military dictatorship in Spain. For them, Madrid had another significance altogether, offering both personal freedom from the ties of their families and home towns and the opportunity for social and cultural encounters and advancement.

There is little doubt that Madrid was at the time one of the most exciting cultural capitals in Europe. Four generations of writers and intellectuals coexisted. Although the Krausist educationalist Francisco Giner de los Ríos had died in 1915, he and his colleagues and disciples in the Free Teaching Institute (ILE) had helped to secure the goals of an independent educational system that attracted students from all around Spain and had also managed to put in place state-sponsored study trips abroad for university students. Thanks to such initiatives, university life and research in Madrid thrived, with the Nobel Prize in Medicine won by histologist Santiago Ramón y Cajal (1852–1934) in 1906 just one recognition of the important contributions that Spain was making at the time to world science. In cultural terms, Lorca and his friends came into contact both with novelist Benito Pérez Galdós (1843–1920), who seemed to them to belong to another age, and with the brilliant *finisecular* generation of Azorín (1873–1967), Ramón del Valle-Inclán (1866–1936), Pío Baroja (1872–1956) and Unamuno (1864–1936, a frequent visitor from Salamanca), although Lorca himself particularly sought out those poets who had been most influenced by Rubén Darío and *modernismo*, including his beloved Juan Ramón Jiménez and Antonio Machado. The intellectual scene was dominated by philosopher José Ortega y Gasset (1883–1955), whose ideas on art and general intellectual authority would have a decisive influence on Lorca's generation. And then there were the younger and more subversive members of the avant-garde, men like Ramón Gómez de la Serna (1888–1963) and Guillermo de Torre (1900–1971) who were helping to import the latest literary and artistic fashions from Europe but also to create a specifically local vanguard culture.

Lorca arrived in Madrid in late April or early May 1919 with a series of letters of presentation that would serve to open many doors and facilitate his acceptance on the cultural scene. The professor of law at Granada University, Fernando de los Ríos, who had heard Lorca playing the piano as a young teenager and had then come across him both in the Rinconcillo and at the university itself, would, for example, ensure that he met up with the notoriously irascible Juan Ramón Jiménez. His main guides at the beginning of his stay, though, would be those friends from the Rinconcillo who had already transferred to Madrid – men like José Mora Guarnido, who booked a room for Lorca in the lodging house where he was staying.[1] As far as his family was concerned, the main purpose of Lorca's first trip to Madrid, which lasted until June, was to find a way for him to complete his university degree. To this end, he soon made contact with Alberto Jiménez Fraud, the director of the Residencia de Estudiantes (Hall of Residence) found in the Calle del Pinar in the north of Madrid.

The Residencia de Estudiantes has quite rightly attained a mythical status within Spanish culture – as a symbol of the intellectual and artistic splendour of Spain from the mid-1910s until the Civil War of 1936–9.

It must not be forgotten that it was first and foremost a hall of residence full of young men in their late teens and early twenties, who were beneficiaries of a first-class education system reserved for the sons of the elite (there was a parallel 'Residencia de Señoritas' available to the 'young ladies' of the middle and upper classes). But it was more than simply a place for students of the University of Madrid to eat and sleep. Influenced by the educational philosophy of Giner de los Ríos and the Krausists and also by the idea of an Oxford or Cambridge college, the Residencia saw itself as an intellectual community in which students of different disciplines lived alongside their professors and also met with a whole host of visiting luminaries, including national figures such as Unamuno and Ortega and international celebrities of the calibre of Albert Einstein, H. G. Wells, Le Corbusier and Paul Valéry. It also offered regular cultural and artistic activities, such as piano recitals and theatre productions (in both of which Lorca would take an active part). It seems that Jiménez Fraud took an immediate liking to Lorca and agreed to provide lodgings for him for the following academic year, commencing in November 1919. After a summer back in Granada and the Vega, Lorca started his lifelong relationship with the Residencia de Estudiantes, which would see him lodge there off and on, with long periods also spent back in Granada, until his departure for New York in 1929.

For Lorca, life at the Residencia had little to do with academic study. He would use the place rather as a base from which to write and to make himself known. According to one of his closest friends of the time, Pepín Bello, Lorca felt that he had no academic obligations whatsoever and would therefore get up late and spend his days reading and writing.[2] Bello, who shared one of the cell-like Residencia rooms with Lorca for a term or two, describes how Lorca would sit bolt upright on his bed with his legs crossed and spend hours in an almost ecstatic state writing and correcting his poems.[3] But Bello and other boarders such as the future film director Luis Buñuel (1900–1983), who soon befriended the newcomer, also make mention of Lorca's high spirits and sense of fun, which meant that he participated in the many student pranks, whether they involved dressing up, acting out his own funeral or parodying professors and other figures of authority. All of these attributes soon made Lorca both the centre of his own little group within the Residencia and a magnet for young writers and artists from across Madrid, who would often congregate in his room. It is really at this moment that the image of Lorca as a vital, exuberant, multi-gifted artist starts to take shape – an image that

Lorca (centre) and friends in front of the Residencia de Estudiantes, Madrid, 1924.

has come, over the years, to stand metonymically in the Spanish psyche for
the cultural vitality and exuberance of Spain herself in the years leading
up to the Civil War.

For Lorca seemed to excel at everything, except his degree. He played
the piano beautifully and sang well too, giving recitals of Granadan and
Andalusian songs in the Residencia's central hall or improvising musical
caricatures of Chopin and Debussy.[4] He acted in the annual production
of Zorrilla's *Don Juan Tenorio*.[5] He recited his poems and also read out
whole plays by Lope de Vega or Calderón, using different voices and

gestures for the different characters.[6] But, above all, there was the simple fact of his physical presence and his magnetic personality, which Buñuel would later refer to as Lorca's true masterpiece.[7]

Many friends and acquaintances have commented upon Lorca's power of seduction. Although his brother Francisco points out that he had a strange and almost clumsy gait, caused perhaps by the fact that his legs were of a slightly different length, and others comment on his tendency towards plumpness,[8] most focus instead on his rich voice with its melodious Granadan accent[9] and his strong facial features – his high forehead, bushy eyebrows and many moles, and, above all, his dark and penetrating eyes.[10] When he was animated, as he often was, he would accompany his words with expansive and highly expressive hand gestures, and those eyes both sparkled and smouldered.[11] At those moments, he struck his friends as a genuine force of nature, someone who, in Buñuel's words, was like a flame full of passion, joy and youth or who, according to fellow poet Jorge Guillén, created a whole atmosphere and weather system around him.[12] The most common words used to describe Lorca's character are joy and laughter, but those who knew him best, including Pepín Bello, the poet Vicente Aleixandre and Granadan friends José María García Carrillo and Emilia Llanos, also insist that there was a darker side to Lorca and that the moments of laughter and inventiveness often alternated with others of deep introspection, when he would lose himself in a brown study, staring into the void and silently moving his lips.[13] Bello also refers to Lorca's terror of death and the multiple superstitions that helped him keep it at bay, such as his belief that window shutters should be closed at dawn, lest death reach in and take the sick and infirm away.[14]

There was also the question of his sexuality. Most witnesses to Lorca's early years in Madrid maintain a discreet silence when it comes to his homosexuality, although few remain completely silent about the sexual opportunities that were generally available in the nation's capital, and Rafael Martínez Nadal makes a brief mention of his close friend's habit of disappearing by himself overnight in search of 'unexpected encounters'.[15] Luis Buñuel breaks the taboo when he reports the shock and horror he felt on hearing rumours of Lorca's sexual preferences and activities. The fact that he was shocked implies that Lorca had learned during his painful school days to hide both his attraction to other men and also, perhaps, his boyish effeminacy – something that Pepín Bello seems to corroborate in his own memoirs[16] – but it also points to the profound ignorance and homophobia that surrounded Lorca even in such a liberal institution as the Residencia de Estudiantes. Buñuel apparently confronted him with the rumour, causing Lorca a great deal of upset, although, in a character-istically generous way, Lorca soon made up with his outspoken and often indelicate friend.[17]

———

Madrid in the early 1920s was a small and intimate city. The Madrid that formed Lorca's playground and that of his group of high-spirited stu-dent friends was even smaller and more intimate – and still exists among the accretions of the second half of the twentieth century and beyond. Its backbone was the Paseo de la Castellana, then still a thoroughfare of grand nineteenth-century palaces, which led northwards from the centre of the city towards the Hippodrome (located where the Nuevos Ministerios now stand) and was flanked on either side by narrower streets of fine middle-class apartment blocks. The Residencia de Estudiantes was found a little way south of the Hippodrome and just to the east of the Castellana, on the higher ground behind the Museum of Natural Science. Beyond it, to the north and east, were fields. Lorca and his friends would walk or take taxis or trams down the Castellana and Recoletos to the Plaza de Emilio Castelar, as the Plaza de Cibeles was then known, and go from there to the art galleries, theatres and cinemas in the centre or to the cafés where famous writers would hold their nightly *tertulias* or get-togethers. They would drop in on playwright Ramón del Valle-Inclán's *tertulia* in the Café Granja El Henar on the Calle de Alcalá, or Ramón Gómez de la Serna's in the Café Pombo on the Calle de Carretas, or they would just gather together in the Residencia or in one of the myriad taverns in central Madrid. The point was to meet and discuss the ideas of the day, with a clear predilection for literary and artistic ideas over political ones. Their visits to the centre would also take them to the streets of the older and more popular quarters south of the Plaza Mayor, where they would enjoy what seemed to them to be the almost medieval way of life and, in some cases at least, visit the houses of ill repute.[18] They also frequented the recently built Ritz and Palace, two ultra-modern and upmarket hotels that still face each other across the Plaza de Cánovas del Castillo, where they would sip cocktails and listen to the live music often played and sung by jazz musicians from the United States.[19] Their Madrid therefore offered them the possibility of immersing themselves both in high and traditional Spanish culture, in the most up-to-date art coming

Lorca and Luis Buñuel outside the Residencia de Estudiantes, Madrid, 1922.

from Europe, and in the latest music and cinema from Chicago, New York and Hollywood – all of which would leave a deep imprint on Lorca's work.

Lorca arrived in Madrid with the explicit mission to complete his university degree but with the secret aim of establishing himself as a writer. He brought two projects with him, one dramatic and one poetic.

Ever since January 1917, when he had started writing in earnest, Lorca had tried his hand at playwriting as well as at prose and poetry. The collection of dramatic manuscripts written mainly between 1917 and 1920 and published posthumously in 1995 shows how they were profoundly related, in both thematic and formal terms, to his essays and poems.[20] His first more substantial dramatic project, *El maleficio de la mariposa* (The Butterfly's Evil Spell), written between spring or summer 1919 and early 1920, takes the form of a folk or fairy tale that is, like the majority of his early work, deeply rooted in his experience of the Vega. It tells a story of unrequited love among a community of cockroaches: the love that a young female cockroach feels for a young male who is a poet and who falls in love, in turn, with a wounded butterfly. Writer Agustín Penón, who visited Granada in 1955 and 1956, mentions a conversation with a group of elderly women in Fuente Vaqueros, one of whom recalled how Lorca would while away the hours as a child talking with the ants, the beetles and the lizards.[21] Lorca would draw on such intimate moments in the Vega when preparing a play that explores the same mysteries of love he had encountered in *A Midsummer Night's Dream* and that gives expression, once again, to the tragic consequences of losing one's heart to someone deemed inappropriate or unacceptable by one's own community. He would also do nothing to hide the sense of threat, as well as the profound beauty, that he found in the Vega, with the insatiable hunger of the character of Alacranito (Little Scorpion), the woodcutter, appearing to represent the sexual appetite and even predation that Lorca forever associated with the woods between Asquerosa and Fuente Vaqueros.

It seems that the idea of staging *The Butterfly's Evil Spell* emerged thanks to a chance meeting that took place in Granada in the months between Lorca's first visit to Madrid and his move there in November 1919. Lorca's Granada friend Miguel Cerón reports that he introduced Lorca that summer to Gregorio Martínez Sierra (1881–1947), a writer and theatre impresario based in Madrid, and Catalina Bárcena (1888–1978), a well-known actress in Martínez Sierra's troupe who was also the impresario's lover.[22] Martínez Sierra had at first been reluctant to meet yet another budding local author, but Cerón took the three of them to the highest tower in the Generalife gardens, where he told Lorca to recite some of his poems. It seems that the poem Lorca chose was 'Los encuentros de un caracol aventurero' (The Encounters of an Adventurous Snail), which tells the story of a snail's meeting with two frogs who are unable to believe in eternal life and with an ant who has fatally injured herself while climbing a tree to see the stars.[23] The impresario and the actress were overwhelmed by the beauty of the place, of the recital and of the poem itself, and they exhorted Lorca to write a play for them. Lorca was able to tell them about one he had already started to compose and which, like the poem he had just recited to them, also dealt with the loves and longings of insect characters.

Lorca's meeting with Martínez Sierra was fortuitous indeed. He and his wife, María de la O Lejárraga (who may in fact have authored or co-authored some of the plays attributed to him), were known as experimental playwrights who resisted the naturalism that dominated the Spanish stage of the time and believed instead in 'total theatre' involving music, dance and elaborate stage design.[24] And the team they put together to stage *The Butterfly's Evil Spell* at the Teatro Eslava, their theatre in Madrid, reveals how the venture served to place Lorca, very shortly after his arrival in the capital, in contact with the cream of the young theatrical and artistic talent of his day. The play was directed by Martínez Sierra himself; the stage sets were designed by Fernando Mignoni (1884–1971), who would later make his name as both a painter and a film director; the costumes were designed by Uruguayan avant-garde artist Rafael Barradas (1890–1929), who would become a close associate of Lorca's group at the Residencia de Estudiantes; and the role of the Butterfly, and the choreography of the dances associated with that role, was entrusted to Encarnación López Júlvez (1898–1945), La Argentinita, who was fast becoming Spain's most famous dancer and singer of regional and popular songs.[25]

Painting, costumes, song, dance and the music of Grieg combined with Lorca's poetry to create what should have been a powerful and truly modern theatrical experience. But the single performance, held at the Teatro Eslava on 22 March 1920, was a complete disaster. Lorca's first attempt to bring the Vega to Madrid did not convince the audience, which ended up laughing at the spectacle of cockroaches falling in love with other insects and addressing lyrical poems to the stars above. Lorca responded by consigning this, his first performed dramatic work, to literary oblivion, together with his first prose work, *Impressions and Landscapes*, doing his best to ensure that no one would henceforth have access to either text. According to Pepín Bello, though, he received the setback with a smile on his lips and was obviously determined not to allow it to dent his pride or his ambition.[26] Indeed, he would sometimes refer back to the whole affair with a certain dry humour, as when he told his friend Carlos Morla Lynch in 1929 that, although the play was not really worth much and the premiere had been full of noise and insults, at least the sight of La Argentinita dancing in a transparent dragonfly costume had managed briefly to capture the audience's attention.[27]

While Lorca's first outing into drama in Madrid ended in failure, he would have a little more success with his first poetic project. The volume he would finally publish in June 1921 under the title *Libro de poemas* (Book of Poems) is made up both of a selection of his earliest verse and of more recent poems that were written specifically for inclusion in the collection. This fact explains the great variety of themes and styles found in Lorca's first published poetic work. But the dates that accompany each of the poems reveal that he has deliberately avoided a chronological structure, which might have suggested some sort of development in his poetic craft and worldview. Rather, as he suggests in the Prologue, he has produced a 'disordered' collection that is therefore better able to offer a faithful reflection of the complex movements of his heart and spirit and of the vagaries of his life as a teenager and young man.[28]

The predominant mood is without doubt the one we already found in the unpublished early poetry, that is, a powerful mixture of Romantic longings and *modernista* melancholy that is communicated through a focus on specific seasons or times of day and on specific elements in the Vega landscape (a tree, a river, a field, an animal, the sky) that can carry the poet's feelings or give form to his emotional, spiritual or metaphysical search. Alongside such poems, there are others that continue openly to explore the mysteries of sexuality, including a couple that can be seen to contain coded homosexual references.[29] And Lorca even has time for historical poems based both on his love of local Granadan history and his travels around Spain with Martín Domínguez Berrueta, poems such as the highly Romantic 'Elegía a Doña Juana la Loca' (Elegy to Joanna the Mad), which presents the queen of Castile, daughter of Ferdinand and Isabella and mother to the future Charles I, as a tragic victim of passion and grief whose remains are kept and treated like a religious relic in the Royal Chapel in Granada.[30]

And yet, amid the toing and froing between high Romantic and more delicate *modernista* poems, there are also signs of a new, and more modern, sensibility emerging in this collection. 'Cantos nuevos' (New Songs), written in August 1920, informs us that

Yo tengo sed de aromas y de risas,
sed de cantares nuevos

sin lunas y sin lirios,
y sin amores muertos.[31]

I thirst after aromas and laughter,
after new songs
that contain no moons or lilies
or loves that are dead.

The poet, very possibly influenced by the latest pared-down and more
philosophical verse of Juan Ramón Jiménez, goes on to say in this poem
that he longs to be able to write a tranquil and luminous type of verse
that knows nothing of sadness or anguish or even dreams, but rather
goes right to the soul of things and is capable of expressing what might
be called their Platonic essence. But New Songs, despite seeming to offer
a new *ars poetica*, only affords an isolated glimpse of what Lorca's new
style might become, and the chronological discontinuities and emotional
oscillations of *Book of Poems* mean that we are soon immersed once again
in the world of the moon, flowers and tragic love affairs that the poem
seems to reject. Rather, the new note that will come more insistently to
the fore in the collection will be fundamentally playful, subversive and
inventive in nature, as can be seen in 'Canción para la luna' (Song for the
Moon), which Lorca teasingly places just two poems after New Songs.
Here the moon is not so much an actor in a cosmic drama of sexual love
or spiritual longings as a simple object whose shape gives rise to a series
of rich and complex images. It is a white tortoise, a pupil part-covered by
an eyelid made of shadow, a chaste St Veronica's handkerchief that cleans
the reddish face of the sun at sunset. And each of these images sets off
a series of further associations that lead Lorca to populate the sky play-
fully with two competing outlooks on life: the religious one, dominated
by the figure of Jehovah, and the political and revolutionary one, dominated by the Anarchists and, above all, by Lenin – the future Ursa Major
(Great Bear) of the heavens.[32]

There is no doubt that the attitudes contained in a poem like 'Song
for the Moon', which was written in August 1920, most probably in
Asquerosa, owe a great deal to Lorca's experiences during his first year
in Madrid. The tone here is lighter, more ludic and even more sardonic,
and clearly reflects the spirit and outlook of his group of friends at the
Residencia de Estudiantes. The emphasis on the creation of novel and
striking images is not completely new in his work but was obviously

accentuated through his contact with the avant-garde writers he was coming across in the café *tertulias*. Both Ramón Gómez de la Serna and the Chilean Vicente Huidobro (1893–1948), whose Creacionismo movement became particularly influential in Spain from 1918 onwards, rejected the old-fashioned Romantic and *modernista* strains in Spanish poetry and devoted themselves instead to a 'hunt' for unusual metaphors. They would also influence a younger group of poets, including Guillermo de la Torre and the Argentine Jorge Luis Borges (1899–1986), who would soon go on to found a similar movement of their own which they would call Ultraísmo.

The few reviews that appeared of *Book of Poems*, most of them written by Lorca's new friends and acquaintances in Madrid, were rather mixed affairs: Guillermo de la Torre himself, for example, expressed the hope that the poet would henceforth cultivate the more avant-garde aspects of his poetic craft and jettison the more conventional and old-fashioned ones, while the renowned music critic Adolfo Salazar, taking a more generous line, recognized that the collection was a work of transition in which the poet was using traditional forms as a means of gradually identifying and exploring new poetic worlds.[33] Even more revealing perhaps is the reaction of Rafael Alberti, who would later become Lorca's friend but also his main rival among the emerging new poets of their generation. Years later, Alberti would recall how he was taken with the simpler and more popular poems contained in the collection, many of which had graceful song-like refrains, but disliked those that reminded him of the rather hackneyed verse that Romantic poets such as José Zorrilla and *modernista* poets such as Francisco Villaespesa (1877–1936) had dedicated to the city of Granada. He could not understand either how, in an age of innovation, a young poet could write a poem about Joanna the Mad. He recognized in the work, however, the voice of a great future poet and longed to meet him – a wish that would finally come true in 1924.[34]

———

Lorca's first forays into performed theatre and published poetry reveal the degree to which his literary inspiration continued to draw on his roots in Granada and the Vega. He would in fact stay closely in touch with his home town throughout his different stays in Madrid, not least with his parents, on whose good will his continued presence in the capital clearly depended. The letters that Lorca exchanged with Federico García and Vicenta Lorca over his first years away from home reveal his parents' increasingly desperate attempts to keep him on a tight rein and his ingenious efforts to break free from it. They make clear that Lorca has given his word that he will devote himself to his studies in order to finish off his degree and that he has been required to check in periodically with certain old family friends currently resident in Madrid, especially Antonio Rodríguez Espinosa, who had been Lorca's headmaster during his school days in Almería.

Despite these promises and safeguards, there were numerous flashpoints, the most serious of which occurred in April 1920. From the letters that Lorca wrote separately to his father and his mother during this month, it becomes clear that Federico García had reached the end of his tether and was suggesting in no uncertain terms that his son should return to Granada in order to complete his studies there. Lorca's reply reveals both what was at stake for him and, implicitly, the full extent and nature of his father's concerns.[35] Using attack as the best form of defence, Lorca does not even mention his studies but rather, addressing his father in an unusually blunt and even aggressive way, tells him that he is not an object that belongs to him but rather a poet who has finally found his path; he has to stay in the nation's capital, since it is only there that he can publish and make a name for himself. He repeats this last point to his mother, knowing in her case, though, that he is pushing at an open door and that she is almost definitely trying to intercede with his father on his behalf. But in both letters Lorca also makes reference to his personal behaviour, assuring his mother that the parties he attends are artistic (and therefore supposedly proper) ones and emphasizing to his father that he is a serious and respectable young man who behaves in Madrid even better than he does in Granada.

Do we here perhaps get a unique reflected glimpse of Federico García's most secret concerns – concerns whose name he probably dared not speak with his son but which shine through this uncharacteristically angry exchange? In this context, it is difficult to ignore the very striking testimony of Francisco Roca, one of Lorca's Granada friends, who told Agustín Penón in the 1950s that Federico García asked all his acquaintances to check on his son during their visits to Madrid; according to Roca, one of them, a captain in the Civil Guard, brutishly reported back to Don Federico that 'En Madrid Federico sigue escribiendo y tomando por el culo' (In Madrid Federico continues writing and being buggered).[36]

Lorca somehow managed to ride the storm of April 1920. And the long summer and Christmas holidays that he spent at home, his growing literary recognition, and the ever stronger encouragement that he received from his mother and also, it must be said, from his father (who ended up financing the publication of *Book of Poems* in June 1921) enabled him to enjoy two consecutive academic years in Madrid. However, by autumn 1921, his father finally imposed his will and made clear that Lorca would not return to the Residencia until he had completed his degree in Granada. Lorca seems to have accepted this decision, which led to him being absent from Madrid until February 1923, with both frustration and resignation. But he also came to see this banishment as an opportunity, because he was fully aware that his creative wellspring was located, in great measure, in his home region. Indeed, over the following years, he would come to associate Granada and Madrid with two separate, if mutually enriching, modes of writing, one more rooted in traditional forms and themes and the other more associated with the modern and the avant-garde. This was the moment in which he could devote himself fully to the exploration of the former.

The draw of Granada for Lorca in fact intensified over these years through his ever-closer relationship with the fourth and final of his key adult mentors (after Antonio Segura, Martín Domínguez Berrueta and Fernando de los Ríos), namely Manuel de Falla (1876–1946), the world-renowned composer who had moved to the city in autumn 1919. In a country that had recently produced Felip Pedrell (1841–1922), Isaac Albéniz (1860–1909) and Enrique Granados (1867–1916), Falla was a giant among giants who had already conquered Europe with works such as the one-act opera *La vida breve* (Life is Short, 1913) and the ballet *El amor brujo* (Love, the Magician, 1915), which combined the sounds and rhythms of Andalusian folksongs with the more modern musical idiom of a Debussy or a Ravel. Falla brought with him to Granada not only his musical brilliance but his connections, arranging visits from foreign luminaries such as Sergei Diaghilev (1872–1929), the founder of the Ballets Russes, which deeply impressed the members of the Rinconcillo.

Lorca probably met Falla soon after the latter set up home in Granada, but their relationship blossomed from late 1920 onwards.[37] As a pianist himself, Lorca was immensely taken by Falla's skills as a performer as well as a composer, while Falla was soon impressed by the young Lorca's writing skills, so much so that he would eventually explore the possibility of using him as a librettist. But what drew both men together from the start was their shared interest in the local Granadan traditions of song, theatre and dance. Lorca, who had long been fascinated with the musical and dramatic traditions of the Vega and Granada and had also started to explore the notion of a specifically Granadan and Andalusian culture and worldview in *Impressions and Landscapes*, saw in Falla a new ally in his fundamentally Romantic drive to record, understand and revitalize the folklore and folk culture of his native region. The two men would together dream up two musical and dramatic projects, one relating to the Gypsy music of Granada and the other to the puppet theatre that Lorca had enjoyed as a child in Fuente Vaqueros. Both would have an important bearing on Lorca's future direction as a poet and a playwright.

Lorca's relationship with Gypsy music is intimately linked to his search for a secret and 'authentic' Granada that he felt lay hidden under the more modern and 'superficial' Granada of the middle classes and the tourists. And, although he had come across this music as a child in Fuente Vaqueros, he would now, as a young adult, seek it out above all in the Albaicín quarter and on the Sacromonte hill beyond. Lorca had already accompanied Ramón Menéndez Pidal (1869–1968), the famous historian and philologist, to these areas of Granada in September 1920 in order to help him record the popular medieval ballads that were still recited there. From just a few months later, Lorca also started to visit the caves of the Sacromonte in the company of Manuel de Falla, as the two men sought out the ancient music of the Gypsies that was mostly despised by *bienpensant* middle-class Granadan society and many musicologists alike.

Soon the idea of a festival or competition was born, an event that could showcase the talents of both singers and instrumentalists and make the world aware of the power and originality of this form of music. A petition was signed in favour of the event and money sought from the town hall. And finally a date was set and a venue arranged: the Concurso de Cante Jondo (Competition of Deep Song), as it would be called, would take place on 13 and 14 June 1922 in the Plaza de los Aljibes in the Alhambra Palace. The preparations and the event itself brought together the energies and talents of a dazzling array of Spanish artists, from the participating singers and guitarists, who came from all over Andalusia, to composers Falla, Joaquín Turina (1882–1949) and a young Roberto Gerhard (1896–1970), poets and writers such as Lorca, Azorín, Juan Ramón Jiménez and Ramón Gómez de la Serna, and the veteran painters Santiago Rusiñol and Ignacio Zuloaga (1870–1945), the latter of whom created the colourful decor for the event.

The organizers of the *cante jondo* festival, Granada, June 1922. Manuel de Falla is seated in the middle, next to the woman in white, and Lorca is seated fourth from the right in the same row. Next to him, holding the guitar, is Ramón Gómez de la Serna.

As part of the publicity campaign for the competition, Lorca prepared a talk entitled 'El cante jondo. Primitivo canto andaluz' (Deep Song: Primitive Andalusian Song), which he delivered in the Centro Artístico de Granada on 19 February 1922. The talk probably revealed to his parents that, despite all the evidence to the contrary, he did in fact possess certain academic and research skills, although it is also clear that he borrowed the majority of his ideas on the origins of *cante jondo* from just one source, Manuel de Falla. Drawing once again on his Romantic belief in the existence of an authentic Granada that is known only to a few, Lorca starts by distinguishing between *cante jondo* and two related phenomena: on the one hand, the more modern 'flamenco' forms such as *malagueñas* and *granadinas*, which started to evolve out of *cante jondo* in the eighteenth century, and, on the other, the debased form of flamenco that has become a staple of literary, tavern and tourist culture in Granada and beyond ever since the mid-1800s.[38] *Cante jondo* is therefore a sort of ur-flamenco that exists nowadays mainly in the form of the *siguiriya*, which is sung by only a very few practitioners dotted around Andalusia and is therefore in grave danger of extinction. Its roots, Lorca goes on to tell us, liberally quoting Falla in the process, lie in the music of the Moors, in that of the Byzantine liturgy that was used by the Spanish Church until the eleventh century, and, of course, in that of the Gypsies, who arrived in the peninsula in the early fifteenth century and soon fused these diverse musical traditions with their own.[39] Befitting of music with such ancient origins, *cante jondo* has something in common both with the sounds of the natural world and with the most primal of human sounds, moving as it does from a terrible initial cry to a sob, which Lorca memorably describes as 'a tear made of sound over the river of the voice'.[40] And its lyrics deal with the deepest realities of human life, those relating to love and death, and give expression to 'the most infinite gradations of Pain and Sorrow'.[41] They are set at night and often project their deep sense of sadness through the mysterious figure of a woman who is surrounded by natural objects, such as a tree or the moon, which are given their own personality and take an active part in the action themselves.[42] This ancient Gypsy poetry and music, Lorca adds in a passage aimed at all the uncomprehending and even racist elements in the Granadan middle classes, is the sound of Andalusia itself, the 'soul of our soul', and has often been better understood outside Spain, by the likes of Glinka and Debussy, than in Spain itself.[43] Its practitioners, the *cantaores*, he concludes, are mediums, immense interpreters of the popular Andalusian soul.[44]

Lorca's research into the origins and nature of *cante jondo* ran parallel to his preparation of a new book of poems on the same subject that he started to write in autumn 1921 and intended to publish before the competition took place. In the end, he would not publish *Poema del cante jondo* (Poem of the Deep Song) until May 1931, although he had completed most of its poems by August 1923. It is quite clear that Lorca did not wish in this collection to compose lyrics for *cante jondo* songs, and the reason for this artistic decision can be found in his talk, where he both states how attractive *cante jondo* is to those poets like himself – who are tired of the over-flowery legacy of Romantic and post-Romantic (*modernista*) verse – and at the same time emphasizes that those poets who try to write popular verse themselves end up muddying the waters of popular inspiration and creating what he calls a paper rose rather than a natural one; they should therefore, he concludes, draw on the essence and colour of popular culture but turn it into something else, something new.[45] Here, in embryonic form, we have a glimpse of the aesthetic outlook that would guide Lorca when writing the majority of his mature works, and it is an aesthetic that he clearly puts into practice when writing *Poem of the Deep Song*.

So, instead of lyrics, this collection provides an imaginative glimpse into the very world of *cante jondo*: its themes, its atmosphere and its

famous practitioners from the past (some of whom, such as Silverio
Franconetti and Juan Breva, are given their own poems in the section
entitled 'Viñetas flamencas' (Flamenco Vignettes)). The first four sections are given the titles of the main forms of *cante jondo*: the *siguiriya*
and three of its derivatives, the *soleá*, the *saeta* and the *petenera*, and the
poems in each of these sections explore certain aspects or characteristics
of these forms by adopting their concision and often their characteristic
imagery too. The seven poems in the *siguiriya* section, for example, deal
with what seem to be the different moments of a recital, from the inspiration that wells up from the landscape of olive trees, to the grief and tears
produced by the guitar, to the cry of the *cantaor* that causes the strings of
the wind to vibrate, to the silence that follows the song, and to the aftermath of the performance in which the *siguiriya*, now personified as a dark
woman with a silver heart and a dagger in her right hand, continues to
echo in the landscape and causes children to ask questions of the moon,
and hearts and dreams to disappear.[46] Each of the poems in the *soleá*, the
saeta and the *petenera* sections similarly takes some aspect of *cante jondo*
– the places it is associated with, the imagery it uses, the sounds it gen-
erates, and the effects it has on the listener, which are often likened to a
dagger penetrating the heart – and explores it in a way that fuses popular
references with modern and often surprising poetic effects. The whole
section on the *saeta*, for example, recognizing the important role that this
type of *cante jondo* plays during the Holy Week processions in Andalusia,
offers descriptions of the statues that are carried through the streets and
of the people who sing their songs to the statues from their balconies,
but it also threads through its eight poems a series of clever references to
archers and to war whose origin lies in the literal meaning of the word
saeta (arrow).[47] At moments such as these, Lorca's poetry is reminiscent
of that of Spanish Golden Age poets Luis de Góngora (1561–1627) and
Francisco de Quevedo (1580–1645), both of whom also aimed in much
of their verse to fuse popular forms and references with complex conceits
often born of wordplay.

Lorca made clear in a letter to Adolfo Salazar in January 1922 that he
was fully aware of the originality of this collection, which he put down
to the fact that no poet had hitherto celebrated *cante jondo* in verse.[48]
More importantly, though, he was managing to achieve new effects of his
own by adopting shorter poetic forms and also exploiting and expanding
cante jondo's field of reference and techniques: its use of a small range of
natural and human objects such as the wind, the moon and the dagger,

and its recourse to personification, which allows the world around to take an active part in the lives and destinies of the human characters. The pantheistic and even quasi-pagan aspect of Lorca's worldview, which can already be glimpsed in his earliest verse, seems to have come into full focus through his study of the contents and dynamics of *cante jondo* lyrics.

At the same time that he was exploring *cante jondo*, Lorca was also immersing himself in another local cultural form, namely the Andalusian tradition of puppet theatre. We have seen how he had been mesmerized by the puppeteers who would visit Fuente Vaqueros when he was a child and also how from an early age he had improvised puppet shows of his own for his friends and family. The influence of puppet theatre can be found in some of Lorca's early unpublished dramatic works.[49] It is clear that Lorca first conceived *The Butterfly's Evil Spell* itself as a puppet play: not only is there a letter from Gregorio Martínez Sierra of 7 January 1920 telling Lorca that the play will definitely be staged but not as 'Guignol',[50] but the opening stage direction of Act II in what is the only extant (and incomplete) manuscript of the play makes reference to the layout and decor of the 'teatrito',[51] a word that is used to refer to a puppet theatre (all of which begs the question of how successful and influential the work might have been if it had been staged in the way Lorca had originally envisaged).

It seems that Lorca's interest in local puppet traditions intensified during the summer of 1921, that is, just when his father had told him that he would not be returning to Madrid that autumn and just a few months before he also started working on his collection of *cante jondo* poems. In a letter written in Asquerosa on 2 August, Lorca informs Adolfo Salazar that he is both learning the Gypsy guitar and asking the locals for their memories of the 'Cristobital', that is, the hilarious and often slightly salacious Punch and Judy-like itinerant puppet theatre that had in the space of a generation more or less disappeared from the Vega de Granada. Lorca enjoys himself recounting some of the scenes that have been described to him featuring the stock characters Doña Rosita, her suitor Currito and her jealous husband Cristóbal, who ends up killing Currito while reciting the words 'Una, dos y tres, ¡al barranco con él!' (One, two, three, down the ravine with him!) accompanied by the sound of a drum coming from the depths of the puppet theatre.[52]

Lorca was obviously as concerned about the future of the Cristobital tradition as he would be about that of *cante jondo*, and his response was once again to cultivate the form himself by mixing the popular elements with more modern elements of his own. The result would be his first major work for puppets, *La tragicomedia de Don Cristóbal y la Señá Rosita* (The Tragicomedy of Cristóbel and his Missus, Rosita), which he would start writing that summer and finish in August 1922. This delightful play tells the story of Doña Rosita, a young and romantic female character who is courted simultaneously by three male figures: her true love Cocoliche, a former suitor named Currito, and the grotesque old man Don Cristobita, who forces her to marry him after convincing her father of the financial benefits of their union. Lorca exploits all the effects offered to him by traditional puppet theatre: the rich and constantly changing stage sets; the brightly coloured clothes and costumes of the puppets; knockabout and farcical moments, including the scene in which the two younger suitors hide in cupboards while Don Cristobita (the Pulcinella or Punch figure) is trying to consummate his marriage with Doña Rosita; the comic but still troubling violence of Don Cristobita; and the popular songs and the earthy and often quite erotic poetry, including the verses that Lorca had heard his neighbours in the Vega recite.

Then there are the more highbrow or modern elements, which Lorca manages to fuse seamlessly with the more popular ones. The moments of intense lyricism that alternate with the humour and slapstick are sometimes expressed through the use of popular songs but at others through a richly metaphorical language, as when Doña Rosita celebrates her love for Cocoliche at the climax of the play by referring to herself as a flower that loses its petals in his hands.[53] There are surreal touches too (some perhaps borrowed from cinema), such as the character Hora (Hour), who appears from within a clock dressed in yellow and wearing a bustle and proceeds to lecture Doña Rosita on the need for patience, or the moment when one of the characters cries into an enormous handkerchief made of blades of grass.[54] And there are also moments when the play calls attention to itself, as when the character Mosquito (yet another insect from the Vega) explains to the audience that he and his troupe have just escaped from the conventional, bourgeois theatre and have come out into the countryside instead in order to talk to more humble people, or when, at the climax, the knife that Currito has plunged into Cristobita's belly makes the puppet come apart to the sound of breaking springs.[55] On closer inspection, though, it is perhaps not so much that Lorca has tried to fuse popular and more modern elements in this play as that he has understood that the Cristobital tradition, with its strange lyricism, surreal humour and metatheatrical touches, is at one and the same time a deeply popular and a deeply innovative theatrical form, one which, he soon realizes, could help renovate Spanish theatre itself.

Little surprise, therefore, that Lorca started talking about the idea of setting up a puppet theatre company. In a letter of 1 January 1922, he tells Adolfo Salazar that, after having serenaded Falla the night before with his own version of the master's 'Canción del fuego fatuo' (Song of the Will-o'-the Wisp), played by four members of the municipal band, he has just received a New Year's Day visit from the great composer, who enthusiastically endorses Lorca's idea of setting up 'un teatro de cachiporra', or what he more specifically calls 'los títeres de Cachiporra de Granada' (Granada Cosh Puppets). Falla, who has offered to write the music for the company's performances, is obviously thinking big, telling Lorca that he can get both Stravinsky and Ravel involved in the project and that the company should plan to tour Europe and Latin America.[56] Lorca is clearly delighted, calling the project the 'dream of my youth' and talking excitedly about it in many of the letters he wrote over the following months, when he was also heavily involved in the *cante jondo* preparations.

In the end, nothing would come of these plans. But Falla and Lorca would work together on a one-off puppet performance that took place at 3 p.m. on Twelfth Night, 5 January 1923, in the García Lorca family home in Granada. Despite the domestic nature of the performance – it was put on for the delectation of Lorca's younger sister and her closest friend – it is difficult to overestimate its significance for both men and also for the expert puppet maker and set designer, Hermenegildo Lanz, who worked closely with them. Lorca adapted two works for the event, Cervantes' *entremés* (farcical interlude) *Los dos habladores* (The Two Talkers) and the thirteenth-century mystery play *El misterio de los Reyes Magos* (The Mystery of the Wise Men), and also wrote one of his own, *La niña que riega la albahaca y el príncipe preguntón* (The Girl Who Waters the Basil and the Nosy Prince). Although nowhere near as long or as complex as *The Tragicomedy*, this last work tells the story of a love affair between a poor shoemaker's daughter and a prince, and once again displays the best puppet theatre effects, including lavish costumes and sets, knockabout comedy and the use of disguises, while also incorporating more lyrical and even mysterious elements, such as the presence onstage in the climactic scene of the sun tree and the moon tree (which also reappear in the backdrop decoration for *The Mystery of the Wise Men*).

The main significance of the event, however, lies in its collaborative nature and in the fact that it allowed Lorca to bring together his

Puppet show at Lorca's home, Granada, 5 January 1923.

literary, dramatic, musical and artistic interests, evidence of which is scattered around present-day Granada. Falla chose and orchestrated the music, which included traditional *villancicos* (carols), arrangements of medieval or traditional songs by Pedrell and Luis Romeu and pieces by Debussy, Albéniz and Ravel for *The Girl Who Waters the Basil* and *The Mystery*, and, for *The Two Talkers*, the Spanish première of Stravinsky's *L'Histoire du soldat* (The Soldier's Tale, 1918). Lorca clearly worked closely with Falla in the preparation of both the plays themselves and the musical accompaniment. The annotated edition of the medieval play *Auto de los Reyes Magos* that he drew upon to create the text for *The Mystery* belonged to Falla's library, which is currently housed in the Falla Archive in Granada, and the score that Falla produced for his orchestration of Pedrell's version of 'Españoleta' for *The Girl*, which is also kept in the archive, shows how the composer has added both repeated phrases and silences in order to underscore the dialogue and choreography of Lorca's play.

Hermenegildo Lanz, meanwhile, carved and painted the expressive wooden heads and created the colourful and flowing costumes for the puppets that would appear in *The Two Talkers* and *The Girl* (and are still kept in Granada by his grandson Enrique Lanz, also a master puppeteer), while he sought inspiration for the cut-out puppets that he devised for *The Mystery* in the beautiful Codex Granatensis that is kept in the library of the University of Granada. It is likely that Lorca helped Lanz with his research into this medieval text, which he describes in loving detail in a talk he gave in Fuente Vaqueros in September 1931 and from which the motifs of the sun tree and the moon tree are taken,[57] but what is sure is that he worked some of the glove puppets during the performance itself and also the Cristobica (Cristobita) puppet, who, armed with his billy club, entertained (and terrorized) the audience during the intervals. Lorca also played an important role in the preparation of the theatre backdrops, some of which are now displayed as paintings in the Huerta de San Vicente (the Lorca museum and former family home located just to the southwest of the city centre). There has been some controversy over the authorship of these lusciously painted panels, which represent an Andalusian square with church and fountain (for *The Two Talkers*) and a patio or garden scene and an interior (for *The Girl*). There is little doubt that the now-disappeared *Mystery* landscape, with its magical sun tree and moon tree, was the work of Lanz alone but, despite the programme-invitation that was created for the event (almost definitely by Lorca himself) declaring that the other backdrops were 'painted by the poet Federico García Lorca', it seems more likely that they were in fact the product of a close collaboration between the poet and the puppeteer and set designer. Their importance as far as Lorca is concerned lies in the fact that they offer some of the very earliest signs of his cultivation of the visual arts: indeed, the strong lines and the schematic and poetically naïve style of his later drawings and paintings can already be found in these backdrops that owe so much to the genius of Hermenegildo Lanz.

The Twelfth Night event held a special significance for Falla and Lanz, who treated it as an opportunity to try out some collaborative ideas that would feed into the Paris premiere, in June 1923, of Falla's one-act puppet opera *El retablo de Maese Pedro* (Master Peter's Puppet Show). For Lorca, it was a chance to immerse himself in the rich world of puppet theatre, both the more knockabout Cristobital tradition and the more delicate and lyrical world of the cut-out figures that Lanz created for *The Mystery*. He made use of his skills as a poet and a musician when writing or adapting the scripts for the plays and collaborating with Falla on the orchestration, but he simultaneously opened himself up to other artistic worlds, those of painting, set designing and, of course, puppeteering. Indeed, this intense immersion in the world of puppet theatre furnished Lorca with an intimate knowledge of all aspects of puppetry: how both glove and cut-out puppets are made and manipulated, how they look, feel and move; how puppet theatres and their sets are designed, constructed and worked; how puppet movement is choreographed and how the puppets interact with their surroundings; how voice, sounds and music are used to punctuate, underscore or offset that movement and interaction; and how the puppeteer relates not only to his puppets but, through them, to his audience. Although he would soon leave the world of puppets behind, only to return to it for a brief moment in 1934, he would draw on all he learned at this time when writing many of the plays and even much of the poetry that would help to make his name over the following years.

Lorca's long stretch in Granada was coming to an end. He had been very busy over these eighteen months, not just with his poems, his *cante jondo* and puppet projects but, to the joy and amazement of his parents, with his studies. He had resumed his law degree in Granada after his failed attempt to engage with an arts degree in Madrid and, by dint of coaching and with a little help from his friends, managed to place himself within sight of the finishing line. His brother Francisco, who was studying the same degree at the same time, provides a good deal of insight into the process.[58] Lorca had already completed some of the easier subjects during his earlier attempt at the degree but now could count on two very important allies in the faculty of law in Granada: his old mentor Fernando de los Ríos and a brilliant economics professor by the name of Agustín Viñuales (1881–1959). Viñuales knew full well that Lorca was both an outstanding writer and a terrible student and so convinced the rest of the faculty, according to Francisco, that Lorca's studies should be assessed using criteria other than traditional academic ones. Francisco was able to coach his brother, and the academic examiners took care of everything else. The only potential obstacle to Viñuales's plan was Fernando de los Ríos, whose professional scruples might have entered into conflict with his obvious loyalty towards Lorca. The great professor and (like Viñuales) future Minister of the Republic dealt with the situation by allowing the oral exam on constitutional law to turn into a discussion on Plato, one of Lorca's favourite philosophers. Lorca earned a simple pass in that subject and in all the others and finally completed his degree in January 1923.

Lorca's academic 'success' provoked much celebration in the García Lorca household and much envy in other quarters, not least in the family of Federico García's distant relative Alejandro Roldán Benavides. As the historians Miguel Caballero and Pilar Góngora have shown, the destiny of these two men had been intimately linked ever since they had quarrelled over the sugar beet factory that Roldán and his partners had been forced to build on Federico senior's land just outside Asquerosa in 1909.[59] Thereafter, Alejandro Roldán seemed to play a strange game of catch-up with Federico García. He moved his family from the Vega to Granada just months after his relative had moved his, and he tried to emulate Federico García in 1917 by becoming a councillor on the Granada town council, only to have his election declared null and void due to charges of political violence and voting irregularities. Alejandro Roldán, who was a member of the Conservative Party, seems to have blamed his old rival Federico García, of the Liberal Party, for his political failure and disgrace. And then his son, Horacio Roldán, would study the exact same degree course as Federico and Francisco García Lorca at the University of Granada, only to be awarded a pass degree in October 1923 while his strict contemporary Francisco passed with distinction – and Federico, of course, had been more or less gifted his degree by Viñuales, Fernando de los Ríos and others the previous January. Unlike Lorca, Horacio Roldán would end up working as a lawyer and would use his position and influence over the coming years to support right-wing political movements. Their paths would cross once again in August 1936, shortly before Lorca's death.

As some of his letters from the second half of 1922 show, especially those to his old Rinconcillo friend Melchor Fernández Almagro, Lorca was champing at the bit and longing to flee Granada. He wants to fly away, he says, to travel, perhaps to Paris, but, above all, to return to Madrid, the only place he can get published.[60] And yet he had also told Melchor just a few months earlier that he found the literary atmosphere and poetic 'decomposition' in Madrid to be quite repugnant and that he dreamt instead of a future dawn that could bring with it the 'ineffable emotion of primitive skies'.[61] In a letter to the guitarist and composer Regino Sáinz de la Maza, also written in February 1922, he acknowledges just how much he and his work owe to Granada and adds that he has been doing things in his home town which, due to 'their Andalusian core and special rhythms', he wouldn't be able to do in the capital: Granada, he says, has given him new visions and filled his heart with unexpected emotions.[62] Lorca therefore returned to Madrid in February 1923 with both a sense of relief and a sense of purpose. He had served an invaluable literary apprenticeship in Granada and would over the following years draw deeply on that time as he produced the works that would finally make his name.

four

Madrid, Granada and Cadaqués: Seeking Success, 1923−7

fter serving his literary apprenticeship over the previous five or
six years, Lorca devoted himself from 1923 onwards to establishing his reputation as a writer. This would prove to be an arduous
and often frustrating process that would not reach its climax until 1928,
around the time of his thirtieth birthday. It would take place mainly in
Granada and Madrid, the two geographical and psychological poles
that he often tended to associate, respectively, with artistic inspiration
and artistic opportunity, although his evolution as a poet and a playwright over these years would also owe a good deal to his two visits, in
spring 1925 and early summer 1927, to Catalonia. There his close friendship with Salvador Dalí and other members of the Catalan avant-garde
opened up new artistic possibilities for Lorca, encouraging him, among
other things, to cultivate further his interest in the visual arts.

In February 1923 Lorca returned to Madrid and the Residencia de
Estudiantes for the first time in over eighteen months. He arrived with
his brother, Francisco, who was about to start his PhD. But if Lorca
thought that his own recent academic success and the presence of his
brother would be enough to keep his parents off his back, he was mis-
taken. The joint letters that the two of them sent home make clear that
they were being required to give a regular account of their activities in
the capital. Their father visited them in March. And in April there was
yet another flashpoint when Federico and Francisco were forced to
respond to an angry, unsigned letter in which their parents called them
'shameless' and 'ungrateful' for not having written for several weeks.[1] It
is obvious that Federico (much more than Francisco) was being kept on
a tight leash and that the parental permission to stay in Madrid could

easily be revoked. It also looks pretty clear that the regularity of Lorca's stays in 1923 and 1924 – which saw him spend the period between late winter and July in Madrid, the summer and autumn in Asquerosa and Granada, and then a further month or so in Madrid before Christmas back in Granada – was the result of strenuous negotiations between the parents and their oldest child.

Lorca's relief and excitement at being back in the Residencia are quite clear from his letters. He met up once again with Pepín Bello, Buñuel and the others, and he also made the acquaintance of an eighteen-year-old Catalan art student, Salvador Dalí, who had arrived at the Residencia the previous autumn. Dalí's long hair and Romantic clothes, including a velvet jacket, a cravat, a cape and often short trousers with stockings, offered a colourful contrast with the fashionably coiffured hair, golf jackets and English suits of most of the other students at the Residencia, and he quickly became the butt of their jokes.[2] But his extreme timidity, driest of dry sense of humour and, above all, his skill as a painter and his cultivation of the latest artistic styles, especially Cubism, soon attracted the attention of Pepín and Buñuel and, on his return, of Lorca also. Thus started what was probably the most important and at the same time turbulent of all of Lorca's artistic relationships, one which would help him forge ever stronger links in his own work between painting and drawing, on the one hand, and poetry and drama on the other.

The years 1923 and 1924 were the halcyon days of this young Residencia generation, which would soon disperse, with Pepín taking up his first job in the summer of 1924 and Buñuel leaving for Paris in search of artistic adventures in January 1925. It was a time of high spirits as these young men tried to make their student days last as long as possible. Pepín and others remember the endless get-togethers that took place in their rooms (often over a pot of tea), Lorca's piano recitals, and the many word games that they all loved to play (some of which made their way into Lorca's poetry). There were also frequent visits to the cafés, cinemas, theatres and museums, especially the Prado, where they would share their enthusiasm for Mantegna, Bosch, Velázquez and Vermeer. It was at this time that Buñuel set up the Order of Toledo, which bestowed fictitious noble titles on all its members and organized weekends away in the ancient city, where Lorca and the others would stay at old hostelries, eat, drink and make merry, and visit the literary and artistic sites, including the house of El Greco. While most of those around him were trying, with varying degrees of enthusiasm, to complete their studies, Lorca threw

Lorca and friends including Pepín Bello (second right) taking tea in the Residencia de Estudiantes, Madrid, 1924.

himself into his writing. These years – especially, it must be said, the summer and autumn months spent back in Granada – were immensely busy ones for Lorca, who was working on three main fronts: his poetry, an operatic project with Falla, and his theatre.

Lorca was working concurrently on three poetic projects. While he continued to put the finishing touches to *Poem of the Deep Song*, he was also writing two other collections: *Suites*, which he wrote mainly between late 1920 and August 1923, and *Canciones* (Songs), some of which dates back to 1921, although the majority belongs to the period between 1923 and 1925. At certain moments over this period, Lorca played with the idea of bringing all three collections out together in a single edition. In the end, *Songs* would be published first, in May 1927, with *Poem of the Deep Song* following it in May 1931, while the multiple manuscripts of the *Suites* were only collected together and published in full in 1983.

There are clear stylistic as well as chronological differences between *Suites* and *Songs*. As its title suggests, *Suites* is made up of some 39 short sequences of poems, each of which is devoted to a specific natural or man-made phenomenon (sea, moon, river, water, wind, night, dawn, sunset, shadows, mirrors, fountains, watches, gardens and so on). Just like

Lorca with Salvador Dalí and Pepín Bello, Madrid, 1925.

musical or painterly suites, they offer different movements or variations on their central theme, and, as if to emphasize the significance of their overall title, Lorca once again, as in his earliest poems, makes full use of musical and painterly references and effects. But there are major differences with his early verse too, as can be seen in the pared-down, almost symbolic treatment of the landscape and the fact that the poems and the line-lengths they employ are now almost invariably short. Lorca is moving here, as he was also doing in *Poem of the Deep Song* and would continue to do in *Songs*, towards a type of poetry that is both more song-like and more enigmatic than much of what he has written to date.

Many of the sequences in *Suites* act almost like riddles, with each poem offering certain aspects or characteristics of the object or phenomenon that is named in the sequence's title. Each of the six poems that make up 'Álbum blanco' (White Album), for example, conjures up different shades of white by referring, in turn, to a cherry tree raining its blossom onto the ground; the river god Kaystros, with the full moon gently sleeping on his wings; cloud-shrouded mountains that seem to long to fly; snow that falls like clothes discarded by the stars; the arrival of dawn, which is seen as the white comb of a golden cockerel; and the blank pages of an album left behind by a young woman who has died.[3] Sometimes, an individual poem within one of the sequences can become even more riddle-like still and, in its compressed language and carefully balanced structure, take on the appearance and dynamics of a Japanese haiku, a type of poetry that particularly attracted Lorca at this time and reminded him of certain types of Andalusian song, including *cante jondo*.[4] Such concise and gnomic verse marks this collection out from Lorca's earlier poetry, although its most impressive trait remains its cultivation of striking metaphors, such as those, scattered throughout the collection, which enable something as elusive as the wind to become a visible, palpable, tangible presence. Through the use of personification and the inversion or transference of meaning, Lorca allows us to feel how the breeze can be wavy like young girls' hair or, when it dies back, become lifeless and wrinkled.[5] It can be a serpent wending its way through a grove of trees or a hand that caresses the very face of space itself.[6] The night, which hangs from the sky, can oscillate in the wind, while the black poplar trees, moved by the breeze, send ripples through the gauze of sound – an effect that any visitor to the poplar groves in the Vega will readily recognize.[7]

Songs, the collection that Lorca focused on principally from the summer of 1923 onwards, when his main work on the *Suites* had come to an end, is also made up of short poems with extremely short lines: although the occasional hendecasyllable makes its appearance, as does the octosyllable of the *romance* (ballad) form, the majority of the poems make use of shorter lines still, while some lines are filled simply with single words made up of one, two or three syllables. The emphasis in this collection, as its title announces, is on the songfulness of the poems, and its main characteristics are elegance, grace, wit and a certain playfulness that is often childlike in nature. Indeed, the section entitled 'Canciones para niños' (Songs for Children), dedicated to the children of some of Lorca's friends and fellow poets, including Pedro Salinas and Jorge

Guillén, contains a series of delightful songs that seem ready-made to accompany a child's games or to act as lullabies.[8]

Other sections explore Lorca's influences, past and present. In 'Tres retratos con sombra' (Three Portraits with Shadow), he celebrates the three artists who had probably done most to forge his sensibility as a young writer and musician, namely Paul Verlaine, Juan Ramón Jiménez and Claude Debussy. He associates Verlaine with Bacchus, in recognition of the French poet's Saturnalian reputation and verse, but emphasizes above all the musicality of his poetry, with Lorca's reference to 'La canción / que nunca diré' (The song / I will never say) hinting both at emotional truths that will remain unsaid and at the song-like beauty of Verlaine's *Romances sans paroles* (Songs Without Words, 1874), a work that had captivated him as a teenager. Juan Ramón is associated with Venus, but Venus as a symbol not of out-and-out sensuality but rather of a more abstract type of beauty, which Lorca describes in terms of a whiteness and a light that cause the artist to search after the infinite. And Debussy and his music are associated with Narcissus and take Lorca straight back to the Vega, where the young poet's shadow walks along the irrigation channels and opens itself up to the colours, sounds and light that surround it; the poet then sees himself as a child who gazes deep into the river in search of a rose, of his own eyes and his own self, all the time running the risk of falling in and losing himself forever.[9]

In the section 'Eros con bastón' (Eros with a Walking Stick), dedicated to Pepín Bello, one finds a more adult type of playfulness that very much belongs to the Residencia de Estudiantes. Indeed, Ian Gibson characterizes the whole of *Songs* as Lorca's Residencia collection,[10] capturing as it does the humorous and sometimes mischievous spirit of Lorca and his student friends, with their love of puns, of wordplay and of in-jokes. The opening poem in this section describes a mysterious moment of misunderstanding that is characterized mock-dramatically as a 'Susto en el comedor' (Fright in the Dining Hall) and ends with an inventive but deliberately overwrought image of the type so beloved of the boarders in the Residencia: '(Grulla dormida la tarde, / puso en tierra la otra pata)', or '(The afternoon, a sleeping crane, / placed its other leg on the ground)'.[11] The following six poems take the form of short erotic vignettes featuring archetypal female objects of desire – Lucía, Virginia, Carmen, an unnamed French woman, Lolita and Leonarda – and employing, alongside some more lyrical and inventive moments, the voyeurism, sexism and even cruelty typical of certain types of male song (all of which begs the

Lorca, photograph taken by Luis Buñuel, 1925.

question of how far Lorca felt obliged to adapt to the very masculine atmosphere he encountered in the Residencia).[12] But the collection as a whole will not be remembered for these uncharacteristically misogynistic moments but rather for the multiple and ingenious ways in which Lorca celebrates the power of song and for the evocative precision of the language he uses. As he seems to recognize in one of the final poems, 'De otro modo' (In Another Way), his very essence as a human being and as a poet is wrapped up in song, and song that is so song-like that his poems actually end up being 'estribillos de estribillos' (refrains of refrains).[13] And his frequent use of lines made up of just one word reveals his conviction that poetry can equally rely on the most complex of metaphors as on the expressive force of a single word, which, once located in its proper place within an overall song, can be made to resonate with great power and suggestion.

While Lorca continued throughout this period to compose and refine his poems, he was also busy with his dramatic writings. Between late 1922 or early 1923 – around the time of their Twelfth Night spectacle – and the end of 1924, he frequently spoke with Falla about not only their puppet project but their collaboration on a short, one-act comic opera entitled *Lola la comedianta* (Lola the Actress). Lorca worked on the libretto for this opera in fits and starts over these years but never managed to finish it; the version that was published in 1981 was made up of what seem to be eleven complete scenes and Lorca's own description of the contents of the final three.[14] The story, which Lorca tells with consummate economy, is set in a wayside inn in Andalusia and focuses on the meeting between a marquis, who has recently returned from a period of exile in England (most probably in the 1820s) and a woman and a man who at first sight appear to be an aristocratic lady and her coachman. In reality, the lady, Lola, is an actress and the coachman a poet, and the two are newlyweds who are spending their honeymoon dressing up and creating comical situations or imbroglios worthy of Cervantes's *Novelas ejemplares* (Exemplary Novels, 1613) or of the nineteenth-century *costumbrista* novels (local novels of manners and customs) of Lorca's fellow Andalusian Pedro Antonio de Alarcón (1833–1891). In the course of this short libretto, Lola presents herself to the marquis in the guise of a beautiful aristocrat who steals his heart, a Gypsy woman who reads his palm, and a Cuban lady who asks him to take revenge on a man who has offended against her honour. On each occasion, Lola sings a fulsome aria: a *romance* for the seduction scene; a Gypsy song for the palm-reading; and a *habanera* for the story told by the Cuban woman. The tone throughout is light – the couple deceive the marquis for amusement rather than material gain, and the only darker element is the marquis's frustrated desire (or, if he is to be believed, broken heart). Lorca obviously has fun playing with the conventions not only of opera itself but of *costumbrista* literature – to the point in fact of allowing Lola to paint a highly stereotypical portrait of the superstitious character and colourful language of a Gypsy woman (some such stereotypes will also find their way into Lorca's later work, *Romancero gitano* (Gypsy Ballads)).

Falla was obviously very taken with the idea of having Lorca as his librettist, and one of the surviving manuscripts of the libretto that Lorca sent to him includes some notes recording his initial thoughts about the music he planned to write. Like Lorca, Falla makes clear that he wishes to parody certain aspects of Italian opera, noting down, for example, that the song in which the marquis expresses his desperate longings for the supposed aristocratic lady (a song which Lorca has sprinkled with words in Italian) should be sung in the style of an Italian cavatina and that 'All the nonsense the marquis says and does must be translated into musical *nonsense*, with lots of roulades, scales, arpeggios, syncopation, lots of yes, yes, yes, ah, ah, ah!, no, no, no. Dialogue with flute, clarinet, etc. Parody of Italian accompaniment.'[15] He also makes it obvious that what has truly attracted him to the project is the possibility, once again, of joining forces with Lorca in the recuperation of Andalusian folklore and folk music. Little surprise, therefore, that he should note down that flamenco and *cante jondo* forms such as the *caña*, the *soleá* and the *siguiriya* should be used both in the overture and for Lola's Gypsy palm-reading song, or that he thinks that the coachman's dialogue should be delivered 'in the Andalusian style', while the Marquis's should be in Italian recitative.'[16]

Lorca seemed at first to drag his feet as far as this project was concerned. In a letter sent to Madrid on 11 March 1923, his mother exhorts him to work hard and not forget his commitments, especially those with Falla, who, she says, had expected to receive the manuscript of *Lola the Actress* before Lorca's departure for the capital a few weeks earlier: you should not forget, Doña Vicenta adds, rather pointedly, that Falla needs to make money with the opera – unlike you, who has a father who provides for your every need.[17] Lorca's own letters reveal that he was hard at work on *Lola* in May 1923, had meetings with Falla about it during August and September of that year, and was still hoping for Falla to start writing the music in July and November 1924.[18] But Falla never did get round to doing so, and the project finally petered out. Some commentators believe that the reason lay in the Catholic and somewhat puritanical Falla's unease with the morality of a tale in which two people play so cruelly with the feelings of another,[19] but others, such as Piero Menarini, think that the problem lay rather in the fact that Lorca provided Falla not so much with a libretto as with a verse drama, and one which, moreover, was already full of a good deal of musical direction.[20] Whatever the truth, it is certainly a pity that this artistic collaboration did not in the end bear fruit, although Lorca would clearly transfer much of what he learned in the process (about the role of acting and deception in human relationships, about plotting, humour and parody, and about the use of poetry and music in drama) to later projects, including *La zapatera prodigiosa* (The Shoemaker's Prodigious Wife).

Another reason for the gradual abandonment of *Lola* might lie in Lorca's urgent determination to succeed in the theatre (the memory of the *The Butterfly's Evil Spell* fiasco was without doubt still fresh in his mind), and, in May and June 1923, he makes his first references to a theatrical project, which, for better or for worse, would consume much of his energy over the following four years until it finally premiered in June 1927: *Mariana Pineda*.[21] Like most *granadinos*, Lorca was very aware of the story of Mariana Pineda, a local noblewoman who had been garrotted in 1831 for having supported the liberal cause against the tyrannical King Ferdinand VII. Ever since he was a boy, he had heard popular songs (*coplas*) and *romances* telling the story of this heroic woman who had embroidered a liberal flag and also resisted the advances of Ramón Pedrosa, the king's violently repressive judge and representative in Granada. It is significant that, for his first full-blown dramatic project, Lorca should turn to his native city and also to one of its most famous offspring. Although he told his friend Melchor Fernández Almagro in September 1923 that he was scared of muddying his delicate (literary) memories of this 'fair-haired and martyred widow',[22] he was obviously committed to the idea of authoring a new version of this local legend and, by doing so, of exploring at the same time his complex feelings about Granada itself.

Lorca gives a first idea of how he visualizes the work and its heroine in the aforementioned letter to Melchor. Although the background of the play will necessarily be political, he says, the story itself is a magnificent Andalusian love story, and Mariana is a passionate woman, even a woman possessed. She surrenders to love for the sake of love itself, while those around her, including her lover Pedro, are obsessed with liberty.

Despite the fact that she is seen by many as a martyr for liberty, Lorca, in a description that seems to announce the drama and tragedy of many of his future female dramatic protagonists, characterizes her instead as a '*victim* of her own heart, which is in love and has grown mad'.[23] The work that Lorca eventually wrote between September 1923 and January 1925 bears this description out. It is Lorca's most Romantic play and focuses on a woman who renounces everything – her interest in her children by her first marriage, her freedom, her life – for the love of a man who has decided to devote himself body and soul to the clandestine struggle for liberty. In this sense, Mariana's politics is love itself, and all of Pedro's talk of liberty only has meaning for her insofar as it can create the conditions in which her love for him can thrive. Indeed, she even tells Pedro during their first encounter in the play that, when he is close to her, she is capable of loving everyone, even the king himself and her principal tormentor Pedrosa.[24]

What is clear is that Lorca is not interested in writing a political play. It is not that he is unaware of the political significance of the story he is telling, and he certainly creates a stark contrast between the idealistic motivations of the liberal conspirators and the base motivations of Pedrosa. But his real interest lies elsewhere: in Mariana herself, in the depiction of Granada, and in the artistic properties of the work. In fact, Lorca's relationship with his play reveals a good deal about his relationship with politics itself during this turbulent moment in Spain's history. He starts writing it in earnest in September 1923, around the time of General Primo de Rivera's *coup d'état*, which brought the period of Restoration politics to an end, shored up the position of King Alfonso XIII, and established a military dictatorship that would last until 1931. The *coup* and the dictatorship divided Spanish intellectuals and writers, with some, like Unamuno, violently opposing Primo de Rivera and even suffering banishment and exile, and others, like Ortega y Gasset, deciding to cut the general some slack to see if he could manage Spain more successfully than the political parties had done. Lorca himself, like most writers of his generation, remained silent on this matter – at least, as we shall see, until the very final years of the dictatorship – but by late 1924 he had obviously become strongly aware of the fact that *Mariana Pineda*, set against the background of a liberal struggle against a tyrannical monarch, would more than likely fall foul of the censors.

In a letter sent to his family from Madrid in November 1924, Lorca makes one of his infrequent references to current affairs, acknowledging that recent events, including the writer Vicente Blasco Ibáñez's anti-dictatorship publications in Paris and the supposed Anarchist invasion of Spain at Vera de Bidasoa (actually, unbeknownst to Lorca, a counter-propaganda event orchestrated by the dictatorship itself), made it very unlikely that the play could be staged in the near future. He expresses his frustration, as well as his determination that preparations for the staging should continue, but then adds that, contrary to the desires of many, including his old mentor and Socialist politician Fernando de los Ríos, the play does not and should not aim for a political success: it is a work of pure art, he says, a tragedy without any political interest, and its success must be poetic in nature.[25] Lorca is obviously resisting the pressure from Fernando de los Ríos and others (including very possibly Manuel Azaña, the intellectual and future President of the Second Republic, who heard Lorca read his play twice over the following years) to make *Mariana Pineda* into an anti-dictatorship (and anti-monarchical) tract. He is adamant that the play, as he had told Melchor back in September 1923, should be more of a madrigal than an ode.[26]

Mariana Pineda is indeed an extended love poem, with its main character placed firmly and agonizingly at the centre of its three acts, suffering as she does from intense anxiety during the course of the first two before descending into quasi-madness in the third. It is in many ways a very late example of a high Romantic play, and its intense lyricism is directly reminiscent of the work of nineteenth-century poets and dramatists such as the Duque de Rivas (1791–1865), Juan Eugenio Hartzenbusch (1806–1880) and, above all, José Zorrilla. The poetry can at times be a little pedestrian and even hackneyed, although Lorca consistently hits a more original note in the final act when capturing Mariana's mixture of desperate attachment to the world and growing sense of detachment from life:

Porque ya estoy muerta.
. . .
Pero el mundo se me acerca,
las piedras, el agua, el aire,
¡comprendo que estaba ciega!
. . .
Este silencio me pesa
mágicamente. Se agranda
como un techo de violetas,

y otras veces finge en mí
una larga cabellera.[27]

Because I am already dead.
. . .
But the world draws close to me,
the stones, the water, the air,
I realize I was blind!
. . .
This silence weighs on me
magically. It grows larger
like a ceiling of violets,
and at other times it feigns in me
long locks of hair.

Alongside Mariana, Lorca is also interested in providing a portrait of the character of his native city, and a pretty ambivalent one it is too. He takes on one of its favourite legends and indeed shows the heroic qualities of the central protagonist, who will until the end remain faithful to her ideals or, rather, to her feelings towards her lover, but at the same time he does nothing to hide her monomania or the fact that her love for Pedro seems to eclipse everything else in her life, even her feelings and duties towards her children. Pedro and his co-conspirators, meanwhile, are not the brave and caring idealists they first appear to be. One of them, Conspirador 4, who, perhaps significantly, given Lorca's own father's origins, is presented as a rich peasant, is not quite as courageous or impulsive as the others and resists the idea of standing up to Pedrosa, while Fernando, the eighteen-year-old who is in love with Mariana and sees Pedro as a rival, begs her at the end to inform on the liberals and thus save her own life – so as to be able to spend it with him. Even Pedro, as Fernando informs Mariana at the climax, has chosen the relative safety of life in exile in England over the danger of attempting to rescue her, news that serves to push Mariana even further into madness. Bit by bit, therefore, both the clear ideological contrasts that lie at the heart of the original Mariana Pineda legend and the supposed heroism of the liberal conspirators become blurred and are replaced with the moving, Shakespearean spectacle of a delirious woman who has been sacrificed as much by an uncaring lover as by a despicable enemy.

Yet, while the play can be seen to be critical of the inhabitants of Granada, whatever their ideological leanings, it still offers a hymn of praise to the city of Granada itself, which is transformed, alongside Mariana, into the central protagonist. It is clear from the stage directions that Lorca enjoys dressing his characters up in typical Andalusian, and specifically Granadan, garb, from the mantillas and carnations worn by some of the young women and Mariana's own brightly coloured dresses and ornamental combs to the velvet hat, embroidered jacket and long leather gaiters of the rich peasant. He adds even more local colour by including, in the first act, a long description of a bullfight that has just taken place in Ronda and, in the second, a popular nineteenth-century song about smugglers. Lorca is providing us with a self-consciously *costumbrista* version of Mariana's legend that is full of local dress, manners and types, although he is also clearly aware that such reliance on typicality could potentially undermine the power of the drama, as can be seen in two of the stage directions in the climactic scene in the second act (when Mariana confronts Pedrosa), both of which exhort the director and actors to avoid caricature and exaggeration.[28] In the end, though, he will avoid the pitfalls and clichés of literary *costumbrismo* through the seemingly paradoxical device of intensifying, rather than attenuating, the *costumbrista* and ultimately artificial qualities of the play. This he achieves through drawing on the essentially visual and plastic nature of his dramatic imagination: Lorca will not simply place his characters in colourful regional dress; he will also insert them into a highly wrought artistic setting that clearly draws upon local Granadan traditions. As early as September 1923, in his letter to Melchor Fernández Almagro, he had said that he visualized *Mariana Pineda* as a 'processional drama . . . like an old Madonna with her arch of cherubim',[29] revealing how he looked both to Renaissance and Baroque painting and to the aesthetics of the Easter processions in Granada when attempting to define the feel and look of his future play and of its dual protagonist (Mariana-Granada). In the end, he will give form to this essentially religious conception of the play mainly in the final act, which takes place in a convent garden, with its Arabic arches, fountains, cypresses and myrtle bushes: we also see, set in a niche in the wall, a statue of Our Lady of Sorrows, surrounded by an immense arch made up of yellow and silver-coloured paper roses, with her heart, just like Mariana's, punctured by multiple daggers.[30]

While he obviously conceived the play in terms of the religious art and iconography of his home town and region, he would eventually draw on another artistic object when thinking about its overall shape and atmosphere, namely the *estampa* (a term that can mean a picture or illustration in a book or a card displaying a religious image). He turns each of the three main acts of the play, both literally and metaphorically, into an individual *estampa*: the first of a white-walled room in Mariana's house, hung with quinces; the second of the main room in her house, with its period furniture and fittings; and the third of the convent garden, with its arches, fountains, trees and statues. Even the short Prologue, in which we watch some girls singing the popular *romance* telling of the execution of Mariana Pineda, takes place in front of a curtain showing an *estampa* of an old Moorish arch and the Plaza Bibarrambla (Bib-Rambla) set in a yellowing frame.[31] This emphasis on illustration (and more specifically, as the stage direction at the start of the second act says, lithography[32]) reveals how Lorca thinks out and plans his literary works in fundamentally visual ways and also how he conceived of each act in this particular play in terms of a static scene that gradually comes to life. But there is more still, since each *estampa* offers a black-and-white illustration onto which Lorca can then apply the colours that will help to create and carry the emotion of the play. The *estampa* reproduced on the curtain in the Prologue is coloured blue, green, yellow, pink and sky blue, and then Mariana will appear in a light mauve dress against the white walls of the first act, in a light yellow dress against the greys, whites and ivory colours of the room in the second, and in a white dress against the riot of colours offered by the convent garden in the third. And, finally, the intensity of these colours is controlled by that most pervasive yet elusive of presences in the play, that is, the special light of Granada itself. The first *estampa* is illuminated by the light of an autumn evening, the light, we are told, that takes so long to yield to night. The second *estampa* takes place at night and therefore relies on the greyish-white tones of the room itself. And the third *estampa* shows us the golden light of evening and then the strange and intensifying pinks, greens and oranges of a Granadan dusk, as the light of day bleeds away from the convent garden while Mariana gradually loses control of her sanity and her life. The overall effect is a symphony of light and colour, the work of a true painter-dramatist.

———

Lorca worked hard on his three poetic projects, his libretto and *Mariana Pineda* over these years and, from July 1924 onwards, also started mentioning in his correspondence other works that he was beginning to write, including two further plays (*The Shoemaker's Prodigious Wife* and *Amor de Don Perlimplín con Belisa en su jardín* (The Love of Don Perlimplín for Belisa in his Garden)) and the occasional Gypsy ballad. These were obviously busy times for Lorca, but they were unsettled and anxious ones too. Most of the moments of crisis we know about seem to take place in Asquerosa and Granada, where he felt more caught in the web of convention and expectation and dwelled most obsessively on matters relating to both his sexuality and his future prospects. In Asquerosa in July and August 1923, for example, he wrote the two final sequences of poems for *Suites*, the incomplete (and overlapping) 'En el jardín de las toronjas de luna' (In the Garden of the Moon-grapefruits) and 'En el bosque de las toronjas de luna' (In the Forest of the Moon-grapefruits), both of which are preceded by prologues that announce an impending journey away from his family into what he calls in the latter's prologue an ecstatic world containing 'all my possibilities and lost landscapes' and in letters 'the garden of possibilities, the garden of what is not but could (and sometimes) should have been'.[33] The overwhelming atmosphere of these poems is that of a dream, as if the poet is sleepwalking through a world of forking paths, virtual realities and alternative existences; indeed, his reference in the prologues to his efforts to overcome common sense and to find a world that lies beyond a mirror,[34] as well as their obvious allusions to Lewis Carroll, imply that he is undertaking a journey into the deepest recesses of his unconscious mind. But the most striking and moving moments in the two sequences are those that seem to express regret: for the family wedding ring that he feels obliged to reject, for the woman who will not be his (and indeed is never actually born), and for the children they will never have – children who will, however, continue to run after him and ask him for his help.[35]

Lorca would carry these regrets with him for the rest of his life and would also explore them through some of the childless characters who appear in his later drama. That they are a response to, or rather have become intensified by, family pressures becomes clear from the letters he sends from Asquerosa and Granada, especially those that date from the summer and early autumn of both 1925 and 1926. Over the previous two years, Lorca had been allowed to spend time in Madrid just before Christmas and to return to the capital once again in January, but things became more restricted in 1925, with Lorca being required to stay at home from July that year until the following March, a pattern that would be repeated again the following year. These enforced and prolonged stays with his family brought about increasingly intense crises during which Lorca lost confidence both in his writings and in the possibility of establishing himself as a professional artist. In his letters from August and September 1925 to Benjamín Palencia and Melchor Fernández Almagro, he says that he is going through an exceptionally difficult time, one that has made him realize that his poetry and his life are mere pastimes or hobbies and that he has no choice but to find himself a proper job (all of which sounds very much like the voice of his parents).[36] A year later, the situation seems to have worsened still, to the degree that he tells Jorge Guillén not only that he needs desperately to find a job (or perhaps spend some time as a lecturer in a foreign university) but that he wishes to get married, although he immediately reveals his confused state of mind by adding, first, that he doesn't think himself capable of doing such a thing and, second, that perhaps he should try nonetheless, as that would be the best way to bring his 'five senses' under control: 'Don't think', he concludes, 'that I am having a *relationship* with a girl, but might that not be imminent?'[37]

Lorca often talks in the letters of this time about his dislike of Granada,[38] where, as he rather cruelly tells his parents, the atmosphere is 'mortal' for his life and prospects and he fears that he will end up having his wings clipped and becoming just another provincial rich kid.[39] He talks constantly about getting away, of travelling abroad and, of course, of returning to Madrid. And yet he also knows that life in Madrid is not perfect either and frequently criticizes the dog-eat-dog atmosphere that dominates literary life there.[40] Moreover, as he tells Benjamín Palencia in August 1925,[41] it is very possible that the 'impure and stupid air of Madrid' is serving to undermine his ancient belief in fatalism, a profoundly Andalusian trait that he wishes to retain and indeed to explore (as he will do in *Gypsy Ballads* and his later plays). The only solution to this sense of disorientation seems to be a period spent in neither Granada nor Madrid, something that he finally achieves in April 1925 thanks to an invitation from Salvador Dalí.

Lorca's week or so at the Dalí family home next to the sea in Cadaqués was to have a profound effect on him and on his work. It is clear that the two men felt a deep attraction to each other. In his autobiography *Vida secreta* (Secret Life), published in 1942, Dalí refers to Lorca as poetry made flesh, bones, blood and fluids, and as a fire that he, Dalí, had attempted to dampen down with his own more controlled and anti-Faustian personality and aesthetics – so that he could then cook up his own work on the embers that were left behind.[42] These words bear witness to both the profound connection and the profound tensions that existed between the two men, tensions that were, at least in part, sexual in origin and nature. In an interview with Alain Bosquet in the 1960s, Dalí refers to a couple of occasions over these years (most probably in Madrid in 1926 and Cadaqués in 1927) when Lorca tried to initiate a physical relationship with him.[43] Dalí, who appears to have been struggling at the time with his own latent homosexual feelings,[44] was both pleased by Lorca's advances and resisted them – on the first occasion, he tells Bosquet rather callously and disturbingly, by inviting a fellow student at his art school, Margarita Manso, to take his place. According to Dalí, this was the first (and perhaps only) time that Lorca made love with a woman.[45] Such tensions would occasionally boil over, with Dalí both drawing attention to Lorca's profoundly jealous nature and confessing that the sight of Lorca's growing popularity among the Residencia group and his brilliance in the café *tertulias*, where he shone like a 'burning, crazy diamond', caused him too, for the one and only time in his life, to feel something akin to jealousy.[46]

For the moment, though, Easter in Cadaqués brought Lorca close to Dalí, to Dalí's family, especially his sister Ana María, and to the landscapes and traditions of Catalonia. It also exposed Lorca further to his friend's current aesthetic worldview, which, as Dalí's description of their relationship above suggests, was based on a rejection of passion and sentiment and an espousal of a cooler, more conceptual and Cubist-inspired perspective that focuses more on surfaces than on depths.[47] Dalí's painting of the time continued to play with multiple perspectives but also revealed a shift towards a more realistic depiction of human figures set against mainly coastal landscapes and the use of increasingly defined outlines and contours, as can be seen in two contrasting paintings that he would exhibit that autumn, namely his portrait of Ana María entitled *Muchacha en la ventana* (Young Woman at the Window, 1925) and the more Cubist work *Venus y marinero* (Venus and Sailor, 1925).

On his return to Asquerosa in the summer of 1925, Lorca's mind was still full of Catalonia and Dalí (which might help to explain the virulence of the emotional crisis he suffered at that time). His letters show a greater impatience with the representatives of convention and conformity, whom he now increasingly refers to by using a term coined by Pepín and often employed by Dalí, namely 'los putrefactos', or 'the putrid ones' (indeed, Dalí and he planned for some time to produce an illustrated book of that name). Under the spell of his friend, he also essays a new sort of writing in the form of short dramatic dialogues which, as he told Melchor in July 1925, are both 'immensely profound because they are so superficial' and more 'universal' than anything else he has written.[48] The most famous of these dialogues, 'El paseo de Buster Keaton' (Buster Keaton's Stroll), certainly shows Lorca focusing on the surface of things and also on objects or phenomena that are separated from their specific contexts and thereby take on a certain strangeness or unreality – all things that he had learned with Dalí. In a homage to Hollywood cinema and to Lorca's (and Dalí's and Buñuel's) favourite comedian, this dialogue exaggerates the incongruity at the heart of Keaton's humour and transforms it into a series of often grotesque scenes, as when Keaton kills his own children, and of surreal stage directions, which draw attention to cinema's ability to play with perspective (as when the landscape gets smaller when seen through the wheels of Keaton's bicycle), to stage the impossible (as when four seraphim are seen dancing among the flowers) or to effect strange metamorphoses (as when Buster dreams of becoming a swan).[49] Other dialogues of the time are more inventive still, as can be seen with the 'Diálogo mudo de los cartujos' (Silent Dialogue of the Carthusians), where the conversation between the monks is made up solely of punctuation marks, or with the 'Diálogo de los dos caracoles' (Dialogue of the Two Snails), where the silent conversation of the snails is marked by detailed stage directions telling the story of a young girl and a rat.[50] In all these works, Lorca seems to be thinking about how screenplays work and also exploring ways in which the conventional theatre could be renewed by importing some of the conventions and techniques of silent cinema.

Lorca would finally give full expression to his admiration for and his debt to Dalí in his 'Oda a Salvador Dalí', which he worked on from May 1925 and published in April 1926 in the prestigious *Revista de Occidente*. Ian Gibson has correctly referred to this ode as one of the greatest hymns to friendship written in Spanish,[51] and Lorca provides a loving portrait of a compulsive, imaginative and vulnerable friend, a 'hygienic soul' who is afraid of the emotion that awaits him in the street and who can only be fully understood in the context of his native Cadaqués and Catalonia. But it is Dalí's work and artistic vision that Lorca is most interested in exploring and extolling. Dalí has fled from both emotion and fantasy in order to focus on surfaces, on things as they actually are. His intelligence projects an ancient light, Minerva's light, onto everything that he surveys; he is the man who looks with his 'yellow ruler' and, once he has looked, copies or stylizes what he sees by imposing forms and limits: 'Amas una materia definida y exacta' (You love matter that is exact and well defined), affirms Lorca, clearly implying that Dalí has allowed the clear contours of Cubism to banish the blurred outlines of Impressionism.[52] And, as he writes, Lorca himself seems to put this self-same aesthetic into practice, offering both multiple perspectives on his subject matter and a series of images and metaphors that are not so much riddles (in the sense that they require or invite the reader to identify an external referent) but rather self-contained (that is, freestanding and clearly delimited and contoured) moments of poetic creativity. In a letter about Lorca's ode from early 1926, Dalí would himself pick out and celebrate such a moment, which he characterized as being purely conceptual and almost arithmetical in nature: 'Las sirenas convencen pero no sugestionan / y salen si mostramos un vaso de agua dulce' (The sirens convince but do not cast a spell / and come out if we show them a glass of fresh water).[53]

———————

Dalí had helped to plant the seeds of a new aesthetic in Lorca's mind, but they would take another year or two to germinate fully. In the meantime, he continued to work on the two plays he had started to write back in July 1924, namely *The Shoemaker's Prodigious Wife* and *The Love of Don Perlimplín for Belisa in his Garden*. These two plays, whose first drafts would not be completed until 1928 and which would first be performed in 1930 and 1933 respectively, show Lorca returning, after the high Romantic drama of *Mariana Pineda*, to the lighter and more comic vein of *Lola the Actress*. They also reveal how despite – or perhaps because of – his continuing failure to have *The Tragicomedy of Cristóbel and his Missus, Rosita* performed, Lorca increasingly introduced aspects of his puppet aesthetic into the drama he wrote for human actors.

    Both plays revisit the age-old theme of the older man (in his fifties) who marries a young woman (in her late teens), a theme which, as Cervantes and many others had shown, already brings with it a good deal of comical and farcical possibilities. In *The Shoemaker's Prodigious Wife*, we see the shoemaker's wife (*zapatera*) both complaining about the passivity of her husband and having to resist the advances of a series of suitors, including the mayor and the younger lads who hang around the shop. At the end of Act I, the shoemaker abandons his wife and leaves the village, forcing her to set up a bar frequented mainly by these lustful men, a situation that sets the local tongues wagging and leads to the creation of songs attacking the *zapatera* and her morals. But, against all expectations, the *zapatera* remains loyal to her absent husband, who returns disguised as a puppet master and proceeds to tell a tale similar to their own. The play ends with husband and wife declaring their love for each other and preparing themselves to face up to the scandal that has been caused by a knife fight between some of the *zapatera*'s suitors.

Lorca, who made clear in a letter of July 1924 that he envisaged the play he was just starting as a comedy in the Cristobital (puppet) style,[54] does indeed treat the characters in an exaggerated and often puppet-like way. The mayor is a grotesque who threatens all and sundry with his stick, while the five neighbour women, who spread the rumours about the *zapatera*, form a coven-like mob, with each of them dressed in a different-coloured frock (red, purple, black, green and yellow). The *zapatera* herself is forever cross and continuously insults and threatens everyone around her, even, at the end of the play, her recently returned husband. But she and her husband are at the same time more nuanced characters who are struggling with the pressures of marriage and of life in a small village, and Lorca provides a devastating portrayal of the destructive power of gossip (a theme he will often return to, not least in *La casa de Bernarda Alba* (The House of Bernarda Alba)). In this context, it is interesting to read a letter he wrote to his brother in July 1926, when he was still busy with this play, in which he complains about life in Asquerosa, where, he says, the stupidly obsessive emphasis on good manners hides a great deal of malice and spite.[55] During that summer, Lorca would in fact more or less cut his longstanding ties with his village and the Vega, as he and his family moved into a house with extensive land, the Huerta de San Vicente, that his parents had bought on the outskirts of Granada itself.

The show that the shoemaker, disguised as a puppeteer, puts on in Act II makes use not of puppets but rather of an *aleluya*, that is, a roll of paper featuring a series of coloured illustrations, which the puppeteer points to in turn as he tells his tale. 'Aleluya erótica' is the subtitle that Lorca gives to his *The Love of Don Perlimplín*, a deeply original play that makes even greater use of farcical and puppet devices than *The Shoemaker's Prodigious Wife*.[56] Perlimplín, with his extreme timidity and naivety, and his young wife Belisa, with her intense sensuality and large sexual appetite, make for excellent puppet-like characters, with their violently contrasting personalities conveyed through their extravagant costumes and the knockabout quality of many of their exchanges. Lorca also makes ironic reference to the narrator of the *aleluya* in his use of the two imps (*duendes*) who draw a curtain across the stage during Perlimplín and Belisa's wedding night and tell us of Belisa's infidelity with five lovers before then re-opening the curtain to reveal Perlimplín wearing a cuckold's horns. But, once again, Lorca adds pathos to the comedy by showing how old Perlimplín finally falls in love with his young wife and, realizing that he is not attractive to her, helps her to arrange what seems to be a tryst with the red-caped suitor who is the main object of her desire. Perlimplín himself plays the part of this suitor and, before he dies at his own hand, has the satisfaction of seeing Belisa both long for him and grieve for him, in a scene that truly marries tragedy with farce and comedy.

———

Both these plays give powerful expression to the anxieties felt by men (albeit, here, older men) in the face both of female sexuality and of marriage – anxieties that Lorca himself experienced during the crises that he suffered in 1925 and 1926. What he needed above all was to establish himself as an artist, since success would be the only passport away from Granada and from the increasing family pressures concerning his personal and professional future. In this sense, he pinned his hopes on *Mariana Pineda* and devoted much of his time during his trips to Madrid between early 1925 and early 1927 to looking for a company to stage the play. In February 1926 Gregorio Martínez Sierra, who had directed *The Butterfly's Evil Spell*, finally gave up on *Mariana Pineda*, mainly because he feared that it would not get past the censors, with the result that Lorca became increasingly frustrated both with what he saw to be the conservatism of the Madrid theatre scene and with the play itself, which he even started to refer to as a 'latazo' (pain in the neck).[57] In October of that year, after he had had little or no response from other companies and lead actresses such as Carmen Moragas (1896–1936), Lola Membrives (1888–1969) and Josefina Díaz de Artigas (1891–1976), he told Melchor Fernández Almagro that he had sent 'la antipática *Mariana Pineda*' (the unpleasant *Mariana Pineda*) to the actress Margarita Xirgu (1888–1969) and that the only reason he wrote it in the first place was to please his parents, who now thought that he was no more than a layabout who should not be allowed to move from Granada.[58] Lorca was quickly losing interest and confidence in his play, telling Melchor in January 1927 that it now represented little more than an excuse to get to Madrid.[59]

Production of *Mariana Pineda*, with set design by Dalí, at the Teatre Goya in Barcelona, June 1927.

Then, in April 1927, Margarita Xirgu, probably the leading actress of her day, finally agreed to take the part and soon invested 30,000 pesetas of her company's money in the production, which was scheduled to premiere in Barcelona in June.[60] Lorca was delighted, not only due to the fame he felt was coming his way, but because the preparations would take him back to Cadaqués and to Dalí, who had agreed to design the sets and the costumes. Lorca's second stay in Cadaqués and Barcelona, which lasted from early May until early August, would both mark the moment when Lorca started truly to taste success and play an important role in his subsequent development as an artist.

An undated letter from Dalí to Lorca gives an idea of how the painter first visualized the decor of his friend's play. The backcloths, he said, should feature simple drawings of the different settings and be almost monochromatic so that they could provide a stark background against which the richly coloured clothes of the characters would stand out.[61] Dalí laid his emphasis on simplicity, as can be seen in the photographs of the actual production, which show how even the convent garden is depicted through just a lone cypress tree and a few white walls and facades, to which some religious motifs have been added – all executed in a schematic and even naive style not dissimilar to the one used by Hermenegildo Lanz and Lorca for the decor of the puppet show back in January 1923 (see illustration on p. 104).[62] Lorca obviously enjoyed helping Dalí with the

Lorca with Dalí in Cadaqués, summer 1927.

design, telling Falla after the production that the decor was full of a marvellous Andalusianness that Dalí had managed to intuit by consulting photographs and, above all, through their many hours of conversation.[63]

As well as advising Dalí on the set designs, Lorca also took advantage of his time in Cadaqués to explore further his own interest in the visual arts. He had been well known among his friends in the Rinconcillo for his satirical drawings and drawings of monstrous humans and animals.[64] He had also started producing coloured drawings around the time of his collaboration with Lanz in January 1923, many of which offer rather stylized representations of Andalusian landscapes, townscapes and rooms, of Granadan women (or Madonnas) dressed in their finery, or of the Harlequin, Pierrot or clown figures beloved of Picasso and others. From

1926 or 1927 he entered a more explicitly Cubist phase, with drawings such as the *Retrato de Salvador Dalí* (Portrait of Salvador Dalí) and *Teorema de la copa y la mandolina* (Theorem of the Glass and the Mandolin), both probably produced in Cadaqués, showing how he superimposes forms or breaks them down altogether in a way that borders on abstraction and recalls the contemporary paintings of Joan Miró and of Dalí himself.[65] During one of his visits to Barcelona that May or early June, Lorca met the art critic Sebastià Gasch and soon presented him with a folder full of his drawings, in the hope that he would help to get them exhibited. Gasch, probably with Dalí's help, convinced local gallery owner Josep Dalmau to organize the exhibition, and Lorca started choosing the 24 coloured drawings that would go on show.

There is no doubting the close artistic collaboration between Lorca and Dalí during these months. Lorca both helped Dalí to visualize his *Mariana Pineda* and learned from him when creating his Cubist-inspired drawings. But by this time Dalí himself was starting to leave Cubism behind and to use his aesthetic of clear outlines and contours to explore instead the contents and workings of the unconscious mind. It was

Lorca in Cadaqués,
summer 1927.

precisely at this point in time, during Lorca's visit, that he created what is taken to be one of his earliest Surrealist-inspired paintings, the now lost *La miel es más dulce que la sangre* (Honey Is Sweeter than Blood). This work, with its strange machines, metal rods, rotting donkeys, mutilated female corpse and human body parts (including most probably Lorca's own head) strewn across sand dunes, deeply impressed Lorca, who, after having left Cadaqués, spoke in a letter to Dalí of the beauty of the blood that leaks from the corpse and of what he called the whole plastic conception of Dalí's physiological aesthetic, which 'has an appearance that is so concrete, well proportioned, logical and true with pure poetry that it attains the category *of that which we need* in order to live'.[66] Dalí had obviously opened Lorca's eyes to the power and beauty of his own personal proto-Surrealist vision, and he would spend the next year or so trying to convince him to adopt a similar aesthetic in his own work.

Lorca's Catalan stay was a huge success on all fronts. On 17 May *Songs* was published in Malaga. On 24 June *Mariana Pineda* opened for a six-day run in the Teatro Goya in Barcelona and received enthusiastic reviews in the press. And Lorca's drawings were exhibited in the Galerías Dalmau between 25 June and 2 July. He had triumphed in three different areas of artistic expression: poetry, drama and, perhaps most unexpectedly, the visual arts. There is little surprise that he left Catalonia in early August with a mixture of regret and satisfaction. He tells Dalí that Cadaqués had allowed him for the first time to feel his blood circulating inside his shoulders, although he also asks his friend to forgive his indecent behaviour, perhaps a reference to his attempt to seduce him.[67] He thanks Gasch for the article he had written about the exhibition at the Galerías Dalmau and registers his pride at being referred to by him as a painter.[68] And he celebrates the new friends he has made among the Catalan avant-garde and makes it clear that Andalusia and Catalonia should work together for the renovation of literature and the arts in Spain.[69]

But 1927 would bring another recognition of Lorca's arrival on the national artistic scene. At the start of the year, he was asked to take part in the celebrations marking the tercentenary of the death of Spanish Golden Age poet Luis de Góngora, whose powerful metaphors he had already identified in a 1926 talk as an essential reference point for modern poets who were trying to escape from the clichés of Romantic and *modernista* verse. Góngora was not to the taste of all Spanish writers – from his exile in France, Unamuno, for example, would declare his disdain both for Góngora's aestheticism and for the young writers of the 'castrated Spanish intelligentsia' who were devoting their time to celebrating that aestheticism rather than fighting against the dictatorship of General Primo de Rivera[70] – but, for those young writers themselves, Góngora represented a rallying call and a badge of identity. At the end of the year, on 16 and 17 December, Lorca, together with fellow poets Rafael Alberti, Jorge Guillén, José Bergamín, Dámaso Alonso, Gerardo Diego, Luis Cernuda and others, took part in an event organized by the Ateneo de Sevilla and local bullfighter and poet Ignacio Sánchez Mejías, in which they celebrated Góngora's poems and read out their own. In this way, a new generation of poets, soon to be known as the 'Generation of 1927', brought itself into being. Lorca was self-evidently one of their number, although he secretly knew that he needed to publish one more work in order to establish his pre-eminence within the group. That work would be his *Gypsy Ballads*.

Lorca's drawing *Verde que te quiero verde* (Green, How I Love You Green), 1930.

five

Granada, Madrid, New York and Cuba: Success, Escape and Return, 1928–30

The *Gypsy Ballads* is probably the best-known collection of poetry in the Spanish language. It also made Lorca the most famous writer in Spain – the pre-eminent poet in what was an exceptionally talented generation. He started to write the eighteen poems that make up the collection back in July 1924, with the last three being written in early 1928. In many ways, these poems represent the summation of all that he had worked towards over these years, allowing him to combine his interest in traditional and avant-garde themes and techniques, to give full expression to his understanding of the personality of both Granada and Andalusia, and to bring together his interests in poetry and other forms of artistic expression, principally painting and puppetry.

Lorca's choice of the ballad (*romance*) form, with its octosyllabic lines and assonant rhymes, is significant. He had often employed the form before, both in his poetic collections and in his drama, especially when he wished to tell a tale or, crucially, to strike a popular note. For the Spanish ballad, from its origins in the Middle Ages, had always been a popular and an oral metrical form, qualities that it would retain even in the hands of Spain's most refined poets, including Lorca's favourite Golden Age poet Luis de Góngora. In the readings of *Gypsy Ballads* that he gave in the early 1930s (the so-called 'Conferencia-recital' that provides so many insights into the collection), Lorca adds that the typical *romance*, with its open-ended structure and emphasis on storytelling, had always been a narrative form and that the more lyrical it became, the more it tended to become something akin to song. He himself has attempted in this collection to do something new – something, one could add, that will ultimately help to explain both its popularity and its originality – that is, to fuse the narrative type of ballad with the more lyrical type and to do so in such a way as to retain the particular qualities of each.[1]

Lorca's words suggest that *Gypsy Ballads* works simultaneously on different levels and that the first and perhaps most obvious one is that of the narrative. The collection is, after all, a collection of *Gypsy* ballads, and its very title suggests that we shall be encountering Gypsy characters and listening to Gypsy tales. And that is indeed the case for most of the ballads, where we hear of how the Gypsy girl Preciosa runs in terror from the wind, how a Gypsy nun embroiders brightly coloured cloth as she dreams of two horsemen, how Antoñito el Camborio (based on a real-life Gypsy from a village next to Fuente Vaqueros) is arrested and then killed, or how the Civil Guard destroys an unnamed Gypsy settlement. Even the religious poems dedicated to archangels Michael, Raphael and Gabriel (popular saints in Granada, Cordoba and Seville, respectively) or to the martyr St Olalla and the biblical figures of Tamar and Amnon are full of recognizably Gypsy references or iconography. When referring to this Gypsy storytelling aspect of the collection in his 'Conferencia-recital', Lorca uses a striking word, 'realism',[2] although he could equally have used the term *costumbrismo*, since *Gypsy Ballads* is actually full of local Gypsy colour and makes occasional use, it must be said, of stereotypes and clichés. As in many nineteenth-century literary and artistic works, Spanish and foreign, Lorca's Gypsies are associated with metalwork and forges, they play guitars and tambourines, and they are deeply superstitious, passionate and violent. By the 1930s Lorca himself would refuse at recitals to read out the sixth poem, 'La casada infiel' (The Unfaithful Wife), with its description of a very cocksure Gypsy lothario, claiming that it was no more than a titillating anecdote and was therefore incapable of speaking in any meaningful way about Andalusia.[3]

Lorca's recognition of the 'realist' element in *Gypsy Ballads* (and his half-recognition of the *costumbrista* element) is only the start of the story, though. He goes on to say in the 'Conferencia-recital' that the realism of the collection is actually fused with a mythical element, which serves to make the poems more mysterious and even 'indecipherable'.[4] It is clear that the collection does contain frequent references to Greek and Roman mythology but, more importantly still, Lorca sets out to create a whole series of Gypsy myths of his own. The two opening poems, 'Romance de la luna, luna' (Ballad of the Moon, Moon) and 'Preciosa y el aire' (Preciosa and the Wind), for example, make use of personification in order to show how the moon becomes a cold, white Death-woman visiting the earth in order to snatch away a young Gypsy boy, and how the wind becomes both a dirty old man and the projection of Preciosa's own fears about her burgeoning sexuality. Even the 'Romance de la Guardia Civil Española' (Ballad of the Spanish Civil Guard), which works on one level as a denunciatory poem highlighting the oppression of the Gypsies, offers up its own mythical reading, as the inhabitants of the settlement seem to be reacting in terror at one and the same time to the invasion of the Civil Guard and to the arrival of night, which seems to come cloaked in the blackness of the law-enforcers' clothes and souls.[5]

Through such myths, *Gypsy Ballads* implies that the Gypsy world-view is essentially pagan or animistic in nature, in the sense that the forces that control the Gypsies' lives are located in the world around them: in the moon, the sun, the landscape and the wind. But Lorca goes one step further in the collection by creating a single, overarching myth, which, he claims, emerges from each and every one of the poems and helps to explain not just the Gypsy way of seeing the world but, more widely, the Andalusian way too. That myth is the myth of 'pena', a word that normally translates as sorrow but which, in his Andalusian context, Lorca wishes to endow with new meaning: it is not exactly melancholy, nostalgia, anguish or pain, he says, but rather a 'struggle between amorous intelligence and the incomprehensible mystery that surrounds it' and, more specifically still, 'a directionless longing, an acute love for nothing in particular, with the certainty that death (a perennial concern in Andalusia) is breathing on the other side of the door'.[6] This conflict between desire and an impenetrable or threatening world is clearly expressed in 'Romance de la pena negra' (Ballad of Black Pena), where Soledad Montoya's search for something she's almost unwilling or unable to put into words but ultimately defines as 'mi alegría y mi persona' (my joy and myself) leads her to abandon the comfort of her house and, against the advice of a mysterious voice that advises her to return home and to wash her body, set off on a journey that may well end up in the sea of death.[7] This is 'pena', the mysterious force that controls the lives of Lorca's characters and of Andalusians in general, and, as if to emphasize its animistic origins, he adds in the 'Conferencia-recital' that it filters through the marrow of their bones and the sap of the trees around them.[8]

Lorca is at pains to point out that, despite its title, *Gypsy Ballads* is about not just Gypsies but the whole of Andalusia – even if, he adds, the

Gypsy element is the deepest and most elevated of all the elements that make up the character of his home region. He even goes so far as to say that the book contains no short jackets or tambourines and is actually 'anti-picturesque', 'anti-folkloric' and 'anti-flamenco' – all of which is patently untrue but does allow him to set up his main point, namely that this is a book which barely expresses the Andalusia one sees but rather where one can feel the tremor of the invisible, secret Andalusia.[9] This statement shows that *Gypsy Ballads* is the culmination of Lorca's drive since at least *Impressions and Landscapes* (1918) to seek out the 'true' Granada and Andalusia that lie beyond all the touristic (and, it must be said, literary) stereotypes, and thereby to contribute to the creation of a richer sense of Andalusian identity that can stand alongside the other regional identities being forged elsewhere in Spain.

Despite its Romantic and even exoticizing origins, what Lorca says about this identity, about the 'soul of Andalusia', is very striking indeed, since, according to him, it is made out of a conflict between two warring elements, that is, between the 'Eastern poison of the Andalusian', on the one hand, and the 'geometry and balance imposed by the Roman heritage', on the other.[10] Just as he had used the two rivers of Granada in the poem 'The River Dauro and the River Genil' (1918) to explore the Moorish and Christian sides of his native city, so he here refers to the Andalusian character in terms of an Eastern (by which he obviously means a Gypsy and probably a Jewish, as well as a Moorish) strain, which he associates with passion and vitality, and a Roman strain, associated principally with order and balance – although he now emphasizes that these two strains do not simply fuse together like conjoining rivers but rather live in tension and even violence. Such a view opens up multiple new possibilities as far as Lorca's understanding not only of the Andalusian character but, more generally, of human nature is concerned, since it implies that Andalusia and humanity are represented not just by Soledad Montoya's overflowing and impulsive desire to find herself or the Gypsy settlement's vitality and colour but also, and at the same time, by the voice that advises Soledad to go home and forget her longings and even the Civil Guard that ransacks the Gypsy settlement. On a symbolic level, Lorca seems to be telling us that life is not predicated solely on the impulse to liberate desire but also, and often tragically, on the impulse to repress and self-repress. Here we find a first mature expression both of the Andalusian fatalism that Lorca had told Benjamín Palencia he feared he might lose in Madrid,[11] and of Lorca's deeply tragic sense of life, according to which both the drive to seek freedom and the drive to take refuge in structure and order can have profoundly destructive consequences.

All this mythologizing about the Gypsy and Andalusian character and insights into human nature itself emerge from the narrative side of the collection, from the stories it tells. But, as Lorca himself informs us, these ballads have a lyrical side too, by which he appears to mean not so much their emotional or song-like qualities as their artistry and inventiveness, precisely those characteristics that will mark *Gypsy Ballads* out as a work of the avant-garde. The success of the collection would ultimately lie in the way in which Lorca melds his more traditional (and deeply Romantic) exploration of regional character with a more modern emphasis on literary and artistic creativity.

At the heart of this creativity lies complex metaphor, which had long been one of the most eye-catching aspects of Lorca's (and indeed his generation's) poetry. Back in 1925, the Spanish philosopher José Ortega y Gasset, who was to have an important influence on Lorca and his peers, had set himself the task, in *La deshumanización del arte* (The Dehumanization of Art), of finding the common elements among all the recent avant-garde movements. He decided that the modern artist does not focus on either the stimulation of the reader's or spectator's emotions or the reproduction of so-called 'reality' (as the nineteenth-century Romantics and Realists had done) but rather on creating art that explores its own language and expressive potential, sets out to create new artistic objects, and is therefore necessarily complex, 'dehumanized' and elitist. For Ortega, the device that allows avant-garde artists to create new realities is metaphor, which, he explains, consists of hiding a (real) object by covering it with the mask of something else. In the old art, he adds, metaphors were no more than adornments that were 'poured over' some reality or other but now, with the new art, 'one sets out to eliminate the extra-poetic or real support and let the metaphor happen, making the metaphor itself into the poetic object.'[12] Just a year after Ortega's essay, and partly under its influence, Lorca would write and deliver a talk entitled 'La imagen poética de Don Luis de Góngora' (The Poetic Image in Don Luis de Góngora), in which he identified metaphor as the key device in Góngora's – and, by implication, his own and his generation's – work. He memorably defines metaphor as 'a change of clothes, purpose or function between objects or ideas from Nature' and also provides an insight into how metaphors actually come into being.[13] Poets, he says, find all the raw material for their metaphors in the natural world, which is why they have to be masters of each of the five bodily senses, in the following order of importance: sight, touch, hearing, smell and taste. Their sense impressions enter the 'camera obscura' of their brains and are gradually transformed there into something new, mainly thanks to the poets' ability to open up 'communicating doors' between the different senses and to 'superimpose' different sensations. The result is the creation of new poetic objects: Góngora's sea, for example, is transformed into an 'esmeralda bruta en mármol engastada' (rough emerald set in marble) and his poplar tree into a 'verde lira' (green lyre).[14]

Lorca's own metaphors draw on all of the senses and also make abundant use of synaesthesia (the opening up of those communicating doors between the senses) and of what we have already seen as other favoured devices of his, such as personification and the transference of meaning. 'Ballad of the Moon, Moon' (and indeed the whole collection) starts off with the moon appearing dressed in her 'polisón de nardos' (bustle made of spikenards), an image that both conveys the whiteness and shape of the light emanating from her and offers just a hint of noise and scent, while Soledad Montoya's body in 'Ballad of Black Pena' smells of horse and shadow and her breasts are 'yunques ahumados' (smoked anvils) that 'gimen canciones redondas' (groan out round songs) – an extended metaphor that combines most if not all of the senses and suggests how her body looks, feels, sounds, smells and possibly even tastes.[15] The blood of the Gypsy bands that have slaughtered one another in 'Reyerta' (Brawl) becomes, as it quietly snakes along the ground, a silent serpent's song, while Christ's five wounds in 'La monja gitana' (The Gypsy Nun) are transformed into five (slices of) red grapefruit and the blood on the shirt of the young man in 'Romance sonámbulo' (Sleepwalking Ballad) becomes three hundred dark-red roses.[16] At times, Lorca builds his metaphors out of popular expressions, as can be seen in the 'Romance del emplazado' (Ballad of the Doomed Man), where he shows how the 'bueyes de agua' (water oxen), a term that is used in the Vega to refer to slow-moving but powerful currents, charge at the young boys 'que se bañan en las lunas / de sus cuernos ondulados' (who bathe in the moons / of their rippling horns).[17] At others, he focuses instead on metamorphosis, with the moon and its reflection on the surface of a lake in 'Burla de Don Pedro a caballo' (Mockery of Don Pedro on Horseback) mutating into a pair of cymbals that a young boy asks the night to play.[18]

The challenge facing Lorca in his ballads was how to blend metaphors such as these into the stories he set out to tell, that is, how to combine the lyrical and narrative sides of his poems. This is an issue he had already touched upon in his talk on Luis de Góngora, who he claimed had been confronted with the following dilemma when writing his poetry: if he were to place the main emphasis on the storyline, the anecdote, his poems would run the risk of becoming simple epics, while, if he did not try to tell any story at all and focused solely on creating a series of strong metaphors, then his poems would lose both meaning and unity and simply fall apart. Góngora's answer, Lorca tells us, was to choose his story and then cover it with metaphors, so that the narrative, that is, the skeleton of the poem, becomes wrapped up in the magnificent flesh of the images.[19]

Of all the eighteen ballads, 'Sleepwalking Ballad', possibly the best known, most clearly illustrates Lorca's point. It tells a mysterious story, which, as its title suggests, seems to function according to the logic of dreams. We come across a young Gypsy woman, who is first seen standing by a railing at the top of her house and then, at the end of the poem, floating on the surface of a well or a cistern, and also two men, very possibly the young woman's father and her fiancé, who have returned home with the Civil Guard hard on their heels and seem either to have been fatally injured or even to be already dead. During the dialogue between the two men that takes up the middle sections of the poem, we hear the younger of the two voice his desire to exchange his nomadic and violent ways for a domestic life with his beloved, and his companion reply that he is unable to offer him any help, as he is no longer himself. There seems to be a growing awareness that the Gypsy woman, whom they desperately seek in the higher reaches of the house, is actually dead, and the story ends with a reference to drunken Civil Guards knocking at the front door. This simple but enigmatic story is introduced by the song-like line 'Verde que te quiero verde' (Green, how I love you green), which is repeated in an almost incantatory way throughout the poem. And the story itself is illuminated by a series of rich metaphors that find their exact place within the economy of the tale. So, the poem locates itself early on at the break of day and makes the dawn breeze palpable by strongly evoking the sense of touch: 'La higuera frota su viento / con la lija de sus ramas' (The fig tree rubs its wind / with the sandpaper of its branches). In one of its middle sections, the poem collapses a visual and an auditory sensation together in order to describe the effect of the wind and the light on the tin lanterns hanging from the roof: 'Mil panderos de cristal / herían la madrugada' (A thousand glass tambourines / injured the early morning). And, in the most powerful image of all, the Gypsy woman's story comes to an end when we find her floating, Ophelia-like, on the surface of the cistern and violently illuminated by a shaft of moonlight: 'Un carámbano de luna / la sostiene sobre el agua' (An icicle of moon / pins her to the water).[20]

It can be seen that Lorca plays with all our senses as he creates his rich metaphors, but it is equally clear that his imagination is primarily visual in nature (as he had implied when placing sight first in the order of importance of the bodily senses). *Gypsy Ballads* is in fact a deeply pictorial, and indeed painterly, collection that includes some direct references to painting and to painting styles: 'Martirio de Santa Olalla' (Martyrdom of St Olalla), for example, is not only arranged as a triptych, focusing on the three key moments in the saint's martyrdom, but contains vivid descriptions of her suffering that are strongly reminiscent of medieval religious art.[21] The collection also widens out its artistic field of reference to incorporate sculpture (which is linked to the second sense in Lorca's list, namely touch), with the three archangels being described as painted and clothed statues standing in their niches or on their plinths or ready to be carried through their city in a procession. Indeed, Lorca actually refers to the whole collection in the 'Conferencia-recital' as 'un retablo de Andalucía' (an altarpiece of Andalusia),[22] which seems to indicate that he conceived each poem as an individual panel within a reredos that is dedicated to his home region and its defining emotion, 'pena'.

Lorca's talk on Góngora, whom he characterizes as an 'essentially plastic poet',[23] provides us with further insight into the visual and painterly way in which he conceives his own poems. His conviction that the narrative represents the skeleton of a poem and the images the flesh can also clearly be read in pictorial terms, with the storyline serving as the canvas onto which the metaphors are then applied. From this perspective, the canvas created by the story of 'Sleepwalking Ballad' offers a particularly rich feast of visual images. Some of these images are figurative in nature, such as the sketches of the three figures at the heart of the story and the description of the interior of the house where the poem takes place, but these figures and forms are surrounded or completed by more abstract details made simply of colour and light. With his insistent chorus of 'Verde que te quiero verde', Lorca covers the canvas of 'Sleepwalking Ballad' with a green wash, onto which he applies a series of primary and secondary colours: the different greens of the Gypsy woman's body and the silver of her eyes in the first stanza; the deep red of the young Gypsy man's roses/blood and the white of his shirt in the third stanza; and the blacks, whites, silvers and yellows associated with the Gypsy woman in the final stanzas. The overall result is a painting that is part-figurative and part-abstract and which, in its mixture of naïve outlines and rich colours, is perhaps reminiscent of the early work of an artist whom Lorca placed among his favourite contemporary painters: Wassily Kandinsky (1866–1944).[24] It must be added, though, that the images Lorca splashes across his canvas are not just visual in nature but tactile, auditory, olfactory and gustatory, since we are also made to feel the rasping touch of the fig tree, hear the clatter of the tin lanterns/glass tambourines, smell the blood of the Gypsy man, and even perceive the rotting corpse of the Gypsy woman, which leaves the strange taste of bile, mint and basil in the mouth.[25]

Finally, the poems of *Gypsy Ballads* do not just function as miniature canvases but also draw on Lorca's long-term interest and immersion in another key art form, namely puppetry. Just as he imported puppet-like characters into plays such as *The Shoemaker's Prodigious Wife* and *The Love of Don Perlimplín*, so he also conceived his ballads with a puppeteer's imagination (in fact, the word *retablo*, which Lorca uses to describe *Gypsy Ballads*, actually translates as 'puppet theatre' as well as 'altarpiece'). 'Sleepwalking Ballad' once again provides a particularly good example. The incantatory line 'Verde que te quiero verde' marks our entry into a world of magic and performance and helps to paint the backdrop of the play an eerie green. The moon and stars will play an increasingly important role in that backdrop, controlling the shifting intensity of the light that is projected onto the stage and picking out certain key objects in turn: the eyes of the Gypsy woman, the tin lanterns on the roofs, and the body of the Gypsy woman on the surface of the cistern. The stage itself has all the magical complexity of the best puppet theatre, with the interior space divided up into a higher level, the domain of the Gypsy woman, and a lower level, where the two Gypsy men have their initial discussion. Indeed, the drawing entitled *Verde que te quiero verde* that Lorca appended to a copy of *Gypsy Ballads* in 1930 reveals how he visualized the setting of his poem not in any naturalistic way but rather as a series of theatrical spaces in which the drama can be played out (see this chapter's frontispiece, p. 106). The protagonists themselves, especially the men with their knives and sashes, are typical of the stock characters that populate puppet theatre. And the descriptive sections that surround the dialogue between the two men contain such lines as '¿Pero quién vendrá? ¿Y por dónde...?' (But who's going to turn up? And which way will they come...?), which create a certain complicity between the poem and the audience that is very reminiscent of puppet theatre (as is the fact that the young man's entreaty to be allowed to climb the stairs is addressed not to the singular 'tú' of his companion but to a plural 'vosotros' that must also include us, the members of the audience).[26]

In short, Lorca's *romances* draw on and make use of all the machinery and conventions of puppet theatre, from setting, lighting and decor to characterization, choreography and the complex relationship between puppeteer, character and audience. Lorca's puppet-characters bring with them and help to establish a deeply original tone, texture and atmosphere, one that lies somewhere between the typical or *costumbrista* and the childlike, playful or even outright surreal. And it is here, in Lorca's dialogue with other art forms such as puppetry and painting, as much as in its cultivation of complex metaphor, that *Gypsy Ballads*, on its publication in July 1928, declared its avant-garde credentials to the world.

———

The first edition of *Gypsy Ballads* soon sold out and was given a rapturous reception in the Spanish press, with fellow poet Ricardo Baeza writing that Lorca had the most original poetic voice since Rubén Darío and was the first obvious successor in Spain to Juan Ramón Jiménez and Antonio Machado.[27] Lorca was now a literary celebrity, and his fame reached well beyond the artistic circles of Madrid, Barcelona and the provincial capitals. Not everyone approved of the work, though, and the most forthright criticism would also be, for Lorca, the most painful. In August or early September 1928, Salvador Dalí sent Lorca a letter in which he called the collection *costumbrista*, anecdotal, traditional and even 'putrid' (using the term that the Residencia group had coined to refer to all that was conventional and old fashioned). You might think you've created some daring images or upped the dose of irrationality in your work, he tells his friend, but in reality your poems are full of the most stereotypical and conformist clichés, the worst example being 'The Unfaithful Wife'. Dalí does in fact identify some more positive aspects, extolling the violence of 'Martyrdom of St Olalla' and the incest of 'Tamar and Amnon' and adding that he is still, despite everything, able to glimpse Lorca in the collection – Lorca the erotic beast, that is, with his sex, his fear of death, and his mysterious spirit. But Lorca has not understood that modern poetry needs now to escape from the old and the conventional and focus instead on all that lies beyond our rational minds; it must adopt what Dalí calls a strictly objective perspective and learn how to look at things as they actually are rather than as our intellects lead us to believe them to be. In short, the way forward for Dalí now was quite obviously Surrealism, and he invites his friend to reject the Gypsy and even infantile image that has been forged of him by the 'putrid ones' and to leap instead into the void that he himself has started to inhabit.[28]

Dalí clearly feels that, despite their discussions about Surrealism during summer 1927, Lorca had failed fully to respond to its challenges. This was also the view of Luis Buñuel, who, from his base in Paris, had for some time been singing the praises of the Surrealist movement and also trying to turn Dalí (and most of the Residencia group) against Lorca. In his letters to Pepín Bello from summer 1927 onwards, most of which appear to have been written in a jealous rage, Buñuel claims that Lorca has 'enslaved' Dalí and that Dalí must join him in Paris in order to escape his disastrous influence: Lorca's extreme narcissism is already enough to make him incapable of friendship, he adds, but, in the end, it's his terrible aestheticism that is finally pushing him away from us all.[29] By this time, Buñuel had in fact just about managed to prise Dalí away from what he saw as Lorca's clutches and in early 1929 both men would start collaborating on a project of their own, namely the Surrealist film *Un chien andalou* (An Andalusian Dog), whose title deliberately aimed to offend and hurt Lorca.[30]

His erstwhile friends' reaction to *Gypsy Ballads* would have a lasting effect on Lorca and his work. It is more than possible that both his later refusal to include 'The Unfaithful Wife' in his recitals and his only partially credible claim that the collection was 'anti-picturesque', 'anti-folkloric' and 'anti-flamenco' were a response to Dalí's criticisms, as was, most likely, his growing discomfort at being known as a 'Gypsy poet' (although he'd already complained to Jorge Guillén about such a tag back in January 1927).[31] Lorca was also clearly intrigued both by Surrealism itself and, even more so, by Dalí's take on it, and would over the coming months increasingly explore the idea of employing an 'objective' aesthetic that would enable him to capture things as they are when freed from the control of the conscious mind – a process that would come to a climax in the poems and plays he wrote during and immediately after his time in New York. He spoke about these matters in two talks he gave at the Ateneo de Granada in October 1928. In the first, 'Imaginación, inspiración, evasión' (Imagination, Inspiration, Evasion), he celebrates the power of the imagination but adds that this particular faculty and its offspring, metaphor, can only work within the realms of reality (and the natural world) and are therefore ultimately controlled by reason and logic. In order to look beyond conventional reality, to be able to gaze at things as they are in the fullness of their being, without concern for explicable causes and effects, the poet must have recourse instead to inspiration, the faculty that allows him or her to evade reason and to gain access to worlds full of virgin emotions. This poetic 'evasion' can be achieved by many means, and Lorca, almost quoting the postscript of Dalí's letter, identifies Surrealism, with its emphasis on dreams and the unconscious, as one particularly obvious means. And yet such evasion of reason and reality through dreams and the unconscious can also give rise to an art that is fundamentally inexact and unclear – and we Latin peoples of southern Europe, he concludes, prefer strong profiles, mysteries that are made fully visible, clear forms and sensuality.[32]

Lorca is a little less ambivalent about Surrealism in his second talk, 'Sketch de la nueva pintura' (Sketch of the New Painting). For this overview of the origins and nature of contemporary painting, he relies as much on Dalí's viewpoint as he had on Falla's when preparing his 1922 talk on *cante jondo*. His main point is that, around 1909, Cubism had replaced the formal imprecision and representational slavishness of Impressionism with a new emphasis on contours and volume and a revolutionary belief in the autonomy of painting and of art in general. By 1926, though, the Cubist revolution had more or less run its course and degenerated into an overly cerebral or intellectual painting style. This was when the Surrealists, taking advantage of the formal advances brought about by the Cubists, started to create paintings that attempted to express the inexpressible, and art entered into a 'mystical, uncontrolled period of supreme beauty'.[33] It is hard not to read this talk as a sort of literary self-portrait on Lorca's part – or at least as a self-portrait painted in the style of Salvador Dalí – especially when one takes into account that in 'Imagination, Inspiration, Evasion', he had created an explicit parallel between his own generation's cult of Góngora and the mature phase of Cubism, which he referred to as a 'painting style based on pure rationality'.[34] But, even though he seems to be implying that he has now outgrown the Gongorine style of *Gypsy Ballads*, it is significant that his main example of a Surrealist painter in 'Sketch' is a 'Latin' like himself – not, though, his hypercritical friend Salvador Dalí but rather Joan Miró, an artist whose work gives rise in Lorca to the same mysterious and terrible emotion that he feels when the bull is killed in the bullring.[35] Lorca appears to be saying yet again that Surrealism may offer a way forward but each artist (and perhaps even each culture) must still find their own way of responding to its challenges and discoveries.

While Lorca was tussling with the future direction that his work should take, he was also trying to cope with a profound personal crisis. The interviews that Agustín Penón carried out in Granada in the mid-1950s offer a unique glimpse into Lorca's sexual and sentimental life at this time. José María García Carrillo, a lifelong friend and, like Lorca and Penón himself, a homosexual, spoke openly about Lorca's love life and emphasized that Lorca was perfectly comfortable with his sexuality and quite happy to discuss it when he felt that he was in safe company, although he would still often use a secret – and humorous – language to do so, as when he claimed that he and his gay friends belonged to the 'masonería epéntica' (epentic Freemasonry). García Carrillo adds that Lorca was a highly sexual being who was particularly drawn to strong young men from the countryside, and he goes so far as to call him 'insatiable' and 'foolhardy', in the sense that he would act quite openly on his desires, even in such a conservative place as Granada: on several occasions he had seen Lorca proposition young men in the streets of the provincial capital, and he had even witnessed his attempted seduction of a young barber in his home village outside the city. By about 1928, though, García Carrillo had become worried about Lorca because of his troubled relationship with a young sculptor in Madrid called Emilio Aladrén. He became so angry at what he saw to be Aladrén's attempts to take advantage of Lorca that he even claimed that he too had slept with Aladrén in a failed attempt to turn Lorca against him.[36]

García Carrillo was not alone in his worries. Ever since Lorca had met Aladrén at Dalí's art school in 1925 and then won him away from his girlfriend, the painter Maruja Mallo, in 1927, his friends had warned him about a man who seemed to them to be interested mainly in his fame and money. Lorca would react angrily to their criticisms and go out of his way not only to protect Aladrén but to try (ultimately unsuccessfully) to promote his career as a sculptor. The truth is that we only have the friends' take on the situation – Lorca's own letters to Aladrén have been lost, and the few letters from Aladrén that have survived do no more than reveal a rather self-conscious and self-deprecating young man who obviously wants to impress his lover.[37] But there is no doubt that their relationship was a source of much pain, as well as joy, for Lorca, especially between the summer of 1928 and his departure for New York in June 1929.

Lorca with Emilio Aladrén, probably 1928.

Lorca gave expression to the start of this new crisis in a series of letters that he sent between August and October 1928 from Granada to Sebastià Gasch, José Antonio Rubio Sacristán, Rafael Martínez Nadal, Melchor Fernández Almagro and a new friend, the young Colombian poet Jorge Zalamea.[38] He says that he is going through the deepest sentimental crisis in his life and that he feels lonely, isolated, listless and desperate. The more he falls in love, the less he understands love itself: it ends up burning him, and perhaps it is better never to get involved with anyone. He spends whole nights looking across at Granada from the balcony of the Huerta de San Vicente and finds the city to be empty and heartless (although he says in another letter that his nights are given over to bacchanalia full of flesh and laughter, adding rather callously that the beautiful flesh of Andalusia always 'says thank you after being trampled on').[39] It is in the letters to Zalamea that Lorca is at his most forthright, since he obviously sees himself as the young Colombian's guide in both sentimental and artistic matters. He advises Zalamea to follow his example by drawing a map of his desire and then living in accordance with it, guided by the two basic 'norms' of beauty and joy. But he also, for the first but certainly not the last time in his life, expresses his fear that other people are trying to 'defeat' him, and he lays part of the blame for this on what he calls 'stupid fame': the man who has become famous, he says using an image reminiscent of the 'icicle of moon' at the climax of 'Sleepwalking Ballad', has his breast 'pierced by blunt flashlights that *others* train on him'.[40] Safeguarding one's intimacy is all-important, he adds, and you must take care not to allow your 'state of being' to filter into your poetry because that would mean opening up what is most pure in yourself to the gaze of those who should never be allowed to see it.[41]

Lorca's crisis, which was clearly existential as well as sentimental in nature, would become even more intense after January 1929, when he found out that Emilio Aladrén had started a relationship with a young Englishwoman (whom he would marry in late 1931). By then, he had also realized that Dalí was not, as he had hoped, going to visit him in Granada but had rather joined forces with Buñuel instead. He attempted to take refuge in his writing, which involved him finishing off both *The Love of Don Perlimplín* and *The Shoemaker's Prodigious Wife* and trying to get them performed (in the end, the former fell foul of the censors and would not be premiered until 1933, while the latter would receive its first performance, with Margarita Xirgu in the title role, in late 1930). He also continued to work on the Granada-based journal *gallo*, a venture that he and his Rinconcillo friends had dreamed up back in 1926 and for which he acted mainly as editor, calling in favours from writers and artists all over Spain. For the first issue, published in March 1928, he had written the article 'Historia de este *gallo*' (History of this *gallo* [Cockerel]),[42] a satirical attack on the tastes of the Granadan middle classes, which, as prominent Falangist Eduardo Molina Fajardo told Agustín Penón in 1955, profoundly displeased many of the city's more conservative inhabitants and marked Lorca out in their eyes as a treacherous undesirable, a sort of enemy within. The second issue appeared in April 1928, and Lorca spent much of the autumn trying without success to organize the third, which he wanted to focus on the art and culture of Catalonia and Andalusia or perhaps even to offer a monograph on Dalí.

It is also clear that Lorca tried at this time of crisis to take refuge in religion. He starts to make many more references to God in his letters, telling Zalamea in autumn 1928, for example, that, despite having had such a bad summer, God has never abandoned him.[43] He talks with his correspondents about his long poem *Oda al Santísimo Sacramento del Altar* (Ode to the Most Blessed Sacrament of the Altar), whose first two parts he would finish by the end of the year (with the rest being completed in autumn 1929). It is, he tells Zalamea, his faith that is helping him to write this ode, in which he opens up his soul before the symbol of the Sacrament.[44] There is little doubt that this poem puts into practice Lorca's new writing style, which is based on the Dalí-inspired principles of objectivity and evasion (the capacity to look at things as they actually are when freed from the control of logic) and his own emphasis on clarity (which enables him to avoid the vagueness he associates with a certain kind of Surrealist writing).[45] Instead of creating metaphors that act like riddles and leave the reader to guess in each case what the referent might be, Lorca now provides a series of precise and vividly evocative images, each of which sheds light on some aspect of the mystery of life (and the Eucharist) and carries a poetic emotion of its own. Lorca is obviously moved by the Sacrament or Host itself, that 'cuerpo de luz humana con músculos de harina' (body of human light with muscles of flour) which is at one and the same time bread and the body of Christ (that is, a living metaphor).[46] At the same time, he returns centrally in the poem to the relationship between the flesh and the spirit, a theme which, as we saw in Chapter Two, had already obsessed him as a teenager. Three of the four parts of the poem are entitled 'Mundo' (World), 'Demonio' (Devil) and 'Carne' (Flesh), and Lorca does nothing to hide the beauty of the flesh, especially male flesh, and even perhaps suggests at times that the body of Christ (Corpus Christi) could signal some new way of melding bodily and spiritual needs. And yet the spirit insistently returns in this poem as the vanquisher of the body, most obviously in 'World', where Lorca provides a vivid and dark portrayal of contemporary life (replete with razor blades on dressing tables, clerks in dingy flats, injured prostitutes and deserted bars) and then turns to the Sacrament as he searches for something that can save him from both the desires of the flesh and the agonies of love:

Sólo tu Sacramento de luz en equilibrio
aquietaba la angustia del amor desligado.
Sólo tu Sacramento, manómetro que salva
corazones lanzados a quinientos por hora.[47]

Only your Sacrament of light in balance
eased the anguish of unbound love.
Only your Sacrament, that pressure gauge that saves
hearts launched at 500 kilometres per hour.

Lorca was very pleased with the poem, believing it to be the best he had written to date and that it represented, along with other odes he was writing at the time, the 'polar opposite' to *Gypsy Ballads*.[48] He published the first two parts in the *Revista de Occidente* in December 1928, dedicating them to Manuel de Falla, himself a devout Catholic. Falla took offence at some of the sexual imagery, and it seems that their friendship cooled somewhat as a result. But Lorca's search for religious solace continued, and, during Easter 1929, he took part as a discalced penitent in the procession of the Cofradía (Brotherhood) of the Church of Santa María de la Alhambra in Granada.[49] As we shall see, he would take his deeply Granadan but at the same time deeply idiosyncratic religious sensibility with him on his trip to New York.

———

By 1929, when he turned 31, Lorca was feeling increasingly desperate and out of place. His relationship with Emilio Aladrén was clearly deteriorating. He seemed unable to find satisfaction either in his sexual or his spiritual life and signally failed to establish any sort of harmony between the two. He had alienated a large part of the Granadan middle class, which probably did not worry him too much, but he had also hurt his old mentor Manuel de Falla and continued to be a cause of concern for his parents and family. And he felt that he was being abandoned by his close friends Salvador Dalí and Luis Buñuel, who found even his latest work, the openly Surrealist-inspired prose poems 'Degollación de los inocentes' (Beheading of the Innocents) and 'Suicidio en Alejandría'

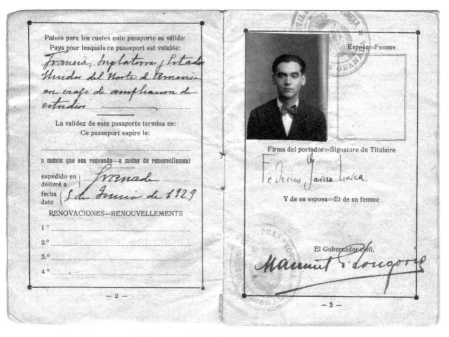

Lorca's passport for his trip to New York.

(Suicide in Alexandria), to have been written with more intellect than instinct and to be as bad, in Buñuel's words, as the 'fetid' *Ode to the Most Blessed Sacrament*.⁵⁰ Buñuel and Dalí had their dream of Paris, and Lorca needed his dream of escape too.

In the end, it would be Fernando de los Ríos, the man who had put him in contact with the Residencia de Estudiantes in 1919 and helped him to pass his law degree in 1923, who would come once again to his rescue. De los Ríos was going to travel to New York on his way to give classes in Puerto Rico and asked his old friends Federico de Onís and Ángel del Río, both professors of Spanish at Columbia University, to sign Lorca up for an English course there. He also used his considerable prestige and charm to convince Lorca's parents of the benefits for their son's health, work and future of a sojourn abroad. The two men, accompanied by De los Ríos' niece Rita Troyano, left Madrid on Thursday 13 June 1929 and, after a day in Paris where they seemed to visit every tourist site possible, took the train and ferry to London on 15 June. Lorca very much enjoyed visiting the British Museum and London Zoo, but seemed to have had an even better time dropping Rita off in Lucton School, near Leominster, and dining with Salvador de Madariaga and his wife in Headington, Oxford, where he also visited University College to see the Shelley monument and kitted himself out with cricket jumpers and Oxford college ties. They finally left Southampton aboard the liner RMS *Olympic* on 19 June and arrived in New York on 25 June.

It seems that Lorca was thrilled by New York and also by life on the Columbia campus in the northern part of Manhattan. He spent the rest of the summer term in a room on the sixth floor of Furnald Hall overlooking the university sports field, where he could watch the men playing tennis or American football far below, and then, after spending a month with friends in Vermont and the Catskill mountains in rural New York State, he moved, in September, into the nearby John Jay Hall, with its views over the Hudson River. His room cost him a little more than $1 a day and his food in the hall canteen some 55 cents (or 75, if he was hungry), so he assured his parents that he could more or less get by on the $100 they wired him every month, although he did frequently ask them for extra money (mainly, he said, for clothes) and also badgered his brother to send across the royalties from *Songs* and *Gypsy Ballads*, which, he claimed, would allow him to go to as many plays as possible in a city that offered the most exciting and revolutionary theatre in the world.[51] Lorca obviously enjoyed this exotic reprise of his Residencia student days. He does seem to have gone to most of his English classes in the short summer term, although his attendance trailed off in the autumn and he soon lost all interest in the idea of speaking English proficiently, pronouncing the few English words he did dare to use in a strong Spanish accent (as when he referred to the *shishpil* [sex appeal] of New York women).[52] He loved keeping his hall neighbours up until the early hours talking about his daily experiences in New York and also continued the Residencia tradition of childish pranks, as when he would feign a limp on the subway in order to be offered a seat only to walk out of the train limp-free at the next station.[53]

But Lorca's life went far beyond that of the normal freshman or sophomore. His literary reputation, above all as author of *Gypsy Ballads*, preceded him, and he would soon be lionized by certain sectors of New York high society. Spain was currently in vogue in the city, and Lorca was invited to soirées at the homes of rich Hispanophiles like writer Mildred Adams and editor Henry Herschel Brickell, where he would often rub shoulders with old friends from Spain such as the dancer Antonia Mercé (La Argentina), folk singer La Argentinita, guitarist Andrés Segovia, bullfighter Ignacio Sánchez Mejías or fellow poet Dámaso Alonso.

Lorca's exuberant personality and above all his recitals at the piano, where he most enjoyed playing and singing Andalusian songs but would sometimes also offer a musical tour through the different regions of Spain, bewitched his audiences. He clearly appreciated the opportunity to share his native culture with his American patrons in this way, but he was also giving them exactly what he thought they wanted, that is, a glimpse of the protean Andalusian artist in action. The role he played for them was clearly a version of the self but it also ended up taking its toll, which might explain the rather ungracious things he sometimes said about his hosts and their guests in his letters home and upon his return to Spain.[54]

While he was playing the role of cultural ambassador at the court of New York's elite, often dressed up in his Ivy League clothes (bow tie and plus fours, or the more casual jumpers and slacks he bought in Oxford), Lorca also took time to explore the city's more unconventional and bohemian locations. According to one of his fellow students, he would sometimes disappear from the Columbia campus for a couple of days and go off on unrecorded adventures; he was also, it seems, a frequent nocturnal visitor to nearby Riverside Drive, a gay cruising ground.[55] A close friend, the Puerto Rican translator Ángel Flores, once took Lorca to see

Lorca with friends at Columbia University, New York, autumn 1929.

Hart Crane in his flat near Brooklyn Bridge and left the two poets, neither of whom spoke the other's language with any fluency, in the company of a group of sailors who were already drunk on moonshine.[56] But Lorca's favourite area of New York was Harlem, just a short walk away from the university, where he often frequented the myriad night clubs, speakeasies and cabarets, some of which offered openly gay shows, and also became fascinated with the life and culture of New York's African American population. He was overwhelmed by the inventive and acrobatic dancing he saw and, above all, by the jazz and blues music that he heard, claiming that it was comparable only to *cante jondo*,[57] but he was also disturbed by the widespread racism suffered by Black communities and by what he believed to be the psychological consequences of that racism.

What Lorca saw and experienced in Harlem brought his understanding of New York (and, by extension, North American) culture into sharper focus. In his letters he presents the city as a place of violent contrasts, where the obscene money of Wall Street, which is fought over daily in an 'international war leavened by a touch of courtesy',[58] stands cheek by jowl with extreme poverty and destitution. His belief in the essentially materialistic nature of the 'American people' (by which he principally meant white people like his fellow students at Columbia and the hosts of the soirées and their guests) led him to claim that Americans were good, friendly, generous, childlike and occasionally brutish, but also emotionally and spiritually stunted, since, as he added in one letter, they 'possess fewer feelings than us Spaniards' and can hardly be said to have souls.[59] Lorca's stay in New York served to bring out a rather conservative, traditional and even xenophobic side in the poet. When he visited Coney Island in early July, he at first enjoyed and then recoiled in horror from the vision of hundreds of thousands of ordinary Americans swimming, enjoying the funfair and eating hot dogs. The spectacle, he told his parents shortly after, was simply 'too popular', while the 'savagery' of the American people can only be explained, he said, by the absence in the USA of social classes.[60] Lorca seems to be giving voice here to a similar fear of social mobility and mass culture to that found in his compatriot José Ortega y Gasset's elitist liberal reading of Western society, *La rebelión de las masas* (The Revolt of the Masses, 1930), although Lorca's vision is also shot through with a rather patriotic bias: Spanish popular culture is as noble and deep as America's mass culture is debased and superficial, he implies, adding to his parents that he is now convinced that Spain is the only 'strong' and 'living' country left in the world.[61]

It is in his reading of the different religions he encountered in New York that we get the full measure of Lorca's patriotic traditionalism at this time and also of his rather stereotypical responses to North American culture. He has no time whatsoever for Protestantism, especially Methodism, which he associates in a negatively Weberian way with a cruel and soulless work ethic and also, crucially, with Prohibition. The word 'Protestant', he tells his parents, is equivalent in his eyes to 'idiota seco' (dry idiot), while, with its 'imposition' of the Dry Laws, the 'hateful' Methodist Church was acting in a much more repressive way than the Spanish Jesuits had ever done.[62] He rejects Protestantism on aesthetic grounds too, finding the sight of a pastor standing in front of an organ rather than an altar and of a congregation doing no more than singing hymns to be not only ridiculous but totally devoid of beauty, humanity and consolation.[63] His Puerto Rican friend Sofía Megwinoff relates that he wanted to run out of an African American Methodist service in Harlem, although she adds that this was more out of a sense of terror than disgust, suggesting some sort of superstitious response to what he witnessed.[64] In contrast, Lorca found there to be power and passion both in the Russian Orthodox liturgy and in the songs he heard in a Sephardic Synagogue (where he thought that all the congregation looked like *granadinos*), although he told his parents that the beauty and depth of Catholicism is infinitely superior to that of the Orthodox Church and that the Jewish rites ultimately lacked meaning for him, as the figure of Christ is too strong to be 'denied'.[65] Only Catholicism and, more specifically, Spanish Catholicism (the North American strain, he felt, had become infected with some of the coldness of Protestantism) has true grandeur and poetry, above all in its adornment of the altar, its adoration of the Sacrament and its cult of the Virgin. It also, as he had already suggested in his *Ode to the Most Blessed Sacrament* (whose final two parts he completed during his first months in New York), has a true sense of mystery that originates in the Spanish people's capacity to feel the living presence of God in Church. In short, as he concludes in a striking (but still reactionary) reversal of the Black Legend, his experience in New York has made him understand 'the *racial* motive behind Spain's great struggle against Protestantism and behind the deeply Spanish attitude of Philip II, that great king who has been so unjustly treated by history'.[66]

There can be no doubting the depth of Lorca's religious feeling in New York, although it is more than likely that some of the exaggerated statements or descriptions found in his letters to his parents also had

Lorca's drawing *Autorretrato en Nueva York* (Self-portrait in New York), 1929.

something to do with homesickness and a sense of cultural estrangement. One of the most impressive drawings he produced at this time, the *Autorretrato en Nueva York* (Self-portrait in New York), shows the poet in two guises. On the one hand, he appears as an ovaloid head with long and flailing arms wedged between strange beasts and skyscrapers with holes, letters and numbers for windows, while, towards the top of the drawing, he presents himself as a flying head with large ears and trailing what look like roots or perhaps nerves.[67] The implication seems clear: however much he enjoyed the excitement, attention and freedom afforded him by the city, he could also feel lost, unrooted and painfully exposed there – and it would be these darker emotions, rather than the more positive ones found in most of his letters, that he would express and explore in the main work that would come out of his North American stay, namely the poetic collection *Poeta en Nueva York* (Poet in New York). Although Lorca continued to refine the poems of *Poet in New York* over the rest of his life (the collection would finally be published posthumously by his friend José Bergamín in Mexico in 1940), the first drafts of almost all of them were actually completed during Lorca's stay in the city. They therefore provide a direct commentary on what he would later, in the 'Conferencia-recital' (Lecture-recital) of *Poet in New York*, refer to as one of the two defining cities in the modern world (the other one being Moscow)[68] and offer a testimony of what he elsewhere called this 'Babylonian, cruel and violent city that is at the same time full of great modern beauty'.[69] It seems from a letter he sent to his family in January 1930 that he originally planned to publish the poems alongside both photographs and drawings,[70] which would certainly have served to reinforce the visual and plastic nature of many of the images they contain. Those images now clearly correspond to Lorca's new Dalinian 'objective' mode of writing, and many of them, especially those that belong to the section entitled 'Introducción a la Muerte' (Introduction to Death), are highly personal, hermetic and surreal in nature. But one can notice other new influences at work in the collection too. Despite being completely uninterested in speaking English in New York, Lorca spent a good deal of time discussing and translating English poetry with friends. Sofía Megwinoff recounts that he asked her one day to read out some poems by Edgar Allan Poe and that, despite not understanding a word, he was hypnotized by the sounds of 'The Bells' and, above all, 'Annabel Lee', whose rhythm he marked both with his hands and by making humming noises.[71] But he was most drawn to the outlook and style of two other North American writers. His friend Ángel Flores showed him drafts of his translation of T. S. Eliot's *The Waste Land*, with its raw depiction of the soullessness of another great city. And, even more importantly still, Lorca continued to be drawn to the vigorous and often sexually explicit poetry of Walt Whitman (which he read mainly in translation), and he would end up emulating Whitman's expansive free verse in some of his own poems. If Lorca and Hart Crane managed to discuss anything literary during their drunken meeting, it was almost definitely Walt Whitman: Crane was at that moment writing his new poetic collection *The Bridge*, whose section 'Cape Hatteras' turns to Whitman as it seeks a poetic idiom capable of capturing (and, in his case, celebrating) the life of the modern metropolis.

As its title makes clear, *Poet in New York* focuses not just on New York but on the poet himself (Lorca started his 'Lecture-recital' by saying that he should perhaps have used the title 'Nueva York en un poeta' instead).[72] Alongside the more descriptive and denunciatory poems, there is also a personal story that informs and helps to shape the collection. As Leslie Stainton has pointed out, Lorca returns here 'for the first time in nearly ten years [that is, since his earliest verse] to a first-person, confessional voice',[73] and what seems to get that voice talking is the very experience of uprootedness and distance from home itself. The first section, entitled 'Poemas de la soledad en Columbia University' (Poems of Loneliness in Columbia University), with its violent images of stunted trees and injured animals, sets the scene of an urban world that is devoid of beauty and cut off from nature but also allows Lorca to start giving expression to his most recent traumas. 'Fábula y rueda de los tres amigos' (Fable and Round of the Three Friends), for example, with its references to Enrique, Emilio and Lorenzo being frozen, burnt, buried and mummified and ultimately murdering the poet himself, may not provide an answer to the pain Lorca continued to feel after the seeming collapse of his relationship with Emilio Aladrén (whom Lorca's friend Rafael Martínez Nadal identified as the Emilio of the poem),[74] but it without doubt starts to lance the boil and clearly serves a cathartic purpose.

More significantly, perhaps, Lorca's sense of physical and emotional estrangement also helped to open up new vistas onto his more distant past. In '1910 (Intermedio)' (1910 (Interlude)), he explores the innocence of the child he once was but also suggests the fears, violence, pain and possibly even abuse that had stalked his childhood world, which he characterizes as 'un jardín donde los gatos se comían a las ranas' (a garden where the cats ate the frogs)[75] – an image that brings to mind the terrifying self-portrait of a drowned child being eaten by rats that starts off 'Infancia y muerte' (Childhood and Death), a poem that, although written in New York, was not ultimately included in the collection.[76] Lorca returns to the theme of childhood in the poems he wrote during his trip outside New York in August and early September 1929, which saw him spend time with his friend Philip Cummings in Eden Mills in Vermont and with Ángel del Río and his family in Bushnellsville in New York State. In 'Poema doble del Lago Eden' (Double Poem of Lake Eden), his experience of the Vermont countryside puts him in contact once again with the 'voz antigua de mi amor' (ancient voice of my love) and leads him, on the one hand, to beg to be allowed to return to Paradise (Eden) and, on the other, repeatedly to demand his right to freedom and human love, while childhood in 'El niño Stanton' (The Little Boy Stanton) and 'Niña ahogada en el pozo' (The Little Girl Drowned in the Well) is associated more tragically with a profound and superstitious terror of illness and death.[77]

These deeply anguished personal poems provide the emotional underpinning for the collection as a whole and for its depiction of New York. When the poet looks head-on at the city, in the sections entitled 'Calles y sueños' (Streets and Dreams) and 'Vuelta a la ciudad' (Return to the City), what he sees is uniformly negative. The pair of poems 'Paisaje de la multitud que vomita' (Landscape of the Vomiting Multitude) and 'Paisaje de la multitud que orina' (Landscape of the Urinating Multitude) give expression to the absolute horror and sense of alienation Lorca felt when contemplating the massive crowds in Coney Island and Battery Park. The former poem focuses on the symbolic figure of a fat woman, the 'enemy of the moon', who leaves death and destruction in her wake as she walks through a landscape that seems to be gradually filling with vomit: it is difficult to imagine, Lorca would later say, just how alone a Spaniard – and especially, he adds, an Andalusian – feels when contemplating the vomiting and urinating masses of New York.[78]

The nightmarish visions offered by these poems, though, are not the most extreme in the collection. On 24 October 1929, Lorca witnessed at first hand the Wall Street Crash, even coming across the body of a banker who had just committed suicide by throwing himself from a hotel window. In his 'Conferencia-recital', he would say that the cold and cruel philosophy of Wall Street, which deals in gold and death, is the perfect product of Protestant morality and that the crash itself revealed a spectacle that was totally alien to him and in fact to all Spaniards: that of death without hope, death that is putrefaction and nothing else.[79] This is the spectacle he tries to capture in 'New York. Oficina y denuncia' (New York. Office and Denunciation) and 'Danza de la muerte' (Dance of Death), which provide a devastating denunciation of the abuses of unchecked capitalism. In the former, he talks of the innocent blood of a myriad slaughtered animals filling New York day by day and then goes on, like a modern-day Old Testament prophet, to spit in the faces of the one side of the city that ignores the other half, the half that suffers. In the latter, he describes a huge African mask (which he says in the 'Lecture-recital' symbolizes a definitive and soulless death that is barbarous and primitive like the United States itself),[80] which dances the Dance of Death over the city and will one day, he concludes jubilantly, destroy Wall Street first with guns and then with the invading lianas of a newly triumphant Nature.[81] This apocalyptic note can also be found in 'Grito hacia Roma' (Cry Towards Rome), where Lorca shows both how the poor and oppressed cry out for social justice and how the Catholic Church seems to have forgotten that Christ can still provide them with water and love.[82] This 'cry towards Rome' is yet another sign, along with the *Ode to the Most Blessed Sacrament*, that Lorca hangs tenaciously on to the belief that the Church, and religion in general, might just still be able to offer consolation for, and even an answer to, the multiple ills of an unjust world.

In this infernal city, only the Black inhabitants show any true sign of humanity: they represent, he says, the most spiritual and delicate side of North America, and their neighbourhoods offer an openness and a vitality that cannot be found in those districts, like Brooklyn and the Bronx, which are inhabited by what he calls 'the fair-skinned Americans'.[83] There is no doubt that Lorca can be patronising in his depiction of African Americans and that he can also easily fall into racial stereotyping. According to John Crow, a neighbour in John Jay Hall, he never really managed to understand the Black population of New York and modelled the African American characters who appear in his poems too closely on his Andalusian Gypsies.[84] It is certainly true that Lorca is often troublingly ready to associate African Americans with all that is primitive and even savage, as can be seen in his depiction of the African mask in 'Dance of Death', but it is also clear that he made an effort to understand the nature and effects of the daily injustices suffered by many. He recounts in the 'Conferencia-recital' that, while he was watching a Black dancer in Small's Paradise, a cabaret in Harlem, he became acutely aware of the fact that she was performing for a mainly white audience (including himself, of course), and he started to notice a certain reserve, distance and even absence in her eyes.[85] It is very likely too that Nella Larsen (1891–1964), who had recently published the novel *Passing* (1929), talked with Lorca during their visits to Harlem about the tendency among some Black people to try and 'pass' as whites by, among other things, powdering their skin and straightening their hair. Lorca talks in the 'Conferencia-recital' about the pain that African Americans feel simply due to the fact of being Black in a hostile world, and he adds that they are forced to live 'de prestado' (a borrowed existence),[86] a disturbing insight that he explores in greater detail in the poem 'El Rey de Harlem' (The King of Harlem), which focuses on the figure of a proud Black man who is imprisoned in a janitor's suit. Here, Lorca once again strikes an apocalyptic note, implying (and seemingly hoping) that one day blood will flow and that Nature will return to destroy the denaturalized and oppressive world that has imprisoned Black people, but he dwells too on the fact that the oppressed can themselves end up acting in a violent and self-destructive way (the king scoops out crocodiles' eyes with a spoon) or wearing masks in order to adapt to their adverse circumstances (the poem's final stanza centres on what Lorca calls 'Harlem disfrazada', or 'Harlem in disguise').[87] As we shall see in the following chapters, Lorca would continue to explore the psychological effects of repression and self-repression and the need to wear masks or disguises in the plays that he wrote over the rest of his life, from *El público* (The Public) to *The House of Bernarda Alba.*

Although Lorca continued to be fascinated by New York (and would later say that it gave him the most useful experience of his life),[88] he was, by early 1930, ready for a change. Having received an invitation from the Institución Hispano-Cubana de Cultura to deliver a series of talks in Cuba, he took the train from New York to Florida on 4 March and then the ferry from Key West to Havana two days later. He was greeted by his old friend the Cuban poet and diplomat José María Chacón y Calvo, together with a large group of Cuban writers, journalists and dignitaries, and throughout his three-month stay on the island he was treated as a literary superstar (he explained to his parents that a poet has more status in Latin America than a prince in Europe).[89] He delivered a series of partly recycled talks (on *inter alia*, imagination, inspiration and evasion, Góngora's poetic images, and *cante jondo*) at the Teatro Principal de la Comedia in Havana on 9, 12, 16 and 19 March and 6 April, sometimes illustrating his points at the piano or finishing off his talk with a poetry recital. The talks were so well received that he was sent further invitations to lecture outside Havana, in Sagua la Grande (23 March), Caibarién (30 March) and Cienfuegos (8 April), and he even used his talk in Santiago de Cuba (2 June) as an excuse to extend his stay on the island.

Lorca experienced his trip to Cuba as a sort of homecoming. He told his parents that Havana was like a mixture of Malaga and Cadiz, although the tropics made it both more animated and more relaxed at the same time: it has a caressing, soft and immensely sensual rhythm, he adds, and a charm that is wholly Spanish or, rather, Andalusian in nature.[90] Later, in the 'Conferencia-recital', he would underline the contrast between his experiences in New York and those in Cuba and, once again making use of a traditionalist, Catholic (and one could add in this case, colonialist) language, claimed that his stay on the island represented an encounter with 'the part of the Americas that has roots, the America that belongs to God, Spanish America'.[91] He fell in love with Havana, where he both shared ideas with the cream of the Cuban intelligentsia, men like essayists and political activists Juan Marinello (1898–1977) and Jorge Mañach (1898–1961), novelist Alejo Carpentier (1904–1980) and poets Nicolás Guillén (1902–1989) and José Lezama Lima (1910–1976), and, according to some testimonies, led a full and free sexual life, including assignations with sailors by the docks.[92] He enjoyed the different landscapes that he encountered on his lecture tours outside the capital and on his pleasure trips to Pinar del Río and Mariel. And he was immensely drawn to the culture, especially the Black culture, of the island.

Lorca's response to the Black population of Cuba was once again shot through with stereotype, mixed, this time, with a certain historical short-sightedness. As in New York, he tended to associate the Black people he met with all that is vital and even primitive, the difference now being that he seemed convinced that the Black people of Cuba, unlike the inhabitants of Harlem, lived in harmony with nature and did not therefore need to disguise their real selves behind masks: they were, he said in a rather condescending way (and seemingly overlooking centuries of slavery and repression), simply 'negritos sin drama' (Blacks without drama). At the same time, he came to believe that the Black and mixed-heritage population of Cuba felt part of the larger Hispanic world, claiming that they were happy to call themselves *latinos*,[93] and he was deeply attracted to those cultural forms that had been born of the meeting of different cultures. He immersed himself above all in Afro-Cuban music and dance, especially the *son*, which combined musical elements from both Africa and Spain. Lorca mused on the possible African roots of both *son* and *cante jondo* and, in the only poem that we know for sure he composed on the island – the 'Son de negros en Cuba' (Son of the Blacks in Cuba), which features as the last poem in *Poet in New York* – he makes use of the rumba-like rhythm of the *son* to pay homage to Santiago de Cuba and to the peoples and landscapes of Cuba as a whole.[94] The insistent chorus of 'Iré a Santiago' (I will go to Santiago) and the references to the illustrations that had appeared on his father's Cuban cigar boxes when he was a boy (the head of Francisco Fonseca and a painting of Romeo and Juliet) reveal not only that his trip to Cuba was the fulfilment of a childhood dream but that it put him in contact once again with the more happy and luminous side of his childhood in Fuente Vaqueros (many of whose fields, coincidentally, were just at that time starting to be turned over to the cultivation of tobacco).

Given the acclaim, freedom and rich cultural experiences that Lorca enjoyed in Cuba, it is not surprising that he boarded the ship that would take him back to Spain with some regret. But his country was living through a revolutionary moment, and Lorca himself was working hard on a new theatrical project whose revolutionary theme and style somehow chimed with the spirit of the times. It was for that reason, perhaps, that he told the friends who accompanied him on 12 June, the day that he left Havana on the *Manuel Arnús*, that 'Hago falta en España' (I'm needed in Spain).[95]

six

Granada and Madrid: Revolution and Roots, 1930–33

L orca returned from New York and Cuba a changed man. He had changed physically, having, as his mother helpfully told him, put on quite a few extra kilograms during his twelve months away.[1] But he appears to have changed as a person too, at least according to his New York friends Mildred Adams and Norma Brickell, who on 19 June 1930 went to see him on board the *Manuel Arnús* as it briefly moored in New York harbour before continuing its journey to Cadiz. Adams would later write that she found Lorca that day to be 'hot, male and triumphant', while Brickell would add that 'The Lorca we knew has disappeared. Havana has produced another, not nearly so nice.'[2] They seemed to have discovered a louder and brasher side to Lorca's personality that the poet had not shown during the refined soirées of the previous autumn and winter, although, as Ian Gibson has pointed out, it is possible too that they had become suddenly aware – or more aware – of his homosexuality, which, after his triumphant and triumphantly joyful stay in Cuba, Lorca felt less compelled to hide or disguise.[3]

The Spain that Lorca encountered when he disembarked in Cadiz on 30 June and arrived in Granada on 1 July was in revolutionary turmoil. General Primo de Rivera had resigned on 28 January, due to not only the increasing opposition of certain sectors of the armed forces and working-class movements and among many intellectuals and university students, but the economic fall-out of the Wall Street Crash, which Lorca had witnessed at first hand. For the time being, Primo de Rivera's replacement, General Dámaso Berenguer (1873–1953), continued the work of the dictatorship but also introduced some timid reforms in an ultimately futile attempt both to placate the opposition and to prop up King

Alfonso XIII. The months leading up to the end of the dictatorship and the fall of the monarchy in April 1931 would be marked by protests, demonstrations, strikes, Republican uprisings and increasing agitation from the far Left, especially the Anarchists.

Lorca, like most artists and intellectuals of his generation, had reacted passively or even apathetically to Primo de Rivera's *coup d'état* in September 1923 and to the first four or five years of his military dictatorship, but, by early 1929, that is, shortly before he left for New York, he had become interested in the new alliance that was starting to form between disaffected students and intellectuals. In April of that year, just a month after the celebration of a large and influential student strike, he became a co-signatory of an open letter calling for the creation of a new and radically liberal political party that could attract young intellectuals and professionals alike. This is one of the earliest examples of Lorca allowing his name to be added to a political or protest letter, although it is very possible that his decision to do so was linked to the banning just a few weeks earlier (for supposed immorality) of his play *The Love of Don Perlimplín*, which was being produced by fellow signatory Cipriano Rivas Cherif (1891–1967). Lorca's comments on the dictatorship during his stay in both New York and Cuba seem to have been restricted to the odd off-the-record complaint about the banning of his play,[4] and there is no sign that he was influenced in any way by the much more radical stance of his friend and mentor Fernando de los Ríos, who was one of the very few intellectuals (and indeed one of the few members of the Socialist Party) to oppose Primo de Rivera from the outset and who had accompanied Lorca to New York precisely because he had just given up his Chair at the University of Granada in protest against the dictator. It is rumoured that, during his stay in Cuba, Lorca did give voice, at least in private, to serious misgivings about the increasingly repressive regime of Gerardo Machado,[5] but, when it came to Spain, what seemed to concern him most was the chaos and violence that might ensue once Primo de Rivera left power. When he finally heard of the dictator's fall in late January 1930, he told his parents from New York that he was in a state of high anxiety and added, rather enigmatically, that he felt that things would now develop dramatically until they reached their definitive solution, without there being anything that anybody could do to 'alleviate' what historical destiny had in store.[6] A month or two later, he summed up the Spanish situation from Cuba with the succinct affirmation 'Aquello es un volcán' (That's a volcano over there).[7]

The truth is that, while Spain was going through its revolution, Lorca was living out a revolution of his own, one that had more to do with sexuality and with art than with politics. The volcanic events in Spain provided the backdrop to this personal revolution and would end up amplifying the intense mixture of excitement and trepidation that Lorca was obviously feeling at this time. It is clear that his experiences in New York and Cuba had bolstered both his confidence as a writer and his sense of identity as a gay man, and it is therefore significant that the work he finished off on the sea journey back to Spain should be his first truly explicit homosexual poem, 'Oda a Walt Whitman' (Ode to Walt Whitman).[8] This poem, more than any of the others that would make up *Poet in New York*, reveals what it was that Lorca felt he owed to Whitman not just as a writer but, more importantly, as an iconic homosexual figure. In this sense, the 'Ode to Walt Whitman' offers a complex and revealing self-portrait of Lorca as a gay man.

Like so many of the other poems in the collection, the 'Ode' is forged out of a simple and even simplistic binary opposition between the dehumanized and denaturalized urban world of New York (associated with mud, barbed wire and death) and the Romanticized world of nature (associated with butterflies, flowers and, of course, the expansive nature-inspired poetry of Walt Whitman himself). Lorca now applies this self-same opposition to homosexuals, making a clear distinction between the young men who work, stripped to their waists, along the East River and yet never wish to become a river themselves and, on the other hand, the figure of Walt Whitman, who dreamt not only of being a river but of sleeping with a 'comrade' capable of filling his breast with 'un pequeño dolor de ignorante leopardo' (the tiny pain of an unknowing leopard). But Lorca goes much further than this, launching a violent tirade against those he terms 'maricas' (queers), gays who may point at Walt Whitman and claim him as their own but are in reality harbingers of death rather than of vitality and life. These 'maricas', he says, inhabit the bars and sewers of the city and expose their flesh to the whip, boot or bite of those who wish to dominate them; they are, he adds in a particularly brutal passage, the murderers of doves,

Esclavos de la mujer, perras de sus tocadores,
abiertos en las plazas con fiebre de abanico
o emboscados en yertos paisajes de cicuta.[9]

Slaves of women, the bitches of their boudoirs,
opening up in squares with the fever of fans
or ambushed in stiff landscapes of hemlock.

These disturbingly homophobic and misogynistic lines, which may,
of course, have their roots in some unknown experience in New York or
Cuba, paint a heartless and rather clichéd portrait of homosexual men
who court a certain type of attention from women or are forced, in one
way or another, to sell or prostitute themselves. Within the overall economy of the poem, they serve to strengthen the central distinction that
Lorca establishes between homosexuals who make an exhibition of themselves, display sadomasochistic tendencies and therefore turn love into
a form of poison or death and, on the other hand, those who, like Walt
Whitman, look for nakedness that has the form and naturalness of a river
and for love that can be passion and compassion, sex and companionship,
at one and the same time. Lorca is obviously drawn to the vitality and
manliness, the 'hermosura viril' (virile beauty), that he has found in
Whitman, and, under the spell of the North American poet, is able to
affirm that man's desire can travel in whichever direction he chooses
and to predict that one day everyone will be able to love freely and with
confidence: 'Mañana los amores serán rocas' (Tomorrow loves will be
rocks).[10]

But that is tomorrow. For now, homosexuals are still not able to
declare their love in public and still have to deal with the psychological
effects of repression and self-repression. In stark contrast to the callous
way in which he treats the 'maricas', whose main sin seems to be that they
expose their complex sexual and psychological needs and perhaps their
self-loathing to the gaze of the world, Lorca proclaims that he would
never speak ill of the boy who writes the name of a girl on his pillow or
tries on a bride's dress in the darkness of his closet or of the solitary men
who swallow with disgust the water of prostitution or whose love of men
leads them to burn their lips in silence.[11] He recognizes that repressed
sexual desire, repressed love, can take many forms, some more benign and
some more harmful or self-harmful, but also suggests that, until the day
comes when desire and love can be liberated and freely expressed, it is
best to keep the complex forms that one's own desire and love can take
to oneself.

While the 'Ode to Walt Whitman' offers a Romantic dream of
strong male love in a utopian future and an apparent call for discretion

in the present, the other unfinished work that Lorca brought back with him from the New World would attempt to gaze through the veil of discretion at the hidden forms of homosexual love beyond. *The Public* is a play that is concerned with opening up and breaking through, with the possibility of carrying out a true revolution in the way that both love and art, in this case theatre, are allowed to comport and manifest themselves, and it gives expression to the mixture of fascination and fear that Lorca appears to feel in the face of potentially violent change. He possibly started work on this play in New York, though the earliest parts of the single extant manuscript are written on notepaper from the hotel he stayed in while in Havana. What we know for sure is that he worked on it intensively on the boat trip home and then during his first two months back in Granada, with the date of completion of the first draft given as 22 August 1930.

The Public is not only Lorca's most original play but his most hermetic one, due in part to the fact that the version that has come down to us is incomplete. Lorca only published two of its constituent scenes (*cuadros*), numbers 2 and 5, during his lifetime; the remaining parts of the play, made up of three further scenes and a poem (at least one other scene is missing), have been reconstructed from the manuscript that Lorca left with Rafael Martínez Nadal on the eve of his final trip to Granada in July 1936.[12] But *The Public*'s hermeticism also derives from its complex and frequently surreal dialogue and settings and from the fact that there often seems to be more than one drama being played out on stage at any one time. In fact, just like the 'Ode to Walt Whitman', *The Public* simultaneously explores two separate but interrelated issues: on the one hand, the search to liberate homosexual love and desire and, on the other, the multiple shapes that homosexual love and desire can assume when faced with the repressive demands of an intolerant society. And it does these things by creating characters who are all involved (as director, actors, prompter, members of the audience and so on) in the preparation and performance of the tomb scene from Shakespeare's *Romeo and Juliet*, a device that allows *The Public* to talk at one and the same time about a possible revolution in both sexual morality and the world of theatre.

The play is built around the contrast between two types of theatre. At the start of the first scene, the character known as the Director declares himself to be an advocate of the 'teatro al aire libre' (open-air theatre),[13] whose main function is to entertain the audience and make money, but he is soon visited by three men, supposedly members of the audience, one of whom, the First Man (Hombre 1), talks of the need to inaugurate a new type of theatre, the 'teatro bajo la arena' (theatre beneath the sand).[14] It is tempting to see the First Man not just as a member of the audience but also as a playwright – and even as a version of Lorca himself, who, as we have seen, had spent many frustrating weeks and months in the mid- to late 1920s trying to convince theatre impresarios, directors and actresses to stage *Mariana Pineda* and *The Shoemaker's Prodigious Wife*. But what the First Man is suggesting is not a historical drama or a comedy but something much more radical, that is, a type of theatre that can plumb the depths of human motivation and sexuality and bring to light what mainstream theatrical audiences will find distasteful and even repugnant. The Director reacts with terror, fearing for his livelihood and also his life: if he were to stage such a drama, he says, he would leave his audience without a safety net and they, in the form of a mask, could turn on him and destroy him.[15] But the First Man insists and gradually, over the following scenes, helps to bring this new theatre into being, first by forcing the Director and his friends to go behind a folding screen, from which they emerge transformed, and then, in the third scene, by helping to relocate the action of the play they are all in to Juliet's tomb.

We are now, by this third scene, not only in the realm of the theatre beneath the sand but, it would seem, in the world of the unconscious and of uncontrolled desires. The central section focuses on the relationship between Juliet and a series of equine characters, whom we first met as representatives of the audience at the start of the first scene and who, here, wish to penetrate and possess her. Juliet resists and ultimately turns the tables on the horses, saying that she is now ready to mount them instead and, like Delilah, rob them of their strength by cutting their manes.[16] She also tells the story of four young men (most probably the transformed versions of the Director and the three men) who have tried to turn her into a man by attaching a clay phallus to her and painting a moustache on her upper lip.[17] When the Director and the First Man return to the stage, the latter celebrates this inauguration of the theatre beneath the sand but also berates the horses for having simply 'swum on the surface' – the implication being that, unlike Juliet, they have not been able fully to understand, accept or express their innermost desires.[18] In the fifth scene, we hear that a riot has broken out: the audience wishes to destroy the theatre beneath the sand, punish the director and the poet who are responsible for what it has just seen on stage, and, above all, kill Romeo and Juliet, since it now realizes that both of these parts were played by male actors and is unable to understand how two men could ever love each other.[19]

Our reactions to the rest of this scene are guided by five new characters, all university students who have witnessed the riot and narrate for us what continues to happen offstage. It is the Second Student (Estudiante 2) who gives a first intimation of what their overall response to the situation will be when he wonders whether Romeo and Juliet really have to be a man and a woman for the play to be truly moving.[20] The students then go off to witness the repeat performance of the tomb scene that a judge has ordered to take place and, upon their return, report that the audience has murdered Romeo and Juliet because, despite the best efforts of the Director, it realized that Romeo was a thirty-year-old man and Juliet a fifteen-year-old boy.[21] Although the audience had in fact been deeply moved by what it saw on stage, the 'letter of the law' (in the form, one imagines, both of the controlling conscious mind and of social convention) has finally been re-established and 'doctrine' has trampled on the 'most innocent of truths', that is, quite clearly, the truth of love itself.[22] But the scene does not end there but rather with what seems to be an epiphanic moment for the First Student and the Fifth Student. When the latter expresses his attraction to Juliet and is informed that she was played by an adolescent boy in disguise, he reacts by saying that he does not care about the gender of the person he loves, so long as that person fills him with joyful desire. He also accepts the First Student's offer of love, and the two men then imagine themselves both expressing their shared happiness, Walt Whitman-like, in the natural world and destroying man-made convention (in the form of houses, families and the priest's missal). Together, they conclude in triumph, they will break open the rocks and allow a volcano to issue forth.[23]

This, ultimately, is the revolution that *The Public* dreams of, a sexual revolution whose volcanic violence mirrors and echoes the volcanic atmosphere in Spain in 1930 (and it is no coincidence that Lorca imagines his sexual revolution being led by students, a sector of society that he knew perfectly well was at the forefront of the struggle for regime change in the country). And yet the play is fully aware that this revolution is a fragile affair, since both the students, with their joyful defence of the right to love freely, and the advocates of the theatre beneath the sand are, as the Director himself had predicted, surrounded on all sides by characters who stalk and threaten them, from the representatives of 'law' and 'doctrine' (such as the judge who decrees the execution of Romeo and Juliet) to the confused and intolerant audience itself that does indeed end up acting as a 'mask' that destroys everything it does not understand. In fact, the story of the students' epiphanic discovery and liberation in the fifth scene is itself intercut with the painful scenes of the long and clinical 'crucifixion' of the now Christ-like First Man, who is being sacrificed due to his love for the Director and his espousal of the theatre beneath the sand. Little surprise, therefore, that the play as a whole should end up focusing as much on the consequences of repression and self-repression as on the ultimately utopian revolution that it appears to announce in the fifth scene.

The Public approaches the matter of repression and its effects on sexual identity through the use of two main motifs. The first is that of the mask, which comes to represent the identities we assume in order to cope with social pressure and convention. The First Man is adamant that he never wears a mask and that he is doing everything he can to rip the Director's mask off too, but the Director retorts that we can never avoid wearing masks: they save us from embarrassment by doing our buttons up in public and they also oppress our flesh when we pick our noses or explore our behinds in the privacy of our bedrooms.[24] Here Lorca returns to the debates over authentic and adopted identities, which had haunted some of his earliest work, such as the short stories 'Friar Antonio (Strange Poem)' and 'Pierrot: Intimate Poem,'[25] and the evidence provided by *The Public* would seem ultimately to corroborate the Director's belief in the inevitability (at least in the world as it is now) of masks: however heroic the First Man's attempt to rip off the Director's mask and to give free rein to his love may appear to be, he ends up being crucified in the fifth scene in the guise of a *desnudo rojo* (red nude) – red-raw, most probably, because he has finally been hounded and flayed by the vengeful mask of convention.

The second motif is that of the costume or disguise. As the First Man takes the preliminary step towards creating the theatre beneath the sand in the first scene, he produces a folding screen that has the effect of bringing about a transformation in those who walk behind it: the Director emerges as a boyish Pierrot figure (to be played, the stage direction says, by an actress) who searches desperately for the love of a woman called Elena; the Second Man becomes a woman dressed in black pyjamas and carrying a lorgnette attached to a false moustache (which presumably allows him/her to re-adopt at will the albeit comic disguise of a man); and the Third

Man appears carrying a whip and wearing a wristband covered in golden nails.[26] Although these new guises disappear at the end of the first scene, they serve to reveal hidden aspects of the sexual identities of these three characters and also to show how each of them is negotiating both their homoerotic desire and the strategies that they have developed in order to express, sublimate or deny it (including taking refuge in a conventional heterosexual relationship or, like the *maricas* in 'Ode to Walt Whitman', openly displaying certain sadomasochistic tendencies).[27] The third scene reveals, though, that, however much one sheds one's costume or identity and adopts another one, it is simply not the case that the latter replaces, or is in any way more genuine than, the former: the characters are joined on stage by the costumes they had assumed in the first scene transformed now into characters in their own right.[28] According to the play, there is clearly no fixed, unchanging, secure identity underlying the multiple disguises we adopt or roles that we play in our sexual or our everyday lives.

———

The Public reveals just how much Lorca had changed both personally and as a writer during his trip abroad, although it also contains signs that the emotional wounds he took with him to New York had not healed altogether. Ian Gibson, who in his reading of the play clearly and perhaps over-insistently associates the First Man with Lorca and the Director with Emilio Aladrén, conjectures that the 'Elena' to whom the Director calls out as a way of evading his homosexual feelings is a direct reference to Aladrén's new fiancée, the Englishwoman Eleanor (Elena, in Spanish) Dove.[29] Lorca appears to have remained in touch with Aladrén throughout his stay in New York and Cuba and to have met up with him again in the autumn of 1930, although their relationship, if they did indeed resume it, would finally be brought to an end with Aladrén's marriage to Eleanor Dove in November 1931 – an event that, according to Lorca's friend Pura Maórtua de Ucelay, made the poet feel desperate and even go 'crazy' for a while.[30] The other old friend very much on Lorca's mind in Granada in the summer of 1930 was Salvador Dalí, to whom he wrote a letter showing off about his time in New York and suggesting that the two of them should spend six months there the following year in order to take advantage of his rich 'idiot friends' who would be more than willing to buy their drawings and paintings: New York, he adds, in an obvious attempt to win Dalí back from Buñuel, would offer him new vistas that Paris, with its 'rotten renovated Romanticism', could never do.[31] Lorca and Dalí (who, unbeknown to Lorca, was also now involved with a woman, his muse Gala) would not in fact meet up again until September 1935.

After a more or less relaxing summer in Granada and Malaga, during which he apparently became romantically involved with a young bull-fighter,[32] Lorca made a triumphant return to Madrid, after fifteen months' absence, in October 1930. He was treated as a celebrity, the author now not only of the hugely popular *Gypsy Ballads* but, as he told journalist Miguel Pérez Ferrero, of three new books of poetry that he was planning to publish soon (but never in fact got round to doing so): the *Odes* and two collections based on his experience of New York.[33] He wrote to his family later in October to say that he was being lionized by the editors and literati of Madrid, with the former wishing to publish everything he had ever written and the latter recognizing his importance and his influ-ence (and, in some cases, he adds, fearing it). He had just made a record with his old friend La Argentinita, accompanying her on the piano as she sang a selection of Spanish folk songs (this being the only sound record-ing involving Lorca that has come down to us: unfortunately, we have no recording of his voice), and would be receiving a tidy sum as a result.[34] He worked with director Cipriano Rivas Cherif and actress Margarita Xirgu on their production of *The Shoemaker's Prodigious Wife*, which received its première in the Teatro Español in Madrid on 24 December to great acclaim from the critics. Rafael Martínez Nadal helped him organize the text of *Poem of the Deep Song*, which would finally appear in print in May 1931. And he undertook a short but successful lecture tour of the north of Spain in early December 1930, apparently with Emilio Aladrén in tow.[35]

The letters of this time reveal Lorca to be in a buoyant mood. It is true that he registered his concern at the political situation in Spain, complaining about the brutal way in which the Civil Guard was repress-ing working-class demonstrations in Madrid and adding that the failed Republican uprising in Jaca on 12 December had left him feeling very anxious, but he was, on a personal level, very proud of his achievements as the new 'niño de moda' (fashionable kid in town) and was also obvi-ously enjoying his freedom in Madrid, especially after February 1931, when he moved into a small flat of his own in the Calle Ayala in the plush Salamanca district.[36] He was particularly excited to hear on 9 December that his sister Concha had just given birth to her first child, and during Christmas, back in Granada, he started his new career as the fondest of uncles, as the family photographs would clearly show over the following years.[37] As far as new literary projects were concerned, he appears to have been more interested at this time in the theatre than in poetry and did his best in late 1930 and early 1931 to get his puppet play *The Tragicomedy of Cristóbal and his Missus, Rosita* produced, going so far as having some of the puppets' heads made by sculptor Ángel Ferrant before the whole project fell through.[38] As he told his parents in late February or early March 1931, he even tried to convince the actress Irene López Heredia to put on *The Public*,[39] a play which, he informed the journalist J. L. in December 1930, represented the true future direction of his theatrical work, although he also suggested in some of his interviews that it might ultimately be unperformable.[40] Perhaps for this reason he spent much of the time over these months and up until August 1931 finishing off another play whose central idea he had also brought back with him from New York and Cuba but whose content would not be quite so shocking (even if its stagecraft would be every bit as innovative). That play would be *Así que pasen cinco años* (As Soon As Five Years Have Passed).

The story at the heart of this play is a relatively simple one: the Young Man (Joven) postpones his relationship with his fifteen-year-old Fiancée (Novia) for five years in Act I, only to find out five years later, in Act II, that she has fallen instead for a very masculine American Football Player (Jugador de Rugby). In Act III, the Young Man declares his love to the Typist (Mecanógrafa), whose approaches he had rejected back in Act I, only to find that she in turn insists now on waiting five years before entering into a relationship with him, news that causes his death at the end of this final act. This haunting play offers Lorca's profoundest examination of the effects that passing time has on desire. All of the characters seem to be made of time itself, although each inhabits different temporal realms. The Young Man's Friend (Amigo), with his talk of pleasure and sexual conquests, and the Fiancée, obsessed as she is with her Football Player, seem to be rooted firmly in the present moment, while the Old Man (Viejo) who accompanies the Young Man sporadically throughout the play appears to waver between the past and the future, both of which he views with trepidation. The Young Man and the Typist themselves never seem to inhabit the same temporal coordinates, with the former living in his future dreams in Act I and in an urgent present in Act III, the exact opposite of the Typist, who ends up repeating many of the Young Man's words from Act I at the climax of the play. And then there is the devastating appearance in the middle of Act I of the dead Boy (Niño), dressed in his white First Communion suit and accompanied by a dead Cat (Gato), both of them waiting to be interred. These characters give expression to an overwhelming terror of death itself, an event that should seemingly lift them out of time altogether and yet in fact seems to leave them in limbo, where all they can do is imagine the coming awfulness of being buried under the ground. Lorca would create few more affecting characters than this dead Boy, who perhaps provides an insight into the fears and superstitions of the child Lorca himself had once been and whose cry of '¡Yo quiero ser niño, un niño!' (I want to be a boy, a boy!) floats over the whole play as a raw and deeply moving *memento mori*.[41]

The appearance of the dead Boy and Cat radically changes the tone and texture of Act I, which up until then, and despite the surreal quality of some of the dialogue between the Young Man and the Old Man, seems to be relatively conventional as far as theme and setting are concerned. Act II, which focuses first on the Fiancée and then on her altercation with the Young Man, also starts off like a drawing room drama but is soon transformed too when, in the second half, the Young Man holds a dialogue with the Mannequin (Maniquí) wearing the Fiancée's wedding dress (a distant cousin of the costumes that appear at the end of the third scene of *The Public*). Act III removes us from conventional drama altogether and takes us to a forest, where Harlequin (Arlequín) and a Clown (Payaso) seem to act as ringmasters of the action that takes place and also to have control over a theatre that has been set up in the middle of the stage. The atmosphere takes on some of the magic of *A Midsummer Night's Dream*, and Lorca revisits the Shakespearean notion of love as chance and fatality that has obsessed him since his very earliest poetry, but the presence of Harlequin and the Clown ensures that the love stories told by the Typist and other characters also take on the strangeness of dreams and occasionally the irreverent playfulness and disturbing pathos of the circus. The Young Man and the Typist are finally forced by Harlequin and the Clown to play out their scene of impossible love onstage and they then continue it in the theatre within the theatre, where they seem to be imprisoned both in their roles and in the specific temporal dimension that each at that point inhabits. Love is therefore transformed literally into theatre, but theatre with a fatal dénouement, as the Young Man ultimately dies as the result of a card game with three shadowy card players who seem to represent the Fates or Death itself.

While *As Soon As Five Years Have Passed* focuses centrally on the relationship between time and love or desire, it also revisits the themes of sexuality and gender identity, although in a far less explicit way than *The Public* (a fact which probably made it a more performable play in Lorca's mind). There is no doubt that there are different forms of masculinity on show, from the (silent) brutishness of the American Football Player, a reflection without doubt of the sportsmen Lorca had lived among and watched from the top floor of Furnald Hall in Columbia University, to the sexual confidence and bonhomie of the Young Man's Friend, to the more sensitive and imaginative, but also timid and fearful, masculinity of the Young Man himself. It might be tempting to read the Young Man's initial desire to postpone his relationship with the Fiancée as the expression of a gay man's fear of women, and his later courting of the Typist as a surrender to convention, but such readings are not suggested by the text itself. There is, however, an important moment in the play that has a direct relationship with an earlier and more directly autobiographical work in which Lorca had expressed some of his deepest desires and regrets as a gay man. As we saw in Chapter Four, the two poems 'In the Garden of the Moon-grapefruits' and 'In the Forest of the Moon-grapefruits', written in summer 1923, open up a dream-like world of virtual realities and alternative existences in which the poet expresses regret for the wife and children he will never have.[42] In a similar way, the exchange between the Young Man and the Mannequin wearing the Fiancée's wedding dress in Act II becomes a duet between a husband and a wife who are never to be and leads the Young Man desperately and movingly to search and long for his child, who 'canta en su cuna, / y como es niño de nieve / aguarda calor y ayuda' (sings in his cot, / and, as a child made of snow, / needs heat and help).[43] It is more than possible that Lorca's joyous new role as uncle to Concha's first-born had served to intensify a similar longing in himself and to make him too feel what the Young Man later claims, that is, that his son 'corre por dentro de mí, como una hormiga sola dentro de una caja cerrada' (runs round inside me, like a single ant inside a closed box).[44]

The months during which Lorca finished off *As Soon As Five Years Have Passed* saw the great change that many in Spain had been fighting for over the previous two or three years. The result of the municipal elections of 12 April 1931, which were seen by many as an unofficial plebiscite on the monarchy, led two days later to both the exile of King Alfonso XIII and the end of the military dictatorship. Thus the Second Spanish Republic was born, a Republic that would immediately represent different things to different people.

From the outset, there were groups at either end of the political spectrum that refused to recognize its legitimacy, including the revolutionary Anarchists on the Left and more radical Monarchists, ultra-conservative Catholics and those with proto-fascist leanings on the Right. There were also elements both in the Socialist Party and in the official conservative and Catholic parties that would become increasingly radical, thereby helping, wittingly or unwittingly, to bring about a growing ideological polarization that would ultimately serve to destabilize the new regime altogether. But, for its first two years at least, the Second Republic would be built and run by a coalition of elements from the more radical liberal-republican parties and the more moderate wing of the Socialist Party, all of which came together in an attempt to create a modern, democratic, reforming State that could tackle issues such as agrarian reform and the relationships between Church and State and between the regions and the centre. This liberal-socialist Republic, led by Manuel Azaña (an acquaintance of Lorca's and the brother-in-law of his close friend and colleague Cipriano Rivas Cherif), in many ways represented the realization of the Krausist dream of intellectuals like Francisco Giner de los Ríos, founder of the Free Teaching Institute (Institución Libre de Enseñanza), whose pedagogical and cultural values had also lain at the core of the Residencia de Estudiantes. Perhaps the greatest representative of this reforming republicanism was Lorca's mentor Fernando de los Ríos, a man who was both a direct product of the Free Teaching Institute himself and a leader of the more moderate wing of the Socialist Party. Fernando de los Ríos would serve first as Minister of Justice (April–December 1931) and then as Minister of Education and the Arts (December 1931 until June 1933) and, briefly, as Foreign Minister (June–September 1933). It was during his time as Minister of Education that he oversaw the opening of thousands of new schools, the training of a whole generation of new teachers, and extensive public investment in the arts, all policies that were designed to put into practice the fundamentally Krausist belief that a country can best be modernized through the fostering of education and culture.

This reforming, educational and cultural Republic would be Lorca's Republic. He said as much in the talk he gave in early September 1931 in his home village of Fuente Vaqueros, where he had been invited, as part of the village fiestas, to inaugurate the new popular library. This talk is the closest Lorca ever came to formulating publicly a clear political position. He starts by praising Fuente Vaqueros as a modern, liberal and progressive village that has always realized the importance of reading and learning, and goes on to remind his audience of all that his family has done for education and culture in the vicinity, starting with his mother, who had taught many local girls and boys to read when she was a schoolteacher and has often read aloud to local people ever since.[45] His main aim in the talk, though, is to defend and proclaim the need for culture. Books like the ones that the new library will contain may be the product of just a few privileged minds, he says, but their contents are for everyone.[46] Culture gives life, which is why he gets angry when he sees politicians and others talking only about the economic needs of the people. Men and women do not live by bread alone, he explains (perhaps forgetting the wretched poverty and even near-starvation that he had witnessed as a boy in Fuente Vaqueros), and it is in fact only culture that can save them from becoming machines in the service of the State or slaves of a 'terrible social organization'.[47] Culture, which Lorca's old acquaintance Ramón Menéndez Pidal had rightly said must be the motto of the new Republic, is the one and only salvation of the people, the only means to bring about their economic and social liberation.[48]

Lorca ends his talk by suggesting that the new library in Fuente Vaqueros should not be stocked following doctrinaire criteria but rather with books of all tendencies and dealing with all topics, from religion to revolution, from the poems of St John of the Cross to the essays of Nietzsche and Marx.[49] Here, in the idea of this eclectic library, Lorca seems to give concrete form to his radically liberal (and deeply Krausist) concept of the Republic as a meeting place where ideas can be acquired, shared and debated, and where the educated and cultured elite can pass on their knowledge and skills. Very shortly after Lorca gave his talk, he received a letter from one of his oldest Granada friends, Miguel Pizarro, who was at that time working as a Spanish teacher in Japan. As Pizarro tries to imagine from a distance what he believes and hopes the new Republic must be like, he paints a picture of a group of friends coming together and holding passionate discussions, just like he and Lorca and the others had done a decade earlier in the cafés of Granada.[50] For Pizarro, and also to some degree for Lorca too, the Republic, it seems, was or should be a version of the Rinconcillo writ large on the body of Spain.

Fernando de los Ríos soon did his best to make Lorca take an active part in the Republic. It has recently come to light that, shortly after becoming Minister of Education in December 1931, he invited Lorca to

accompany him as one of his private secretaries on his first official visit
to the Spanish Protectorate in Morocco.[51] But he had already given the
green light to a project that would involve his young friend in a much
more substantial role. Back in May 1931 the then Minister of Education,
Marcelino Domingo, had overseen the creation of the Misiones Pedagógicas (Pedagogical Missions), whose job it would be to take culture,
in the form of lectures, drama, film showings, mobile libraries and
even copies of masterpieces from the Prado Museum, out into the provinces. In early November a group of students from the University of
Madrid, most probably inspired by the idea of the Misiones, invited
Lorca to become the artistic director of a student troupe that would
perform the classics of the Spanish theatre both in Madrid (during
term-time) and in towns and villages throughout provincial Spain
(during the holiday periods). Both the Misiones Pedagógicas and the
Teatro Universitario (University Theatre), or La Barraca (The Stall), as
this travelling theatre company soon became known, were clearly
Krausist-inspired ventures that aimed to put into practice the belief, so
clearly shared by Lorca himself, that culture represented the 'salvation
of the people'. Lorca not only accepted the invitation but interceded with
Fernando de los Ríos, who, once Minister of Education, secured state
funds for the undertaking.

Lorca thus threw himself into an adventure that would take up a
large part of his time over the next four years. He chose the texts to be
performed, with a clear predilection for some of the best-known works
by Lope de Vega – *Fuenteovejuna* (1619) and *El caballero de Olmedo* (The
Knight from Olmedo, 1620) – and Calderón (*La vida es sueño* (Life is
a Dream), 1635), and set about adapting and preparing them for performance. He helped to choose the actors from among the student volunteers
at the university by imposing a strict regime of auditions that involved,
first, the reading out of a piece of prose and a piece of poetry, second, the
recital of a piece of the student's own choosing, third, the acting out of a
role from a play and, finally, the acting out of all the characters from a play
(this being something that Lorca himself had delighted in doing during
his Residencia days).[52] He then taught the chosen actors how to declaim,
gesture and move around the stage and would often also direct the plays
(and even act in some of them), working closely with a tightly knit group
of set designers, painters and technicians.[53] La Barraca made its first outing
between 10 and 22 July 1932, with performances in Burgo de Osma, Soria
and other towns and villages in Old Castile, followed by a tour of Galicia

Lorca at the Huerta de San Vicente, Granada, 1932.

and Asturias (21 August–10 September), one-off performances in Granada and Madrid in October and December, and then tours of Alicante, Elche and Murcia in the first days of 1933, of Valladolid, Zamora and Salamanca in April 1933, of the provinces of Valencia, Albacete, Ciudad Real and Toledo in July and, finally, of León, Santander, Pamplona and other towns in the north in August 1933. Although Lorca found the whole process to be exhausting and exasperating at times – as is witnessed by a letter he sent to the secretary of La Barraca in August 1932 asking how on earth he could be expected to find and train a replacement actor just three days before the upcoming performance[54] – he also found it to be exhilarating. And there is no doubt that he carried out his work with a clear sense of mission, the mission, that is, as he told the journalist V. S. in December 1931, to 'educate the people using the instrument that was made for it but has been shamefully taken from it, that is, the theatre'.[55] La Barraca, he says in other interviews of the time, does not have a political bias of any sort but rather simply aims to educate the inhabitants of 'our beloved Republic' through the restoration of their own theatre. The performances themselves, he would later say, confirmed that Calderón and Cervantes could still speak clearly to all of La Barraca's audiences, whatever their social class or condition.[56]

In between these tours with La Barraca, Lorca led an intense social life. He entertained a good deal at his flat in the Calle Ayala but also spent many evenings in café *tertulias* or at soirées in friends' or acquaintances' residences. His favourite soirée was the one held at the home of Chilean diplomat Carlos Morla Lynch and his wife Bebé, who first lived in the Calle Velázquez in the Salamanca district and then in the Calle Alfonso XII by the Retiro Park. Morla Lynch, who knew Lorca from March 1929 onwards, has left us in his published diaries an extraordinarily intimate account of Lorca's visits, which, during some periods over these years, were almost nightly. He captures not only his friend's inventiveness and joie-de-vivre but his occasional acts of selfishness, for example when he disappeared for a month around the time of La Barraca's first outing in July 1932 without telling any of his friends that he was going to be away.[57] He was also witness to several of Lorca's first readings of his works, and to the theatre company's performance of Calderón's *Life is a Dream* in the Great Hall of the University of Madrid on 25 October 1932, in which Lorca both played the role of the Shadow and whispered orders and advice to the other actors around him. Later that same night, Lorca, dressed in the proletarian overalls worn by the troupe, turned up in Morla Lynch's flat and, still high on adrenaline, recited poems, told stories, played and sang songs at the piano and made up a popular song (*copla*) on the guitar.[58]

There is no doubt that Lorca and Morla Lynch formed a special bond, which led the former to feel able to open up about his deepest fears, including his terror of death, and the latter to share the deep sorrow that he had felt on the loss of his baby daughter a few years earlier.[59] Although the diary is extremely discreet on the matter, there are signs too that Lorca spoke openly with Morla Lynch about his homosexuality

Collage of photographs of Lorca and others performing Calderón's *Life is a Dream* for La Barraca.

and even involved him in his adventures, as when the two of them and the poet Luis Cernuda took a young man Lorca and Cernuda had found on the streets – whom they called their 'chiquillo vagabundo' (little vagabond boy) – to a *zarzuela* (operetta) performance in May 1932.[60] The many letters that Lorca sent to his friend over this period reveal just how much the whole Morla Lynch household had come to mean to him, to the point that he wrote from Granada in summer 1931 to say that the place he had most felt at home was their bathroom that time when he lay in the bath while Carlos brushed his hair, his son put brilliantine on his, and Bebé called to them all to say that lunch was ready.[61] If, as the evidence of the diaries might suggest, Carlos Morla Lynch was in fact homosexual or bisexual himself, could it be that Lorca found in this household a vision of what might to him seem to be a perfect family situation in which a man could both freely express his sexuality and at the same time enjoy married life (or, at least, the presence of a maternal figure) and, perhaps more crucially for him, have children?

Lorca's own personal situation would in fact become more complicated from December 1932, when his parents acquired a flat in the Calle de Alcalá in Madrid and demanded that their son give up his own place and join them there. Lorca remained strongly attached to his family but had also, as we have seen, been trying for more than a decade to establish his personal and financial independence. Now he would be able to enjoy home comforts in Madrid as well as during the family's summer and Christmas stays in Granada, but he would have to live under their direct surveillance too. It seems both fortuitous and perfectly appropriate, therefore, that Lorca should just at this moment be experiencing ever stronger feelings for a young man who lived back in Granada. Between late October or early November 1932 and April 1933, he sent six passionate love letters to Eduardo Rodríguez Valdivieso, a bank clerk he had first met in early 1932 during the carnival celebrations in his home city.[62] Each of these letters expresses a growing yearning to be with Eduardo, the only friend he feels he still has in Granada or perhaps anywhere in the world. 'I may have crowns of glory', he tells him, 'but I do not yet have those of love; my triumphs mean that many people claim they love me but their love is not genuine, which is why I look back to Granada and to you.'[63]

In one of the letters to Eduardo Rodríguez Valdivieso, Lorca mentions the work which, more than any other, would indeed crown him with glory: *Bodas de sangre* (Blood Wedding).[64] He seems to have conceived this theatrical masterpiece in mid-1931 and then finished it off in the Huerta de San Vicente in Granada in one intense burst of writing in August 1932. For this play, which tells the story of a young bride who runs off with a former suitor on her wedding night and of the subsequent mutual killing of her husband and the suitor, Lorca returns to his native Andalusia. Most of the characters, just like those in *The Public* and *As Soon As Five Years Have Passed*, will have generic names – Madre (Mother), Novia (Bride), Novio (Bridegroom), Mujer (Wife), Vecina (Neighbour) and so on – but these characters now very much belong to and are rooted in a recognizable place, that is, the villages and landscapes of the rural south.

Back in February 1931, just at the same time that he was starting to proclaim that *The Public* was most probably an unperformable play, Lorca said in an interview that theatre can be bold but must always also be accessible to everyone, and his subsequent experiences with La Barraca had clearly confirmed this belief, which he puts fully into practice in

The Huerta de San Vicente, Granada, summer 1931.

Blood Wedding.[65] Lorca based the play loosely on a real-life event that had taken place in 1928 near Níjar in the province of Almería, although he appears to set it in what is for him a much more familiar landscape still, that of the Vega de Granada. Indeed, the story unfolds above all in two contrasting places – the rich and well-watered land belonging to the Bridegroom and the dry and less fertile land belonging to the Bride – which clearly reflect the topography of Asquerosa, a village that was situated, according to Francisco and Isabel García Lorca, between the fertile land by the River Cubillas to the southeast and the dry lands to the north where only capers could grow.[66]

But in *Blood Wedding* Lorca draws on his knowledge of not only the Vega and its people but of his own family's relationship with the land. His father spent his whole adult life buying and selling land, cultivating the most lucrative of crops, mainly sugar beet from the 1890s onwards and then tobacco from the 1930s, and investing in larger industrial concerns such as the sugar beet factories that became a notable feature of the landscape of the Vega at the turn of the century. At the start of his career above all, Federico García frequently bought land together with his own brothers, with the brothers of his first wife or with members of some of the other local landowning clans such as the Roldáns and the Albas, with whom the García family often intermarried in an attempt to consolidate land and wealth. His increasing commercial success also meant, though, that he ended up being seen as a rival and even as an enemy by some of these other landowners, above all his distant relative Alejandro Roldán Benavides, whose own part-owned sugar beet factory was located on land belonging to Lorca's father and uncles and therefore depended on the latter's good will when it came to the control of the water supply or plans for expansion. The enforced closure of the factory in 1931 and 1932 due to its contamination of the irrigation ditches in the surrounding land, a measure that had the effect of increasing the output of Lorca's father's own part-owned factory a few kilometres away, served to intensify the animosity of the Roldán family towards Federico García just at the time that his son was starting to write *Blood Wedding.*[67]

Land, and above all land as commodity, lies at the very heart of the play. The Bridegroom's Mother and the Bride's Father conceive their children's marriage almost exclusively in terms of the union of their lands, a union that will be more symbolic than real given the large distance that exists between their estates. When they first meet in Act I, the Father recognizes that the Bridegroom and his Mother's land is more fertile than his own and that, with their recent acquisition of vineyards, they are better off than he can ever be. He wishes that he had had sons who could have made his own land more fertile and that the Bridegroom's vineyards could now somehow be replanted on his land. He also, in what may be an indirect reference on Lorca's part to his father's recent dispute with Alejandro Roldán Benavides, talks with frustration about a more fertile area found in the middle of his own land that belongs to other landowners who have long refused to sell it to him.[68] For their part, the Bride and the Bridegroom clearly share their parents' identification of them with the land they have been brought up on. At the climax of the play, after the Bridegroom and her suitor, Leonardo, have killed each other, the Bride talks of all three of them as if they were not just products of the land they inhabited but actually part of it: the Bride herself says that she was a 'mujer quemada' (scorched woman) full of wounds and the Bridegroom a stream of water that she had hoped would bring her children, land and health, while Leonardo had been a dark and raging river that both offered soothing frost for her burnt flesh and ended up dragging her away against her own will.[69] Language such as this reveals that Lorca, as might be expected from the poet of *Gypsy Ballads*, presents the characters of *Blood Wedding* as the playthings of feelings and forces that lie beyond their control and are located in the natural world that surrounds them. The Bride's passion originates in the dry land that cries out for water, while Leonardo will ultimately lay the blame for their elopement and his impending death on the land itself – a clear reference both to the fact that his own poverty and lack of land had prevented him from marrying the Bride in the first place and to the fateful forces which, as Lorca had said when talking about the emotion he called 'pena', inhabit the sap of the trees as well as the marrow of the characters' bones.[70]

Lorca therefore once again explores in this play that profound sense of fatalism that he believed lay at the heart of the Andalusian character and which, in the case of the Bridegroom, is represented by the knife that he will ultimately feel obliged to use, like some character from the *cante jondo* tradition, in order to avenge his own and his family's honour. But in *Blood Wedding* Lorca does not simply explore this sense of fatalism through the words of the main protagonists, but actually provides it with an onstage presence in the immensely powerful third act of the play. Influenced by ancient Greek drama and also by some of the allegorical Golden Age plays he was performing with the Barraca, Lorca shifts in this final act from the relative naturalism of the settings portrayed so far to a clearly supernatural location where events are narrated and enacted by allegorical characters, including the Fates, who appear here in the form of three Woodcutters (Leñadores), and Death, who takes on the shape of an old Beggar Woman (Mendiga). As at the end of *As Soon As Five Years Have Passed*, we find ourselves here in a magical forest but, in this case, an almost recognizable one, since its description seems to take us right back to the woods between Asquerosa and Fuente Vaqueros that had haunted Lorca's earliest verse. The Woodcutters appear to be readying themselves to cut down the poplar trees on either side of the River Cubillas, while the Beggar Woman herself is reminiscent of the poor and often starving women Lorca had seen wandering through the fields near Asquerosa in search of sustenance.[71] This Beggar Woman embodies the sinister and threatening character of these woods at night and orders the Moon, who, unusually for Lorca, appears here in the guise of a man (a fourth Woodcutter), to illuminate the eloping lovers and thus reveal their whereabouts to the pursuing Bridegroom.[72] The Moon, in a direct echo of the 'moon icicle' that pierces the Gypsy woman at the end of the 'Sleepwalking Ballad', refers to himself as a knife that reaches down to Earth and longs to heat himself up by penetrating human flesh and bathing himself in blood.[73] Death and her helper finally achieve their aim at the very end of the penultimate scene, when the Beggar Woman stands in the centre of the stage with her back to the audience and her arms raised and cloak opened, looking for all the world, according to the stage directions, like a large bird with huge wings illuminated by the Moon, who stands next to her. Offstage two heart-rending screams announce the deaths of Leonardo and the Bridegroom.[74]

In *Blood Wedding*, Lorca reaches new heights as a dramatic artist. The action of the play is conveyed with great economy and balance, and Lorca makes very effective use of verse throughout, from the lullaby that Leonardo's wife and mother-in-law sing to his baby son in Act I to the wedding songs in Act II and the *romances* used by Leonardo, the Bride and the Moon.[75] Above all, he captures with profound insight the complex feelings that lie at the heart of the multiple relationships between the different characters, whether it be the atavistic and ultimately self-fulfilling fears that dominate the Mother's relationship with her son, the anxieties, suspicions and guilt displayed in the meetings between the Bride and the Bridegroom and between Leonardo and his Wife, or the simultaneous attraction and repulsion that the Bride feels as she flees with Leonardo. But it is in the final scene, with the operatic meeting between the Mother, the Bride and Leonardo's Wife, that the play is at its most sublime. The Mother has just told her Neighbour that her son's death means that she must live out the rest of her days in public silence and private grief, when the Bride suddenly appears and demands to tell her story as a victim of forces and feelings beyond her control. The Mother reacts by hitting the Bride, who says that she has come precisely in order to be killed so that she can join the two dead men, but the violence of the scene gradually gives way, after the entrance of Leonardo's Wife, to a much more elegiac concluding passage in which the three women start to sing of their dead son, husbands and lover. The Mother, the Bride and the Wife stand apart but their voices come together as they mourn the dead and, in the words of the Mother, reach deep down into the wounds of their loved ones and arrive at that place 'donde tiembla enmarañada / la oscura raíz del grito' (where trembles / the dark and tangled root of the scream).[76]

Blood Wedding, with Josefina Díaz de Artigas in the role of the Bride, received its première in the Teatro Beatriz in Madrid on 8 March 1933. Carlos Morla Lynch tells us that the première was attended by the leading writers of the day, including, among the older generation, the playwrights Jacinto Benavente, Eduardo Marquina, Serafín and Joaquín Álvarez Quintero, as well as Miguel de Unamuno, and, among the writers of Lorca's own generation, Vicente Aleixandre, Luis Cernuda, Jorge Guillén and Pedro Salinas.[77] The play was an immediate success, both among Lorca's peers and in the press, where Lorca was increasingly being seen as representing the future of the Spanish theatre. It was also, to Lorca's great delight, successful at the box office too, enjoying 38 performances in all and, for a short while, running alongside his *The Love of Don Perlimplín*, which received its première in the Teatro Español in Madrid on 5 April. When he was asked by journalists what sort of theatre he wrote, he replied that it was aristocratic in style and spirit but always remained in contact with the people and was nourished by the 'popular sap'. And, when asked about his future plans, he explained that *Blood Wedding* was the first part of a projected trilogy dealing with 'la tierra española' (the Spanish land or earth).[78] For the moment, though, as well as his work for La Barraca, it would be *Blood Wedding* that would remain uppermost in his mind, as the Argentine actress Lola Membrives had decided to put the play on in Buenos Aires and insisted that Lorca join her there. He finally left Spain on 29 September 1933, just days after Manuel Azaña's government, with Fernando de los Ríos as Foreign Minister, had resigned. By the time he returned in April 1934, the Spanish Republic would have taken on a very different hue, having lurched radically to the Right.

seven

Argentina and Madrid: Triumph and Trepidation, 1933–6

Lorca's six-month stay in Buenos Aires, between 13 October 1933 and 27 March 1934, was wildly successful and helped to turn him into the most famous writer in the Spanish-speaking world. In his letters home, he said that he was as celebrated and popular as a visiting bullfighter and was having to cope with constant press interviews and with crowds lining up for his autograph.[1] The *Gypsy Ballads* had already made his name as a writer, but it was Lola Membrives's production of *Blood Wedding*, which had premiered in the Teatro Maipo in Buenos Aires in late July, that had prompted such expectation and excitement among the Argentine public.

During the first months of his stay, Lorca and the stage designer Manuel Fontanals, who had accompanied him on the trip from Spain, worked with Lola Membrives and her company on a reprise of *Blood Wedding*, which celebrated its one-hundredth performance at the end of November, and on new productions of *The Shoemaker's Prodigious Wife* and *Mariana Pineda*, which premièred in the Teatro Avenida on 1 December and 12 January, respectively. He also gave several public lectures, including a revamped version of his *cante jondo* talk from 1922 and two new talks that focused on other aspects of his native Andalusian and Granadan culture: *duende*, that is, the magical spirit that inhabits and inspires the greatest Gypsy singers and whose origins, he claims, lie in a heightened awareness of death, and, on the other hand, the songs, sounds and smells that mark the changing seasons in his native city.[2]

The royalties and fees that he received for the plays and the talks were substantial. He admitted in the press that his parents' generosity meant that he had never needed to write for money, explaining to one journalist,

'Thank God I have parents. Parents who sometimes lay down the law but are very good and always end up paying out.'³ But his letters home reveal just how proud he felt to be earning considerable sums at last. He would use the conference fees as spending money and put the theatre royalties aside as savings, he said, but he also bought his mother expensive gifts (including a fox fur coat) and insisted that the money he was sending home really belonged to his parents, who should feel free to spend it on themselves. Lorca's insistent references to his new wealth seem to suggest at times a certain relief that he would henceforth be less financially (and perhaps therefore emotionally) dependent on his parents.⁴

From his very first interviews, Lorca made clear that he had come to Argentina not just to work and make money but also to enjoy himself: 'The only thing I'm interested in,' he told the main Argentine daily *La Nación* on the day of his arrival, 'is having a good time, going out, talking for hours on end with friends, meeting girls.'⁵ Lorca had in fact sailed to Argentina with something of a heavy heart, having left behind a 21-year-old student called Rafael Rodríguez Rapún, who had become the secretary of La Barraca earlier in the year and with whom he was just starting a relationship that would last for the rest of his life. It seems that Lorca's response to Rapún's absence was indeed to have a good time, which meant immersing himself fully in the night life of Buenos Aires, often in the company of a new friend, the Chilean poet Pablo Neruda. In his memoirs, Neruda describes how Lorca kept watch one night while he and an unnamed local poetess enjoyed a drunken sexual (or, as Neruda modestly put it, 'erotic-cosmic') encounter.⁶ By all accounts Lorca himself had a number of affairs over these months, including with the poet Ricardo Molinari and possibly Maximino Espasande, a young man who had a bit part in *Blood Wedding*.⁷ The Peruvian novelist Santiago Roncagliolo has also recently chronicled Lorca's close relationship at this time with writer Enrique Amorim, whom he refers to as Lorca's 'Uruguayan lover'.⁸

Lorca comes across as relaxed and content in his many press interviews. Although he sometimes complains about the price of fame,⁹ he is obviously relishing both the attention and the freedom that he has found in Buenos Aires. The interviews offer a surprisingly intimate glimpse into Lorca's life in the capital, not least because he tended to receive the journalists in his rooms in the plush Hotel Castelar in the Avenida de Mayo around midday, when he was often still in his pyjamas and dressing gown or even coming out of the shower and getting dressed and ready to go out. The journalists themselves were without exception seduced by his openness, approachability and cordiality, qualities which were to become the leitmotif of their articles after they witnessed how Lorca, on stepping off the boat in the harbour to meet his reception committee, had gone first to embrace a group of emigrants from Fuente Vaqueros, including the daughter of the Compadre Pastor, the farmworker who had told him so many stories when he was a boy.[10] They were struck by Lorca's physical presence, with some pointing out that he was not very tall and not traditionally handsome either, with his round face, bushy eyebrows, high forehead and rebellious black hair, but that he had

Lorca with Pablo Neruda (left) and others at a party in Buenos Aires, 1934.

the rude health of a peasant and eyes that shone and burned as he spoke, while his small and eloquent hands made the most emphatic or delicate of gestures to help illustrate his points. What most impressed them was his vivacious and exuberant personality: the intriguing ways in which he would jump from topic to topic, finding the most ingenious links between them, his mixture of deep seriousness and surreal and sometimes caustic humour, and, above all, the sense of joy that he communicated to those around him. Almost every interviewer described Lorca as being childlike, as possessing a child's frankness, enthusiasm, imagination, amazement at life, spontaneity, impulsiveness, wide smile, occasional naughtiness and infectious laughter.[11]

He also indulged in a good deal of fabrication and myth-making in his interviews. Knowing full well that many of the journalists were intent on presenting him to their readers as a genius poet who was in contact with the cosmic and telluric forces he had uncovered in *Gypsy Ballads* and brought onstage in *Blood Wedding*, he was happy to talk of his profound rootedness in the land, of the irresistible and overwhelming need he sometimes felt to write, of just how young he had been when he composed some of his masterpieces (apparently he had written *Mariana Pineda* when he was just twenty), and even, despite all his previous protestations on the matter, of his deeply Gypsy nature and of the *duende* that animated his work.[12]

Lorca in Montevideo, January/February 1934.

Some journalists did manage to get beyond the public image, none more so than Uruguayan poet Alfredo Mario Ferreiro, who spent a day with Lorca and Enrique Amorim in Montevideo, where Lorca spent the first couple of weeks of February holed up in the exclusive Hotel Carrasco trying to get some writing done far from the crowds of Buenos Aires.[13] As they drove around the streets of Montevideo and then to the coast at Playa Atlántida, Ferreiro noted the surprise and delight that Lorca felt on encountering new people and landscapes, commenting memorably that 'this immense child travelling with Amorim and me arrives everywhere new, like a clean sheet'. He also heard this 'immense child' confess that he longed to be loved by everyone and that this was his main motivation when writing his poetry and drama. But Ferreiro managed to shed invaluable light on the darker side of Lorca's character too, on those moments commented upon by Vicente Aleixandre, Emilia Llanos and other close friends when he would suddenly go quiet and withdraw into himself.

Ferreiro was witness to an unusual moment when Lorca, rather than sinking into silence, actually gave voice to the deep fear that had suddenly taken hold of him. As the three new friends sat on a hotel terrace overlooking the sea and a stormy sky, and just at the moment when two boys passed by spurring on a pair of horses with improvised whips, Lorca suddenly exclaimed that he lived surrounded by death – his own death, Ferreiro's death, Amorim's, even the death of the two boys in front of him, whose faces he imagined being destroyed by a kick from the horses they were driving. 'Tell me: why does death haunt and circle me?' asked Lorca, 'What need do I have of the death of those children who are following the horses? Have I come here for that?' His words imply not only a profound terror of death itself but a sense that he was in some way responsible for the fate of those around him. This brief event, sensitively caught by Ferreiro, suggests a deeply superstitious side to Lorca's character, as if this immense child spent his life not just doing everything he could to earn the love and attention of those around him but trying to ward off the images of death and destruction that occasionally took hold of his mind.

Lorca's triumphant visit to Argentina and Uruguay was coming to an end. The reaction to his stay had been almost unanimously positive and enthusiastic, although Neruda does report that some envious soul tried to disrupt the banquet that was put on in their honour by the PEN Club, while one increasingly famous local writer, Jorge Luis Borges, would forever after complain that Lorca had appeared to him to be always acting out a role, that of a 'professional Andalusian'.[14] The truth is that, just as with his visit to Cuba in 1930, where his readings from *Gypsy Ballads* had helped spark a renewed local interest in popular poetry and the *romance* form, Lorca would leave a strong legacy behind him in Argentina and indeed throughout Latin America – with the productions of his plays creating a new interest in poetic drama and revealing novel ways of combining music and theatre.[15] Lorca told his parents that, as a result, his influence was spreading throughout the continent and that he hoped that people back home realized just how much he was contributing to the prestige of Spain.[16]

He would produce two parting gifts for his hosts. On 4 March, the actress Eva Franco appeared in his version of Lope de Vega's famous drama *La dama boba* (The Lady Simpleton, 1613), co-directed by Carlos Calderón de la Barca and Lorca himself. The enthusiastic reviews emphasized that this was very possibly the first time that a Latin American national company had put on one of the Spanish classics and also praised the ingenious production, which saw the imaginative stage designer Manuel Fontanals (who would continue to collaborate with Lorca over the coming years) transform the interior of the Teatro de la Comedia into a courtyard theatre of the sort used by the dramatists of sixteenth- and seventeenth-century Spain.[17]

Then, on 25 March, Lorca organized a puppet show in the foyer of the Teatro Avenida as a way of thanking the actors, journalists and writers who had made his stay in Buenos Aires such a success. This event represented the realization of Lorca's decade-old dream to share the Andalusian tradition of puppet theatre with the world, and it is not surprising that he should make use of some of the texts that had featured on the programme of the puppet event that he, Manuel de Falla and Hermenegildo Lanz had prepared for Lorca's sister Isabel on Twelfth Night in 1923. Lorca wrote a new puppet play for the event, the *Retablillo de don Cristóbal* (Don Cristóbal's Puppet Play), which, just like his 1922 *Tragicomedy of Cristóbal and his Missus, Rosita*, shows how the ageing Punch-like figure Don Cristóbal buys the affection of Rosita, only to find this time that she entertains three men while he sleeps and ends up giving birth to five children as a result.[18] The play also features a Poet and a Director, who explain to the audience that the piquant language used by the characters is typical of Andalusian villages and whose comically stormy relationship provides a humorous and affectionate commentary on Lorca's experience working with various actors and directors over the previous six months. It seems that, despite its one-off nature, Lorca's puppet spectacle inspired a number of artists who attended the function that night, men and women like Ernesto Arancibia (1904–1963), who designed the glove puppets following Lorca's instructions, Javier Villafañe (1909–1996) and Mane Bernardo (1913–1991), who would in the following years draw on Lorca's (and, it must be said, Falla's and Lanz's) ideas, and the Andalusian tradition of puppet theatre on which they were based, as they set out to create an Argentine and, more generally, Latin American puppet tradition of their own.[19]

———

Lorca returned on 11 April 1934 to a very different Spain. The liberal, education-focused Republic that he had left behind was no more, and the government was now in the hands of the Radical Party led by Alejandro Lerroux, with support from José María Gil-Robles' Confederación Española de Derechas Autónomas (CEDA; Spanish Confederation of Autonomous Right-wing Groups): a coalition of Catholic, conservative and often monarchist parties that were hell-bent on repealing most of the reforms of the previous two years, especially those relating to land ownership, workers' rights, the autonomous regions and the relationship between Church and State, and, in many cases, on undermining the Republic itself.

Lorca had followed the November general election from Buenos Aires with great trepidation, expressing his fear about the possible result and his concern for his old friend Fernando de los Ríos, who, as a leading Socialist and a former government minister, was in the front line of the political battles.[20] In December 1933, when he heard about the violent Anarchist backlash against the new government that involved the planting of bombs in Madrid and the burning of convents in Granada, his main concern was understandably the safety of his family, but he also went on to say in his letter home that he actually felt very pleased with what was happening, since the Anarchists' actions would serve to show those on the Right that they could not 'take Spain by force' – adding that this was the opinion of everyone around him.[21] Such statements are revealing of Lorca's relationship with politics and with the political situation in Spain. They make clear that he felt a strong antipathy towards the new right-wing government and also give voice to the same striking mixture of fear of, and fascination with, political violence that he had shown on his return from Cuba in 1930, while the final words suggest that Lorca was perhaps easily influenced by the political views of those who surrounded him. As time went on, his letters became filled more with fear than with fascination, and he once again started to talk of Spain in terms of a 'volcano' but also now of an 'open wound': something is going to happen, he announced ominously in late January 1934, since 'la pasión está desatada' (passion has been let loose).[22]

Apart from an early reference to the fact that the freedom-loving Spanish people were on the Left of the political spectrum,[23] Lorca was more discreet when it came to his public pronouncements in the Argentine press. What we find, though, not only in Argentina but after his return to Spain, is that Lorca channelled his political frustrations and anxieties into an increasingly virulent attack on the cultural philistinism of the middle classes and the bourgeoisie. In one of his earliest interviews in Buenos Aires, after making clear that he was not affiliated to any political party, Lorca told the strange story of how, shortly after the proclamation of the Republic, the 'peasants' of Granada burned down the social club belonging to the rich and powerful of the city and how, as they watched the flames, Lorca's father (who was a member of the club) lamented what was happening while Lorca and his brother exchanged furtive looks of delight at the destruction of what was to them a detestable institution.[24] This anecdote offers an interesting insight into not only Lorca's complex relationship with a father whose love he cherished and whose authority he often resented, but his hatred of the Granada bourgeoisie, with its stultifying rules and conventions, and, more widely, of the Spanish bourgeoisie that filled the theatres and would vote for the right-wing parties that won the 1933 general election. Little surprise, therefore, that, from late 1933 onwards, Lorca should intensify his attacks on this 'frivolous and materialistic bourgeoisie', which, he says, has destroyed or prostituted the theatre in Spain, nor that he should once again, as in the 1920s, establish a strongly Romantic distinction between the interests and instincts of the bourgeoisie and those of the noble 'people' of Spain (which happened to coincide, he suggested, with those of the cultured minority of the nation).[25]

La Barraca and his own dramatic projects formed the core of Lorca's programme of work on his return to Spain. After a stay in the Huerta de San Vicente, he arrived back in Madrid on 10 May and spent a couple of months at the Residencia de Estudiantes, where he met up with old friends and started to prepare La Barraca's summer tour. Carlos Morla

Lynch found Lorca, who would stay in his friend's bedroom until four in the morning talking of his experiences in the New World, to be 'sunburnt, jubilant, exuberant' and full, as always, of stories, jokes and pranks. On 12 May, a group of friends put on a special reception in his honour at the Hotel Florida in the Gran Vía that included a one-off reprise of the puppet show from Buenos Aires. Then, on 1 June, Pablo Neruda arrived in Madrid to take on the role of Chilean consul alongside fellow poet Gabriela Mistral and, the following night, Carlos Morla threw a welcoming party for him, during which Lorca did a celebratory Eastern dance wrapped up in his host's office rug and then sang Andalusian *peteneras* on the guitar before the two poets recited poems – Neruda from his *Residencia en la tierra* (Residence on Earth) and Lorca from his *Poem of the Deep Song*. Neruda immediately became one of Lorca's closest friends and drinking partners, both in the bars and cafés of central Madrid and at the frequent get-togethers in Neruda's flat in the so-called 'Casa de las flores' (House of Flowers) located in the Argüelles district of the capital.[26]

Lorca and Rafael
Rodríguez Rapún,
Madrid, 1935.

Lorca also renewed his relationship with his lover Rafael Rodríguez Rapún, with whom he worked closely on the upcoming Barraca productions of Lope de Vega's *Fuenteovejuna* (1619) and Tirso de Molina's *El burlador de Sevilla* (The Trickster of Seville, *c.* 1630). Carlos Morla, who first met Rapún in April 1933, writes that he was a handsome and athletic student of engineering and the son of working-class parents, adding that he possessed a strong personality, made up in equal parts of boldness and reserve, a strong moral compass that was unusual in someone so young, and a clear and passionate commitment to socialism.[27] Whether or not Ian Gibson is right to claim (on rather scanty evidence, it must be said) that Rapún was not in fact a homosexual but rather someone who was simply unable to resist Lorca's spell and attention,[28] it seems clear that Rapún, like Dalí and Emilio Aladrén before him, was also sexually attracted to women. Lorca had once again chosen a partner who had none of the effeminacy of the *maricas* he had so violently attacked in the 'Ode to Walt Whitman' but who could also potentially abandon him for a heterosexual relationship.

With rehearsals well advanced and the Barraca tour set to start in mid-August, Lorca returned to the Huerta de San Vicente on or around 18 July in order to finish off a play that he had first mentioned to Carlos Morla in late May 1933 and whose third and final act he had signally failed to write during his retreat in Montevideo.[29] *Yerma* would be the second of his rural tragedies and, if anything, an even more 'popular' work than *Blood Wedding* – in the sense that it looks more closely still at the life, atmosphere and beliefs of a small Andalusian village. The story told here is that of a young wife in an arranged marriage with an older man, Juan, who is more interested in his material comforts and in making money with his crops and sheep than in having children. Although Yerma feels some affection and, above all, respect for her husband – bound as she is by the same honour code that features so centrally in the Golden Age plays Lorca was adapting for La Barraca – her longing for a child intensifies as the acts go by, and she feels an ever-stronger attraction to a younger and more virile man, Víctor. She ends the play by strangling her husband out of sheer frustration at his indifference to her desires, fully aware that, by doing so, she is also killing off any possibility of having a child: her final words are '¡No os acerquéis, porque he matado a mi hijo, yo misma he matado a mi hijo!' (Don't come close, as I have killed my child, I myself have killed my own child!).[30]

Yerma is shot-through with, and driven by, the popular beliefs of the village. Lorca once explained that each of the three acts was set in one interior and one exterior location and that, while the interior locations focus on the spiritual torment of the individual protagonists, the exterior locations are inhabited by Greek tragedy-style choruses, that is, by collective or archetypal characters who give voice to the cosmic forces or social rules that shape the lives of the villagers.[31] It is an unnamed Vieja (Old Woman) who, by referring to the fertility of Yerma's forebears and the reproductive laziness of Juan's, reveals at the climax of the play the full extent of the biological determinism that informs the village's understanding of both human and animal life, while it is the washerwomen at the start of Act II who, with their colourful stories, prurient humour and cruel references to Yerma as the 'casada seca' (dry wife), demonstrate the destructive power that gossip can wield in a small community (as Lorca himself had discovered in Asquerosa and already shown in *The Shoemaker's Prodigious Wife*).[32]

But the village can also offer potential solutions to Yerma's predicament, from the mixture of herbs and prayers prescribed by the wise woman to the pilgrimage that features in the climactic scene and which Lorca based on a real-life event that takes place each year in the village of Moclín, about 25 kilometres (15.5 mi.) from Asquerosa. This pilgrimage, during which local women have traditionally asked Christ and the local saint for children, is shown by Lorca to be both a deeply Catholic and a deeply pagan affair, with his addition of a highly erotic Masque played out by the figures of the Macho (Male) and the Hembra (Female) serving to transform the religious festival into a sexual orgy and an invitation to the women to couple with the local men who hang around offering a more earthly answer to their prayers.

Yerma provides a moving portrait of a woman who, we are led to believe, is not infertile herself but rather unable to conceive with her husband (her name, deriving from an adjective that is mostly applied to the land, translates not only as 'barren' but as 'uncultivated'). The play seems to suggest that the intensity of her longing for a child originates in a powerful commixture of deep, instinctual drives and internalized social expectations. Lorca made clear in an interview he gave in late 1935 that he was fully aware of the most recent (that is, Freudian) theories concerning sexual desire and that he had received letters from eminent gynaecologists and neurologists (by which he probably meant his close friend the writer and physician Gregorio Marañón) authenticating the 'case study' he had provided in the play, but he added that he had deliberately avoided intellectualizing his subject matter or analysing his characters, choosing, instead, to allow them to speak with their own voices and to express their anxieties and longings in their own way.[33] Yerma uses popular expressions, most of them profoundly physical and bodily in nature, both when she celebrates her desires and instincts and when she speaks with the conventional and repressive voice of her society. She equates joyful sexual relations with singing and with the sensation of being a 'mountain of fire' and clings desperately to the hope that her belly will ultimately carry children, just as the cloud carries sweet rain, while, on the other hand, she laments the fact that her breasts are dry and 'blind' beneath her dress and adds, devastatingly, that a childless woman in the countryside is as useless as a bunch of thorny bushes.[34] As her yearning hardens into an obsession, she provides a powerful insight into her feelings and mental processes when she talks of the humiliation she experiences on observing the fertility of the corn, sheep and dogs around her and of her fear that her frustrated maternal longings will end up making her believe that she is her own child.[35]

The poetry generated by Yerma's intense desire for children is sonce again reminiscent of that found in Lorca's early poems 'In the Garden of the Moon-grapefruits' and 'In the Forest of the Moon-grapefruits', where

Premiere of *Yerma* in the Teatro Español, Madrid, on 29 December 1934.
The scene shown is that of the Masque featuring the figures of the Macho (Male) and the Hembra (Female).

the poet had given expression to the deep regret he felt for the children he would never have.[36] But he claimed that the play was not just about infertility, regret and frustration but that he had also intended it to be 'the living poem of fecundity', since the tragedy itself depended on the contrast between sterility and life.[37] *Yerma* is Lorca's most explicitly sexual play. Men in the village, as Yerma claims and even Víctor confirms, may have another life involving their flocks of sheep, their trees and their conversations, but the women's lives derive meaning solely from having and raising children.[38] Yerma herself thinks that the sexual act is linked exclusively to procreation but also believes – like other female characters in the play – that conception can only occur when there is true desire and pleasure involved.[39] In this sense, and despite Yerma's own increasing feeling of frustration and failure, the play does indeed celebrate the sexual urge, not least in the concluding Masque scene, during which the characters of the Male and the Female openly describe and enact a sexual encounter. The stage directions make clear that these characters are anything but grotesques: rather, they display a great beauty and spring from the land itself. Here, and also in the preceding scene in which Yerma, in a reversal of the Annunciation, asks God to open his rose in her flesh, Lorca skilfully and imaginatively draws out the sexual undertones of the part-Catholic, part-pagan rites that continued to play such an important role in the life of the rural *pueblo*.[40]

Lorca felt very happy with the play. Even before he had finished Act III, he had said that with *Yerma* he was being fully himself and writing what and how he wished to. After he had completed it, he would add that he had given the people an 'authentic' drama and a true tragedy, whose popular theme and tone could help to banish twenty or thirty years of 'art theatre' from the Spanish stage.[41] Lorca must have worked hard over the three weeks he was in the Huerta de San Vicente – and also played hard too, at least according to a letter to Rafael Martínez Nadal in which he says that 'epentismo' (his secret word for gayness and gay activity) had reached 'epidemic proportions' in Granada.[42] He returned to Madrid on or around 8 August 1934 in order to prepare for La Barraca's trip to Santander on 13 August, and had time to read *Yerma* to actress Margarita Xirgu, who agreed to put the play on in the autumn. On 11 August, he had heard the news of the goring in Manzanares (Ciudad Real) of Ignacio

Sánchez Mejías, the bullfighter and poet who had helped to arrange the
Góngora celebrations in Seville in December 1927 and had since become
a close friend. Lorca initially put off his trip with La Barraca but, despite
asking for news from friends, did not pluck up the courage to go and visit
Ignacio in the Madrid hospital to which he had been transferred. As soon
as he heard of the bullfighter's death on the morning of 13 August, he left
for Santander, telling Jorge Guillén that he did not wish to see the body.[43]

The International Summer University in Santander, where La Barraca
performed in 1933, 1934 and 1935, was a redoubt of liberal Republican and
Krausist values in an increasingly polarized nation. The performances that
August of *The Trickster of Seville* and *Fuenteovejuna*, staged in the grounds
of the Magdalena Palace, the Summer University's headquarters, received
enthusiastic plaudits from audiences that included old friends such as
Unamuno, José Ortega y Gasset, Pedro Salinas and Dámaso Alonso.
Carlos Morla tells us that Lorca was in a jubilant mood, despite the sadness he felt over Sánchez Mejías' death, and that Rapún proved to be a
very energetic member of the troupe, acting as secretary and helping to
assemble the stage and repair the decor. Morla, though, also recounts a
private conversation in which Lorca talked about the transitory nature of

Lorca (front row, first left) and other members of La Barraca, 1933. Rafael Rodríguez
Rapún is holding the briefcase.

happiness and about the lack of understanding that can make those who love each other torture each other too, implying perhaps that all was not well between the two lovers.[44] The Santander performances attracted a good deal of international attention and, in late September, Lorca told Italian academic Ezio Levi that he had received an invitation from playwright Luigi Pirandello and inventor Guglielmo Marconi, President of the Italian Royal Academy, to participate in the Theatre Congress organized by the Volta Foundation in Rome. He was feeling both excited and nervous at the prospect of taking part, although one of his main questions to Levi was whether he could interpret the invitation, which had been directed to Lorca and 'his wife', as meaning that he could take the secretary of the Barraca, who, he added, was also his own personal secretary, with him instead. In the end, he would graciously turn down the invitation, adducing unavoidable prior obligations.[45]

During the month of September, which he spent in Granada, and then during his autumn stay in Madrid, Lorca continued to think about his friend Sánchez Mejías. There was something about the death of this man, both the circumstances of the death and his own response to it, which played on his mind and ultimately led him to write what would perhaps be his single greatest poem, the *Llanto por Ignacio Sánchez Mejías* (Lament for Ignacio Sánchez Mejías).[46] This four-part lament, which he finally published in March 1935, functions in many ways as a classical elegy, giving expression in turn to a sense of stunned surprise, desperate loss, admiration for the man who has died, and a search for consolation of some sort. Much of the imagery is unsurprisingly derived from the world of bullfighting, as Lorca explores another aspect of his beloved Andalusian culture and allows it to colour and transfigure his own store of mythical *cante jondo* references – so that the knife that is so central to deep song becomes the bull's horn or the bullfighter's sword, the moon becomes the accomplice of the night that engulfs the scene of the goring, the wind becomes an agent of decomposition or the voice of mourning, and death, that ubiquitous presence in Andalusia and Andalusian culture, stalks both the bullring and the aseptic infirmary where Ignacio's life blood seeps away.

But there is something different here in Lorca's treatment of death, something less mythical, more personal and more urgent. The first three parts of the poem focus obsessively on the cold and precise facts of the goring and the events following it: the exact time of the encounter

Ignacio Sánchez Mejías, Cadiz, 1930.

between bull and man, captured in the incantatory line 'a las cinco de la tarde' (at five in the afternoon) that echoes throughout the first part; the blood shed on the sand in the second part; and the lifeless body laid out on the stone representing Ignacio's tomb (and, before it, the stretcher and the infirmary bed) in the third. And these palpable facts relating to Sánchez Mejías's agony and demise are what crowd in on the poet as he tries to comprehend and come to terms with death not so much in its guise as a mythical being but rather as a stark and inexorable reality.

The *Lament* offers us the shape of Lorca's emotions at a moment of acute and painful existential self-awareness. The story he tells is that of his own terror and cowardice in the face of death, his own fear of looking at the blood that has been shed or of staring death – Ignacio's death – in the face. '¡Que no quiero verla [la sangre derramada]!', '¡No me digas que la vea!' ('I don't want to see it [the spilt blood]!', 'Don't tell me to see it!') are the cries that form the chorus in the second part, while, in the third, the poet searches for 'ojos redondos' (round eyes) that might allow him finally to gaze on the body. Those eyes, he tells us, in language that recalls what he had said about Walt Whitman in his 'Ode', belong to the strong men with hard voices who tame horses and rivers – manly men who can teach Lorca how to look at and respond to life and death.[47] And it seems to be the wisdom, companionship, sight and insight of these strong men – men like Ignacio himself, who refused to close his eyes when the bull's horns were near – that allow Lorca, in the fourth part, to accept the reality of his friend's death, the finality of which is conveyed in the relentless repetition of the line 'porque te has muerto para siempre' (because you have died forever). As the title of this final part, 'Alma ausente' (Absent Soul), implies, there is no transcendence here, no consolation: the most Lorca can hope for is summed up in the line 'Yo canto para luego tu perfil y tu gracia' (I sing for later your profile and your grace), where that telling adverbial phrase, replacing the perhaps more expected 'para siempre' (forever), reveals how Lorca is desperately trying to turn Sánchez Mejías's bravery in the face of death into an exemplum that he might be able to emulate in his own final hour.[48]

––––––––

Lorca's main job over the autumn of 1934 was to work with Margarita Xirgu on the rehearsals for *Yerma*, which finally premiered in the Teatro Español in Madrid on 29 December. If Lola Membrives's *Blood Wedding* made Lorca's name in Argentina and throughout Latin America, it would be this production that would finally make Lorca a prophet in his own land, the leading representative, as far as many fellow writers and critics now claimed, of the future of Spanish theatre. But the premiere actually gave rise to violently polarized opinions in the press, which divided very much along ideological lines, with certain right-wing newspapers complaining bitterly about the immorality of a play that dealt so explicitly with issues of a sexual nature and featured a character, the Vieja (Old Woman), who dared to declare herself an atheist and to suggest adultery as a possible solution to Yerma's predicament.[49]

The conservative and reactionary press had in fact been making snide comments about Lorca ever since the creation of La Barraca, with one newspaper, *Gracia y Justicia*, referring to him in the title of an article published in July 1932 as 'Federico García Loca' ('loca' translates roughly as 'queer') and La Barraca becoming known in reactionary circles, according to Lorca's close friend Pura Maórtua de Ucelay, as 'Sodoma por carretera' (Sodom on wheels).⁵⁰ The attacks on *Yerma* were of a different order, however, and were motivated in large part by the tragic events that had shaken Spain over the first three weeks of October 1934.

On 1 October, a political crisis led Prime Minister Alejandro Lerroux to give certain ministerial posts to members of the CEDA (Spanish Confederation of Autonomous Right-wing Groups). In response to what they saw as the increasingly powerful influence on government of this coalition of reactionary and, in some cases, anti-Republican and even fascistic parties, the more radical elements in the Socialist Party and on the Left called for a general strike and armed insurrection. Between 5 and 19 October, there was open conflict throughout Spain, but especially in the mining province of Asturias and also on the streets of Barcelona, where, for just 24 hours, a Federal Catalan Republic was proclaimed. The army brutally repressed the insurrection, which left some 2,000 dead, and the authorities imprisoned many thousands of left-wing supporters and also other less radical but, for them, equally uncomfortable political figures such as the former prime minister Manuel Azaña, who happened to be staying in Barcelona in early October at the house of his old friend Margarita Xirgu.

This link between the actress and the politician did not go unnoticed in the reactionary press in the lead-up to the première of *Yerma*. The fact that Azaña had been released from prison the very day before the première and Xirgu had once again offered him her house as a refuge may have been one of the motivating factors behind the noisy protest organized at the start of the performance by right-wing activists.⁵¹ From this time on, Lorca, whose name was often coupled with that of Socialist minister Fernando de los Ríos, would also be associated by some on the hard Right with the figure of Manuel Azaña, their true *bête noire*.

Lorca was being caught up in the ideological battles that polarized opinion and led many writers of the time, in Spain and internationally, to sign up to parties or movements at either end of the political spectrum. He had in fact become the target of criticisms from the Left as well as the Right, with an article that appeared in the Santander newspaper *La Región* in April 1934 characterizing him as a bourgeois and anti-Marxist writer who, with his love of Andalusian saints and madonnas, was helping to revive the 'sensual and religious poetry of the Andalusian countryside' and clearly placed his own class interests above those of the proletariat. He was thus the polar opposite of Rafael Alberti, that 'formerly bourgeois writer' who had come to despise bourgeois culture and to place his work at the service of the revolution and the future Socialist society.[52] The author of this article may well have been responding to an interview that had appeared in the León newspaper *La Mañana* back in August 1933, in which Lorca had claimed that his old friend and rival Rafael Alberti had returned from his recent trip to Russia a Communist and a writer, not of poetry, but of 'bad newspaper literature.'[53] Lorca was in fact restating here, albeit in an uncharacteristically personalized way, his long-held belief that poets and dramatists should be artists and creators first and foremost, since hitching one's work to a political cause was tantamount to prostituting one's art. Over the first years of the Republic, he had questioned the politicization of literature, just as he had done back in 1924, when Fernando de los Ríos and others had tried to persuade him to turn *Mariana Pineda* into a play with a clearer political message. Art certainly had a social function but La Barraca, he stressed time and again, did not have a political agenda, and he himself strongly disliked both propagandistic literature and the experience of being constantly hounded for his opinion on the political issues of the day.[54]

The events of autumn 1934 would not radically change Lorca's self-perception as an artist, nor his conviction that his work served more of a social than a political purpose, but they did deepen both his awareness of the hard Right's animosity towards him and his own anti-bourgeois animus. On occasions, his pronouncements seemed on the surface to take on a more political edge, especially when read in the context of the heightened political tensions of the time. On the eve of the premiere of *Yerma*, for example, he told the Madrid newspaper *El Sol* that he was and would always be 'on the side of the poor' and explained that, if the pain and sacrifice of middle-class intellectuals like himself were placed in one weighing scale and justice for all in the other, he would slam his fist (clenched, one might imagine, to form the left-wing salute) down on the latter.[55] More often, though, his response to the increasingly fraught situation consisted simply in intensifying his anti-bourgeois rhetoric or continuing to *épater les bourgeois*. We find him in late 1934 and the first months of 1935 telling his interviewers with a certain glee that he was working on a play called *La destrucción de Sodoma* (The Destruction of Sodom) that would complete the trilogy that he had started with *Blood Wedding* and *Yerma*.[56] Very little is known about this play, beyond the fact that, according to two of Lorca's friends, it was going to deal with incest as well as sodomy and that he was imagining some of the scenes as if they were paintings by Giotto or Piero della Francesca,[57] but Lorca obviously derived great pleasure from agreeing with his interviewer in *El Sol* on 1 January 1935 that the title was a daring and even a 'compromising' one.[58]

As things turned out, though, Lorca would in fact spend much of 1935 on two far less controversial and more urgently personal artistic projects, one poetic and the other dramatic. In the midst of the *Yerma* scandal, and in the same interview in which he declared himself to be on the side of the poor, Lorca said that his involvement with the theatre did not mean that he was neglecting what he calls his 'poesía pura' – a telling term to use when many around him were openly abjuring 'pure poetry' in favour of socially or politically committed verse.[59] He was in fact hard at work on two collections, both of which he had started several years earlier: the *Seis poemas galegos* (Six Galician Poems), which were written in the Galician language and would be published at the very end of 1935, and *Diwán del Tamarit* (The Tamarit Divan, or Collection), which would only see the light of day posthumously. What links these two collections is that they are both, in their own way, 'regional', that is, rooted in the culture, poetic forms and language of Galicia and Andalusia, respectively. In this sense at least, they can be seen as poetic outcroppings of Lorca's very first work, *Impressions and Landscapes* (1918), where he had set himself the task of understanding and celebrating the rich cultural diversity of the whole of the Iberian Peninsula.

Six Galician Poems was actually a joint venture between Lorca and Galician poet Ernesto Pérez Guerra da Cal (1911–1994), who was the co-author of at least one of the poems and advised Lorca when it came to the latter's use of the Galician language. He also received some help from another Galician writer, Eduardo Blanco Amor (1897–1979), who visited Lorca in Granada on a couple of occasions in 1934 and 1935 and appears to have had a close sentimental relationship with the poet.[60] The poems themselves are all given Galician settings, including Santiago de Compostela and Buenos Aires, a favoured destination for the Galician diaspora of the early twentieth century, but those settings are more literary and stylized than real and act as the background for a series of recognizably Lorcan erotic, religious and existential dramas: the lover who cloaks his melancholy in the persistent rain of Santiago, the religious procession through the Galician countryside that is joined by a multitude of the dead in the form of mist, the body of the drowned adolescent that floats on the river and is gradually being taken out to sea.[61] Lorca has found in Galicia the same natural agents that control the lives of his Andalusian gypsies and peasants: the river, the sea, the wind, the moon, the forest. But he has found these agents in a literary source too: the medieval Galician-Portuguese tradition of *cantigas* (songs), especially the genre of the *cantiga de amigo* (song of a friend), where a young lover, normally a woman, laments the absence of her beloved in haunting poems made up of simple verses and a repeated (or slightly varied) refrain. The final poem in the collection, 'Danza da lúa en Santiago' (Dance of the Moon in Santiago), is a modern *cantiga de amigo* in which a young woman watches the moon dancing through one of Santiago de Compostela's central squares, the Praça da Quintana dos Mortos, and debates with her mother whether what she is seeing is actually a beautiful but injured ghostly white youth. The moon, previously a female agent of death in *Gypsy Ballads* and a male accomplice of Death the Beggar Woman in *Blood Wedding*, here becomes an ethereal, seductive but also vulnerable – and at times threatening – object of desire for this young Galician maid.

Lorca and his mother in the Huerta de San Vicente, Granada, 1935. Photograph taken by Eduardo Blanco Amor.

In *The Tamarit Divan*, we find the first and practically the last glimpse of Lorca's mature lyrical poetic voice. He returns in this collection to his native Andalusia, and in particular to the city of Granada itself, and, as the titles of the two sections into which it is divided announce, he does so by adopting the spirit and often language of two poetic forms that recall Granada's Andalusian Arabic past: the *gacela* (ghazal) and the *casida* (qasida).[62] Following tradition, his twelve *gacelas* focus mainly on the joys and pains of love and the nine *casidas* on loss and death, although love and death are in fact inseparable presences throughout. Lorca continues his journey, which we had first noted in *Poet in New York*, back to a more subjective and personal mode of writing, although the *yo* (poetic self) that appears here is now fully immersed once again in what is for the poet a clearly recognizable, if still mysterious, poetic universe, that of Andalusia. In poems such as 'Gacela del amor imprevisto' (Ghazal of Unforeseen Love) and 'Gacela del amor desesperado' (Ghazal of Desperate Love), Lorca fuses the eroticism and sensuality of his Arabic models with the compressed metaphors that had characterized his pre-New York verse in order to celebrate the contours, smells (magnolia, jasmine) and taste (blood) of his beloved's body or to show how he and his beloved will come together despite all the obstacles, cosmic or social, that are put in their way.[63] Elsewhere, he evokes the personality of Granada itself, above all through its complex relationship with water. In this city that is distant from the sea and has covered over its river, Lorca seeks water underground, in its wells, or in the ponds and Arabic cisterns found in squares and houses, or in its fountains, where the jets of water spurting up from below become swords of love that can injure and kill those who come into contact with them.[64] Granada in these poems is a place of supreme beauty that can provide refuge and solace for lovers, but it is also a place of hidden depths and threats: what the poet can hear from his balcony is 'llanto' (sorrow and weeping), and even the beloved tree-lined groves that link the Huerta de San Vicente with the Huerta del Tamarit (the neighbouring property belonging to one of Lorca's uncles that gives its name to the collection) are full of barking dogs, groans and sighs.[65]

The Tamarit Divan in fact takes the highly personal and anguished voice found in *Lament for Ignacio Sánchez Mejías* in new and unexpected directions. Granada and its surroundings become the site of private and primal terrors, such as the fear of drowning that has appeared in Lorca's work since his earliest Vega poems and resurfaces here in 'Gacela del niño muerto' (Ghazal of the Dead Child), as it had in the 'Noiturnio do adoescente morto' (Nocturne of the Dead Adolescent) in *Six Galician Poems*.[66] Death haunts each and every poem, even the most sensual and erotic of them, since it seems to form a part of the sexual act itself and is seen eating away at the body of the beloved, ultimately turning him into no more than a memory in the mind of the poet.[67] But the most striking aspect of the collection is the poet's obsession with his own death: its place, its time, its circumstances, the sensations it might cause him. He asks the birds and the sun and the moon to let him know where his grave will be.[68] He expresses his desire for 'una muerte de luz que me consuma' (a death made of light that can consume me) or for an afterlife that takes place far from the commotion of cemeteries and is like the sleep of a child.[69] He talks of his fear of what the moon, the grass, the ant and the scorpion might do to his buried body, but also tries to imagine what the moment of death will feel like, even confronting one of his most basic fears by putting himself in the place of the drowned boy:

> *Quiero bajar al pozo,*
> *quiero morir mi muerte a bocanadas,*
> *quiero llenar mi corazón de musgo.*[70]

> I want to go down the well,
> I want to die my death in mouthfuls,
> I want to fill my heart with moss.

And, most movingly, he longs for a hand to accompany him and to act as a guardian that can, on the night of his death, shut out the moon and keep it at bay.[71] Moments such as these reveal how Lorca is now harnessing his profound acquaintance with love and death, his metaphorical brilliance, and his immersion in the lyrical traditions of Spain and his native Andalusia to create poetry that is both deeply innovative and deeply affecting.

The other job that took up much of his time during the first half of 1935 was the completion of his next play, *Doña Rosita la soltera* (Doña Rosita the Spinster), which tells the story of a young Granadan woman whose fiancé leaves to make his fortune in the Americas and ends up, despite all his pledges and promises, marrying another woman and never returning. Each of the three acts is set a decade or so apart – 1885, 1900, 1911 – and reveals how Rosita, like the *rosa mutabilis* cultivated by her uncle, blooms, matures and declines under the effects of disappointment and age. In his interviews, Lorca suggests that he conceived the work as a bourgeois comedy that would use caricature to poke fun at the prudishness and tweeness ('mojigatería' and 'cursilería') of the Granadan middle classes, and there is no doubt that the play, digging deep into Lorca's Rinconcillo past, does in fact derive a good deal of almost schoolboy humour from its parodic depiction of Rosita's pretentious suitors (who seem to be based on teachers or professors from Lorca's school and university days) and of some of her close female friends, with their social ambitions and insecurities and their love of frippery and kitsch.[72] However, apart from such moments, the bulk of the play does not act as an outlet for Lorca's newly intensified anti-bourgeois prejudices but rather transforms into something altogether more subtle: both a love poem to the Granada of his youth and a moving portrait of what he calls the drama or tragedy of spinsterhood.[73] Lorca reproduces in luscious detail the interiors, furnishings and dress of the Granadan middle classes of the turn of the century, making use of the testimonies of his parents' generation for the first two acts and his own childhood memories for the third. And, after having focused on the unbridled feelings of his peasant characters in *Blood Wedding* and *Yerma*, he shows great skill and sensitivity when charting the bridled emotions of Rosita and her aunt and contrasting their decorous language with the demotic bluntness of the Ama (Housekeeper), whose lively expressions, superstitious nature and fierce devotion to Rosita's family act as an affectionate homage to the housekeepers and maids whom Lorca himself had known and loved as a boy, most of them brought from the Vega by his parents.[74] Lorca felt that his story of a spinster who is meek on the outside and burns with repressed passion within was that of a multitude of Spanish women who had been 'sacrificed by the social ambience which envelops them', and he was sure that his play would, as a result, contain (and cause) more tears than any of his previous dramas.[75]

Despite the growing political tensions, Lorca enjoyed both his success and the fruits of his success throughout 1935. In March he had three plays running concurrently in Madrid: *Yerma*, *Blood Wedding* and *The Shoemaker's Prodigious Wife*, and he was soon talking about the idea of buying a house for himself on the Mediterranean. His new wealth triggered some envious responses in Granada, and Eduardo Blanco Amor reports how, during a visit in July to the social club, which Lorca hated so much (and which had been rebuilt after the fire in 1931), some of the members, including friends of Lorca's own father, made openly insulting

Lorca (photograph
dedicated to Rafael
Rodríguez Rapún), 1935.

remarks to Lorca both about the money he had brought back from
Argentina and about the fact that he was a 'maricón' (queer).[76] In August,
Lorca joined La Barraca in Santander for the start of their summer tour,
and Eric Hawkins, the British linguist and educator, remembers how the
troupe performed on a makeshift stage illuminated by lorry headlights
and how Lorca recited *Lament for Ignacio Sánchez Mejías* in his rich,
dark and disturbing voice.[77] This would in fact be the last time that Lorca
toured with La Barraca. It seems that his success as a playwright in his
own right, and his increasingly active involvement in the multiple productions of his plays, gradually distanced him from the project. When,
in December, the student union that oversaw its running replaced some
of its key officers, including Rapún as secretary, Lorca seized the opportunity to cut his remaining ties.[78]

Lorca spent the autumn conquering Catalonia. He arrived in Barcelona
on 9 September and, apart from several short trips to Madrid and Valencia,
would stay there until 24 December. During this time, actress Margarita
Xirgu and director Cipriano Rivas Cherif put on a series of plays written
or adapted by their Granadan friend: his version of Lope de Vega's *The*

Lady Simpleton, which premiered in the Teatro Barcelona on 10 September; *Yerma*, which ran at the same theatre from 17 September until 14 October and then at the Teatro Principal in Valencia from 5 to 11 November; *Blood Wedding*, which received its Barcelona première at the Teatro Principal Palace on 22 November; and, finally, the world première of *Doña Rosita the Spinster*, which ran at the same theatre between 12 December and 6 January 1936. The Catalan intelligentsia took Lorca to its heart in a way that seemed to fulfil Lorca's call, made after his visit to the region in summer 1927, for a close cultural dialogue between Catalonia and Andalusia.[79] And Lorca, who remembered his 1925 and 1927 trips to Catalonia with great fondness, was delighted to be able to renew his acquaintance with Salvador Dalí, whom he had not seen since early 1929. Little is known about what the two men discussed at their meetings on 28 September and thereafter, but we do know that Dalí could at last present his partner Gala to Lorca and that Lorca once again started talking about Dalí in the press with great enthusiasm and admiration.[80]

In a series of talks and interviews over these months, Lorca provides a glimpse both of his ambiguous relationship with politics and of his intimate state of mind. In late September, he gave a talk to a group of Catalan workers in which he can clearly be seen adapting his message to his audience. He presents himself as the son of a Fuente Vaqueros 'peasant' who sides with the 'pariahs' against the 'señoritos' (rich and privileged) of his region. He attacks the tyranny of Fascist Italy and Nazi Germany, where artistic freedom is repressed, and sings the praises of the USSR and its literature (in an interview a week or so later, he qualified his position somewhat by adding that the Soviet regime had in the first years tried to control art and literature but had since realized how futile that had been).[81] He also says that he would love to visit Moscow, which represents in his mind the 'polar opposite' of New York. In this context Lorca underlines the fact that art cannot turn its back on the drama of social life and that the main mission of theatre is to orient and educate the 'masses'. At the same time, though, and despite showing some appreciation for the German Marxist dramatist Erwin Piscator, he complains about the dogmatism of much political theatre and adds that while Sergei Eisenstein and others are showing that there is such a thing as epic cinema devoted to and aimed at the masses, theatre, on the other hand, needs to address and resolve intimate, individual problems.[82]

We find a similar ambiguity in an interview that Lorca gave in Valencia in mid-November. Here he avoids making any political references and, perhaps as a response to the negative reviews of his plays that had appeared in the right-wing Barcelona press, has recourse instead to his more usual anti-bourgeois rhetoric. He says quite openly that he wishes to scandalize and strike fear into bourgeois audiences and critics and even to create a reaction of revulsion so that all that is bad in contemporary theatre can be 'spewed out once and for all'. That's why he's writing a play about incest whose crudeness and violent passions will make *Yerma* sound angelical. Theatre today, he explains, can only be interested in social or sexual problems, and he personally is more interested in the latter. He even underlines that he is a Christian and has no qualms about exploring traditional concepts like honour or his own personal concerns about the afterlife. He is not therefore interested in the idea of a popular revolutionary theatre and, when pushed on this point by the interviewer, evades the issue altogether by talking instead about the revolutionary and subversive forms and techniques that he employs in his own plays. In short, Lorca reverts here to his old idea that the true function of theatre is to educate and influence the *pueblo* (people), a word that he deliberately employs in the place of 'masa' (mass).[83]

While Lorca was struggling to cope with the political pressures being placed on him, he was also struggling with issues of a personal nature. It seems that during his short trip to Valencia in mid-November, he was upset to find that Rapún did not join him there as planned.[84] In an astonishingly frank series of articles published in 1957, the director Cipriano Rivas Cherif reported that, shortly before the opening of *Blood Wedding* in Barcelona on 22 November, Lorca failed to turn up to rehearsals the morning after an all-night party. When Rivas traced him to a café near his hotel off the Ramblas, Lorca seemed distracted, even crazy, and proceeded to tell his friend, who claimed not to know until this point that Lorca was gay, that Rapún had left the party with a beautiful Gypsy singer. Lorca was once again, as had happened with both Emilio Aladrén and Salvador Dalí, confronting the possibility of losing his partner or closest friend to a woman, and that possibility, although it never in fact became a reality in the case of Rapún, had a profoundly unsettling effect on him. According to Rivas Cherif, Lorca took advantage of their unexpected encounter to share some deeply intimate thoughts. He had never had sexual relations with a woman, despite the fact that he was surrounded by so many admirers. He put his deep attachment but lack of sexual attraction to women down to the profound respect and affection he felt towards his mother. He liked manly men rather than *maricas* (the 'queers' he had so brutally attacked in the 'Ode to Walt Whitman'), whose effeminacy he found entertaining but not attractive. In his opinion, neither heterosexuality nor homosexuality should be seen as the norm: the only normality should be 'limitless love', the basis of a stronger and better morality than that offered by any dogma, including that of the Catholic Church. In his form of love, neither lover dominates the other or submits to him; there is only abandon and mutual joy and pleasure. But for such love to triumph, as Walt Whitman had made clear, a true revolution and a new morality are needed: the morality of full and complete freedom.[85]

At the very end of 1935, it appears that Lorca's immediate plan was to accompany Margarita Xirgu and her company on their tour of Cuba and Mexico, starting in late January.[86] Rivas Cherif claims that Xirgu did all she could to sign Rapún up to her company, in the knowledge that Lorca would not go without him. In the end, Rapún stayed in Spain in order to take his university exams, and Lorca stayed with him.[87]

The following months were deeply unstable ones in Spanish politics. After Alejandro Lerroux's government collapsed in late 1935, following a series of corruption scandals, President Niceto Alcalá-Zamora called a general election for 16 February. Liberal Republicans and more moderate Socialists and left-wingers came together to form the Popular Front, which would eventually win the election with a narrow majority. The election campaign and result would serve to polarize Spanish politics even further and give rise to increasingly violent confrontations between radical factions on the Left and the Right.

Lorca lived these months, both before and after the elections, with a mixture of expectation and exasperation and, above all, a growing sense of trepidation. There seems to be little doubt that he relished the possibility of a change of government, as a photograph taken on 22 February 1936, shortly after the election result had been declared, suggests. There we see Lorca, along with friends and fellow writers such as Rafael Alberti, María Teresa León and Vicente Aleixandre, celebrating the visit of several Argentine journalists with grins on their faces and their fists clenched in the Popular Front salute.[88] He had also been working for some time on a play known as both *El sueño de la vida* (The Dream of Life) and *Comedia sin título* (Play Without a Title), whose single extant act features, rather like *The Public*, a revolution that appears to represent necessary, though troublingly violent, change. The character known as the Author verbally assails his bourgeois spectators, who, he says, have no sense of solidarity with those who suffer, and warns them of his intention to destroy the theatre in order to allow the truth of the outside world in.[89] His spectators recoil in horror at this prospect and, once the revolution actually starts, one of them, claiming to serve an unforgiving and militant God, takes great pride and pleasure in shooting the first worker who appears on stage.[90]

This indeed is Lorca at his most subversive and his most angry, as he vents his spleen against the selfish and superficial middle-class world that he feels turns a blind eye to social injustice. When he described parts of the play and the revolution it depicts in a press interview in April, he seemed to be almost taken aback by what he himself was saying and asked his interviewer, rhetorically, whether he was sounding like a Socialist.[91] But the truth is that even here, in this apocalyptic play, there are signs that the revolution Lorca is interested in is not just about the fight against inequality and hunger but also about the future of theatre itself and about sexual freedom. The actors we see onstage are preparing to rehearse *A Midsummer Night's Dream* (rather than *Romeo and Juliet*, as had been the case in *The Public*) and are seen debating an issue that had dominated Lorca's work ever since his second oldest poem, that is, the idea that the identity (and therefore gender) of those we fall in love with is no more than a matter of pure chance.[92]

At the same time that Lorca was expressing a certain glee at the prospect of radical change, there are also signs that he was tiring of the political pressures he was being placed under. He had been courted over the years by both Right and Left, there being rumours that the founder of the fascist Falangist movement, José Antonio Primo de Rivera, impressed by Lorca's anti-bourgeois rhetoric and his ability to reach the noble 'people' through the work of La Barraca, had tried to recruit him to his cause.[93] According to Carlos Morla Lynch, however, many of Lorca's close friends, among them the closest of all, were in fact on the Left of the political spectrum, including the Socialists Rafael Rodríguez Rapún and Rafael Martínez Nadal and the Communist Rafael Alberti.[94] Morla Lynch, a rather conservative figure himself, may have had his own axe to grind when pointing out the ideological leanings of Lorca's friends, but it is clear that Lorca's fame and artistic influence, as well as his pronouncements on social injustice, made him a prime target for those who wished to sign him up to their own political cause. Lorca seemed happy to continue

Lorca with other members of his artistic generation (including Luis Buñuel, Rafael Alberti, Miguel Hernández and Pablo Neruda), Madrid, May 1936. Second left is Rafael Rodríguez Rapún.

to add his signature to left-wing manifestos – celebrating Workers' Day on 1 May, for example, or criticizing the regime of Portuguese dictator António de Oliveira Salazar[95] – but he showed increasing caution when it came to his own public statements and took to revising the text of his interviews in order to root out any potentially compromising statements before they were published.[96] In early June, for example, after giving an interview to the political cartoonist Bagaría for the Madrid newspaper *El Sol*, during which he lamented the loss of the Moorish civilization in Granada and claimed that his home city was now run by the 'worst bourgeoisie in Spain', he wrote to his old friend Adolfo Salazar, a colleague of Bagaría's, in order to ask him to do his best to delete his 'indiscreet' answers on Fascism and Communism.[97]

In such trying circumstances, Lorca's artistic imagination took him away from Madrid and back home to Granada and, in particular, the Vega. He worked during these months on two plays, one in a major and the other a minor key. In the only extant act of *Los sueños de mi prima Aurelia* (The Dreams of My Cousin Aurelia), he turns the clock back to 1910 and recreates the warm and imaginative atmosphere that he had found in the household of his real-life cousin Aurelia in Fuente Vaqueros.

Lorca himself appears as a young boy who sings songs and is fascinated by his cousin and aunts, who live their lives surrounded by music and literature and telling stories using the lively and inventive language of the Vega.[98] The atmosphere of *The House of Bernarda Alba* could not be more different. While *The Dreams* is set in happy and well-watered Fuente Vaqueros, the references in *The House of Bernarda Alba* to a small and poorly irrigated village that is ruled by gossip very much brings the Asquerosa of Lorca's teenage years and young adulthood to mind.[99] Moreover, in order to tell the story of a mother who intends to keep her five daughters locked up at home for years while they mourn her recently deceased husband, Lorca makes deliberate use of local surnames, such as Alba and Benavides, and even employs the name of a real local lothario (and another distant relative) for the character of Pepe el Romano, who is never seen onstage but whose offstage presence helps to drive the drama and cause the tragedy that brings the play to a close. Crucially, Alba and Benavides, together with Roldán, are the names of the local families from the Vega with which the Garcías had long intermarried and with whom Lorca's father had both formed commercial alliances in the past and, more recently, suffered bitter disputes over the ownership of land and their investment in the local sugar beet factories.[100]

This 'photographic documentary', as Lorca describes the play,[101] focuses on the sexual rivalry and frustrations of the five sisters, from the oldest, 39-year-old Angustias, who is being offered in marriage to Pepe el Romano, to the youngest, twenty-year-old Adela, who ends the play by hanging herself when she is mistakenly led to believe that Pepe, her lover, has been shot and killed by her mother. The play tells the story of a revolution of sorts, as the repressed feelings of the sisters – above all Adela's desire, as she puts it, to own her own body and to give it to whomever she pleases – finally erupt, with violent and tragic consequences.[102] The housekeeper, La Poncia, tries to help the sisters realize what is going on inside them and to communicate the gravity of the situation to Bernarda, but she too is ultimately forced to become an agent of Bernarda's oppression and ends up advising the sisters to repress, rather than express, their desires. In sharp contrast to the close and intimate relationship between the Aunt and the Housekeeper in *Doña Rosita the Spinster*, Bernarda often reminds La Poncia of her inferior social status and of the fact that she is a servant rather than a part of the family.

Bernarda herself comes across as a tyrant, as someone who is obsessed with status, appearances and the reputation of her family, especially that of her daughters. She claims to despise gossip and yet is the first to want to know what goes on in the village and even, at the end of the second act, calls on the local men to lynch a young woman who, the rumours say, has just killed her illegitimate newborn baby.[103] There are few more powerful indictments of the destructive power of gossip in Spanish literature and, in this sense, the play seems to show Lorca settling scores with a village, Asquerosa, which had long been his base in the Vega but which he had latterly come to associate with this particularly pernicious form of social control. Bernarda's first and final word is '¡Silencio!' (Silence!), and the play does at times seem to ask us what exactly it is, beyond her daughters and her maids, that she is trying to silence.[104] Although she has a good deal in common with the Mother in *Blood Wedding*, especially in her obsessive and controlling nature, we know of no traumatic event from her past that can explain the way she is. But her insistence on silencing emotions or, more precisely, on keeping them private – as she has done over the death of her husband and will do at the end after the death of Adela – suggests that her monstrous oppression of others springs from unspoken but deep-seated fears of her own.

Lorca finished *The House of Bernarda Alba* on 19 June and read it out over the following weeks to several old friends, including Pepín Bello, Gregorio Marañón and Carlos Morla Lynch.[105] He told Morla that his plan was for the play to be put on in the autumn. What Morla most remembered about his meetings with Lorca at this time, though, was that his friend's mood seemed to alternate between elation and deep anxiety. On a visit to the countryside near Alcalá de Henares on 5 July, he was full of life and plans but, just three days later, at a dinner with Fernando de los Ríos, Morla found him to be subdued, silent and absent. He only came out of his reverie at one point in order to stress once again that he was 'on the side of the poor', but he immediately added that he was actually 'on the side of the *good* poor' – implying, perhaps, that he had no time for those who used violence in their fight for social justice.[106]

Stage designers José Caballero and Santiago Ontañón report that Lorca had first-hand experience of the political violence of these weeks, since he found a stray bullet embedded in the wall of his family's flat on the Calle de Alcalá and also witnessed how a church in the Plaza de Santa Ana had been set alight.[107] Other friends, including Pepín Bello and Rafael Martínez Nadal, affirm that Lorca was by now terrified that Spain was about to descend into civil war and that he was also deeply anxious because he did not know if he would be better off remaining in Madrid

Lorca with a group of friends at the Verbena (Festival) de San Pedro y San Pablo, Madrid, 28 June 1936. Lorca's hand rests on Rafael Rodríguez Rapún's forehead.

or joining his parents in Granada.[108] The thought of leaving Rapún behind doubtlessly created yet more uncertainty in Lorca's mind, although it has recently been confirmed that Lorca was also in a relationship at this time with a nineteen-year-old student and actor called Juan Ramírez de Lucas, possibly another powerful reason for staying in Madrid.[109] In the end, it was the murder on 12 July of the left-wing police officer José Castillo, most probably by members of the Falange, and the revenge killing, by Leftist

Lorca with Manuela Arniches on the terrace of the Café Chiki-Kutz, Paseo de Recoletos, Madrid, July 1936. This is one of the very last photographs of Lorca.

militiamen, of leading anti-Republican politician José Calvo Sotelo the following day, that made Lorca's mind up. He left for Granada on the night of 13 July, seemingly convinced that he would be safer away from the capital and surrounded by his family.

eight

Granada: Refuge and Death, July–August 1936

Since the early 1950s, several historians have tried to piece together what happened over the following month, the last in the life of Federico García Lorca.[1] Thanks above all to the interviews carried out by Agustín Penón in 1954 and 1955 and by Ian Gibson and Eduardo Molina Fajardo over the following decades, we also have the direct testimonies of many of Lorca's relations, friends and even enemies in Granada.[2]

On his arrival in the Huerta de San Vicente on the morning of 14 July, Lorca announced his intention of staying just a few days, mainly in order to celebrate his father's and his own Saint's Day on 18 July, before then joining Margarita Xirgu in Mexico. In his last extant letter, which was dated 18 July and contained a fresh jasmine flower pressed between its pages, Lorca gently encouraged his new lover Juan Ramírez de Lucas to 'overcome all difficulties' – most probably a reference to the young actor's attempts to persuade his parents to let him accompany Lorca to Mexico.[3] But Lorca was having difficulties convincing his own parents of his plans too. His close friend Emilia Llanos and the family maid Cordobilla Angelina report that Lorca's father was opposed to the Mexico trip and insisted that his son spend the summer with them in Granada instead.[4] Over the first days of his stay, Lorca read *The House of Bernarda Alba* to his family and to friends at various houses around the city, and it seems that both his mother and his father took exception to his use of the Alba and Benavides surnames and to his references to members of the Roldán family and that they tried, unsuccessfully, to get him to change or remove them.[5]

The 18 July festivities, which Lorca had told Rafael Martínez Nadal a few days earlier tended to be a lavish affair attended by numerous relatives and friends,[6] turned out to be very subdued, because news came through that very morning that General Francisco Franco and the Spanish army in Morocco had risen against the Republic. Granada itself remained relatively quiet until 20 July, when local army officers, Falangists and militiamen associated with the reactionary CEDA coalition took violent possession of the city, arresting, among many others, the Socialist mayor, Manuel Fernández Montesinos, who was married to Lorca's sister Concha and was father to his beloved nephew and nieces. All active resistance within the city itself had been crushed by 23 July, but the insurgents, aware that much of the surrounding area remained in the hands of Republican loyalists, initiated a campaign of terror that aimed to cow the population through mass arrests and also mass executions.

Lorca kept as low a profile as possible at the Huerta de San Vicente, just 1 kilometre (half a mile) or so from the centre of Granada. He was in a state of high anxiety and unable to work, spending much of his time smoking, drinking brandy and listening to radio broadcasts, especially those from the Republican side. One of his cousins remembered how he panicked when someone on the radio read out the signatories to a manifesto attacking the military uprising, fearing that his friends in Madrid might have added his name to theirs.[7] When Republican planes bombed the city, he would take refuge under the piano with his family and the maids. On 6 August, he received his first direct proof that the insurgents were taking an interest in him when a group of Falangists searched the house for a radio transmitter with which he was supposedly sending information to the 'Russians'. They left, but another group came three days later searching for the brothers of the Lorca family caretaker, who were incorrectly suspected of having murdered a right-wing politician in the Vega. On seeing how this much more aggressive group of Falangists and CEDA supporters mistreated the caretaker, Lorca protested and was pushed down the stairs, hit with the butt of a rifle and called a *maricón* (queer) in front of his family.[8]

This visit brought home to Lorca that the danger he was in was not simply political or ideological in origin. Among the group that terrorized the Lorca household that day was his distant cousin Horacio Roldán, with whom he had played as a boy. Horacio was the son of Lorca's father's relative Alejandro Roldán Benavides, another rich Asquerosa landowner whose relationship with Federico García had soured over the years due to their commercial disputes.[9] Alejandro Roldán had moved to Granada shortly after the García Lorca family had done so and had attempted to emulate Lorca's father even further by entering into politics, in his case as part of the Conservative Party, only to find his political career beset by accusations of violence and corruption. Horacio had studied the same law degree as Federico and Francisco García Lorca but ended up with a worse result than they did, mainly, the Roldáns believed, due to the unfair support that the Lorca boys received from Fernando de los Ríos. Horacio went on to work as a lawyer in the service of the Acción Popular (Popular Action) party, which formed part of the CEDA. The historian Miguel Caballero has claimed that Horacio's uncle José Benavides Peña, the real-life Pepe el Romano, was most probably also part of the thuggish group that visited the Huerta de San Vicente that day, and that all of the branches of the Alba-Benavides-Roldán family were probably aware by then of how Lorca had portrayed them in *The House of Bernarda Alba.*[10]

Lorca realized that he was no longer safe in the Huerta de San Vicente and telephoned a close friend, the young Granadan poet Luis Rosales, for advice. Rosales, whose brothers were all committed Falangists and who had himself enlisted in the Falange when news of the uprising came through, went straight to the Huerta de San Vicente and heard Lorca and his parents debating the different options open to him. Lorca rejected the idea of travelling the few kilometres to cross into Republican territory, something that was still easy to arrange at this point in the war (Lorca's father had in fact already offered to help one of his son's friends to do this), saying that he did not want to escape and did not feel that his life was in danger.[11] He also decided not to take refuge in the house of Manuel de Falla, of whom he had seen little ever since the composer had taken exception to Lorca's 'Ode to the Most Blessed Sacrament'. Rather, he accepted Luis Rosales's invitation to stay at his own family home in the centre of Granada: where better to find safety, after all, than in the house of Granada's leading Falangists?[12]

That very night, 9 August, the family chauffeur drove Lorca to the Rosales house in the Calle Angulo and later remembered that all Lorca took with him were a few clothes wrapped up inside his pyjama top.[13] He was given a room on the second floor and, as Luis and his brothers spent most of the day in the Falangist headquarters or at the front, he was looked after mainly by his friend's mother, sister and aunt Luisa, whom he fondly called his 'divine jailers'. He continued to be very anxious, smoking incessantly and listening obsessively to the radio, but he did gradually find the presence of mind to start reading again, especially the works of the medieval poet Gonzalo de Berceo, whose religious verse, shot through with vivid popular expressions and refrains, he had always enjoyed.

He would spend some of the evenings in discussion with Luis Rosales, who told Agustín Penón in 1955 that Lorca deep down wanted the Nationalists (supporters of Franco's uprising) to win the war, as he was tired of all the turmoil of the previous months and was, moreover, a conservative at heart.[14] In an off-the-record interview with Ian Gibson in 1966, Rosales would go into more detail: Lorca was not a man of the Right, although he did have a 'right-wing mentality'; he had been a friend of Manuel Azaña but also of José Antonio Primo de Rivera; and, in those last days, he supported the idea of a military dictatorship that could bring the political violence to an end.[15] Rosales's claims have long been ignored or disputed by historians, and Rosales himself avoided making any such comments in later interviews,[16] and yet they should not perhaps be simply dismissed out of hand as the self-interested ideas of a Falangist. Lorca, as we have seen, was a rich and complex personality whose subversive and anti-bourgeois instincts coexisted with a profoundly religious sensibility and a passionate devotion to popular, and traditional, culture. It must not be forgotten too that half of his Rinconcillo colleagues would end up supporting the Franco regime, as would quite a few of his closest friends from his Madrid days, including Salvador Dalí (in his own idiosyncratic manner) and also Pepín Bello: indeed, Pepín would later claim that he had been so furious to witness how the Republican side had turned the 'apolitical' Lorca into a 'martyr' that he had told a Falangist friend after the war that the Falange should do its best to claim Lorca for itself.[17]

All this by no means confirms what Rosales said, and it is clear that, since the start of the Republic, and especially the 1933 elections, Lorca had shown much more sympathy for the Left than for the Right. But it is also clear that Lorca, like a large proportion of the Spanish population, was left stranded by a civil war that tested loyalties to the limit and divided families and friends in often irreparable ways. In this context, it is instructive to remember Pura Maórtua de Ucelay's story of how Lorca responded to a friend who had asked him shortly before he left Madrid what 'side' he was on: I salute some people in this way, replied Lorca, using the stiff-arm Fascist (and Falangist) salute, and others like this, he added, raising a clenched fist in the Communist (and Popular Front) style, but, with my friends, I simply open my arms and embrace them thus.[18]

Luis Rosales also reported that Lorca tried to write during these days and that among the papers that he later returned to Lorca's parents were the poems that would be published in 1984 under the title of *Sonetos del amor oscuro* (Sonnets of Dark Love).[19] Lorca had made little use of the sonnet form since his earliest verse but, with this group of eleven, he created one of the most beautiful (if probably unfinished) love cycles in the whole of Spanish poetry. He had started writing them in Valencia in November 1935, and it is very possible that several of them reflect the anxiety that he was then feeling about his relationship with Rafael Rodríguez Rapún.[20] All of the sonnets use complex and delicate metaphors that have been inspired both by Lorca's Golden Age master Luis de Góngora and by the Arabic poetry that he also drew on when writing *The Tamarit Diwan*, and we once again encounter in them a powerful mixture of sensuality and pain, presence and absence, love and death. It is impossible to know whether each of the poems is addressed to a particular lover, be it Rapún or perhaps Juan Ramírez de Lucas, or whether Lorca composed any of them in the Rosales house or simply re-read or revised them there. It is obvious, though, that the references to the absence of the beloved, to the memory of his body, or to the feeling that the lovers are under threat or being watched ('¡Mira que nos acechan todavía!', or 'Look how they stalk us still!') must have taken on a special significance for the poet during this time of enforced confinement.[21]

Around 4.30 p.m. on Sunday 16 August, three men, backed up by assault guards posted around the adjoining streets and even on the surrounding rooftops, went to the Rosales house with, they said, an order for Lorca's arrest.[22] As the Rosales menfolk were not at home, Luis's mother asked the leader, Ramón Ruiz Alonso, to go and speak first to her son Miguel, who was at that moment at the Falangist headquarters nearby. As Ruiz Alonso was not a Falangist himself but rather a member of Acción Popular and a subordinate of the Rosales Falangists, he did as Luis's mother requested and soon after returned with Miguel, who tried to put Lorca's mind at rest by saying that he would accompany him and the arrest party. Lorca was already in a state of deep shock, having just heard that morning about the execution of his brother-in-law Manuel Fernández Montesinos. He was given time to get changed and to say a prayer with his 'divine jailers' before he was driven to the Civil Government building in the Calle Duquesa, just 300 metres (1,000 ft) away from the Rosales' home.

Miguel Rosales and also his brother Luis, who went to the Civil Government building late that night after returning from the front, later affirmed that Ramón Ruiz Alonso never produced an arrest warrant but rather claimed sole responsibility for Lorca's arrest.[23] For the Rosales brothers, this was proof that Ruiz Alonso's main motivation had been personal spite and ambition, since this former member of parliament for Acción Popular had twice applied for membership of the Falange only to be turned down on both occasions.[24] There could be no better way of taking revenge, they implied, than bringing to light the fact that the leading local Falangist family was giving refuge to an 'undesirable' such as Lorca. The truth of the matter went much deeper than this, of course, since it is clear from the way that Lorca had been treated over the previous weeks that he was already a marked man. The Franco regime would spend the next forty years trying to cover up what was for it a very embarrassing and diplomatically damaging episode, and would periodically send agents to Granada to try and find out what had really happened. In 1965 the Granada police, under pressure from Madrid, prepared a report that only came to light half a century later, according to which Lorca had indeed been killed but in circumstances that were still unclear. It then proceeded to provide a list of possible reasons for his death, including the fact that there were rumours (but no proof) of his homosexual practices, rumours (but no proof, beyond his friendship with Fernando de los Ríos) of his Socialist leanings, and supposed proof (which has never been forthcoming or corroborated) of his having been a freemason.[25]

This disturbing document reveals just what little evidence was needed in the dark days of the war and post-war in order to carry out, sanction or justify an extrajudicial execution. What it doesn't reveal is that, alongside all the reasons and motivations behind Lorca's death mentioned above, there was another, more atavistic one that has only recently started to come to light fully. Ramón Ruiz Alonso was in fact a close associate of fellow Acción Popular activist Horacio Roldán, as was one of the other men who accompanied him to the Rosales house on 16 August, that is, Juan Luis Trescastro, who was also yet another distant relative of Lorca's father.[26] Lorca's fate was obviously being decided by a deadly mixture of ideological disputes, local gossip, prejudices, envy and family resentment.

It seems likely that Lorca spent no more than ten hours in the Civil Government building. Shortly before midnight on 16 August, he was taken by car to the village of Víznar, about 8 kilometres (5 mi.) northeast of Granada. This village, 1,000 metres (3,280 ft) up in the Sierra de Huétor mountain range, was at the time situated just a few kilometres behind the front line and, together with the main cemetery in Granada, was proving to be a very useful place for the mass executions of Republicans and Leftists. The military head of the sector, the Falangist Captain José María Nestares, remembered ordering one of his subordinates to

La Colonia, Víznar, where Lorca spent his final hours before being shot. The photograph of this now demolished building, which shows the Peñón Colorado in the distance, was taken by Ian Gibson in 1966.

accompany the car to a building known as the Colonia, which was found about 1 kilometre outside Víznar, on the road to Alfacar.[27] This building was being used to house both those who were to be executed and those prisoners whose job it was to bury them. One of the guards that night, a young man called Eduardo González Aurioles, was devastated to see Lorca arrive, as both men's mothers were close friends and Lorca had once saved him from drowning.[28]

Some time around 4.30 a.m. on Monday 17 August, Lorca and three other prisoners – a local schoolteacher and two bullfighting *banderilleros* who had anarchist affiliations – were driven a kilometre and a half further along the Alfacar road, past the Víznar ravine, which Gerald Brenan would find still 'pitted with low hollows and mounds' in 1949,[29] and on to a flat area to the right of the road that was used for military exercises. Here they were forced to walk 50 metres (165 ft) to the place they would be executed and buried. In front of them was the steep bluff of the Peñón Colorado. Behind them, 20 kilometres (12 mi.) due west down in the flat plains of the Vega, was the village of Fuente Vaqueros, nestled behind the sphinx-shaped mass of the Sierra Elvira. In the firing squad that day was a member of the Benavides family, who later bragged that he had put two bullets into the skull of that *cabezón* (swollen head).[30] Among those who hounded Lorca, arrested him and killed him, there were distant family members: like countless others in civil wars the world over, Lorca was the victim of feuds both personal and political.

REFERENCES

OC: Federico García Lorca, *Obras completas*, ed. Arturo del Hoyo, 3 vols
(Madrid, 1986)

Introduction

1 Arturo Barea, *Lorca: The Poet and his People* (London, 1944).
2 Gerald Brenan, *The Face of Spain* [1950] (London, 1988), pp. 126–50;
   Marta Osorio, ed., *Miedo, olvido y fantasía. Crónica de la investigación
   de Agustín Penón sobre Federico García Lorca, 1955–1956* [2000]
   (Granada, 2009); Claude Couffon, *Granada y García Lorca* [1962]
   (Buenos Aires, 1967); Marcelle Auclair, *Enfances et mort de García Lorca*
   (Paris, 1968); Ian Gibson, *The Assassination of Federico García Lorca* [1973]
   (London, 1983).
3 Paul Binding, *Lorca: The Gay Imagination* (London, 1985). See also
   David Johnston, *Federico García Lorca* (Bath, 1998); Ángel Sahuquillo,
   Federico García Lorca and the Culture of Male Homosexuality
   (Jefferson, NC, and London, 2007); and Ian Gibson, *Lorca y el mundo gay*
   (Barcelona, 2010).
4 For a vivid account of the 2009 search for Lorca's remains and of the
   media attention it attracted, see Ian Gibson, *La fosa de Lorca: Crónica
   de un despropósito* (Alcalá la Real, 2010).
5 See Leslie Stainton, *Lorca: A Dream of Life* (London, 1998); and Ian
   Gibson, *Federico García Lorca* [1985] (Barcelona, 2011) and its English
   version *Federico García Lorca: A Life* (London, 1989).
6 Two particularly striking examples of this type of biography, both of which
   create a link between Lorca's sexuality and his supposed tragic 'destiny', are
   Jean-Louis Schonberg, *Federico García Lorca. L'homme – l'oeuvre* (Paris,
   1956) and Francisco Umbral, *Lorca, poeta maldito* (Madrid, 1975).

1 La Vega: His Own Private Arden, 1898–1909

1 Federico García Lorca, *Poesía inédita de juventud*, ed. Christian De Paepe
   (Madrid, 2008), p. 72.
2 On Vicenta Lorca's training and career as a schoolteacher, see Amelina
   Correa Ramos, '*Mater et magistra*: Reconstrucción de la trayectoria
   profesional de Vicenta Lorca, con la aportación de algunos documentos
   inéditos', *Analecta Malacitana*, XXXVI/1–2 (2013), pp. 135–60.

3 Federico García Lorca, *Prosa inédita de juventud*, ed. Christopher Maurer (Madrid, 1994), p. 431.
4 Ibid., p. 436.
5 Isabel García Lorca, *Recuerdos míos* (Barcelona, 2002), p. 70.
6 See Eutimio Martín, *Federico García Lorca. Heterodoxo y mártir. Análisis y proyección de la obra juvenil inédita* (Madrid, 1986), pp. 83–143.
7 *OC*, II, p. 1122.
8 Ibid., pp. 1122–3.
9 Lorca, *Prosa inédita de juventud*, pp. 440–42.
10 Ibid., p. 438.
11 Isabel García Lorca, *Recuerdos míos*, pp. 58–9.
12 Lorca, *Prosa inédita de juventud*, p. 435.
13 Ibid., p. 438.
14 Ibid., pp. 448–50.
15 Ibid., p. 448.
16 *OC*, III, p. 344.
17 Lorca, *Prosa inédita de juventud*, pp. 449–50.
18 Ibid., p. 461.
19 *OC*, III, p. 431.
20 Isabel García Lorca, *Recuerdos míos*, pp. 54–5.
21 Francisco García Lorca, *Federico y su mundo* (Madrid, 1981), p. 19.
22 Isabel García Lorca, *Recuerdos míos*, p. 53.
23 Lorca, *Prosa inédita de juventud*, pp. 251–6.
24 Lorca, *Poesía inédita de juventud*, pp. 387–9.
25 Ibid., pp. 476–7.
26 Ibid., pp. 159–60.
27 'Tarde de abril' (April evening); ibid., pp. 257–60.
28 'Aria de primavera' (Spring Aria); ibid., pp. 272–9.
29 See 'Que nadie sepa nunca mi secreto' (Let No-one Ever Know My Secret) and 'El poeta y la primavera' (The Poet and Spring), ibid., pp. 283 and 485–92.
30 See 'Mañana' (Morning) and 'Letanía del arroyo' (The Stream's Litany), ibid., pp. 445–8 and 285–7.
31 Ibid., pp. 398–9.
32 Ibid., pp. 90–92 and 117–18.
33 Ibid., pp. 357–61.
34 Ibid., pp. 404–5.
35 Ibid., pp. 462–5.
36 Ibid., pp. 393–6 and 379–81.
37 Ibid., pp. 163–4.
38 Ibid., p. 441.
39 Ibid., pp. 297–8.
40 Ibid., pp. 99–104.
41 Lorca, *Prosa inédita de juventud*, pp. 413–15.
42 *OC*, I, pp. 1048–9.
43 Lorca, *Poesía inédita de juventud*, pp. 549–50.

2 Granada: A Paradise Closed to Many, 1909–19

1 Federico García Lorca, *Poesía inédita de juventud*, ed. Christian De Paepe (Madrid, 2008), pp. 197–9.
2 See Francisco García Lorca, *Federico y su mundo* (Madrid, 1981), pp. 67–75 and Isabel García Lorca, *Recuerdos míos* (Barcelona, 2002), pp. 35–42.
3 Francisco García Lorca, *Federico y su mundo*, p. 76.
4 Ibid., pp. 88–9.
5 Ibid., pp. 78–82.
6 *OC*, II, p. 951.
7 Francisco García Lorca, *Federico y su mundo*, pp. 87–8.
8 See Ian Gibson, *Federico García Lorca* (Barcelona, 2011), p. 87.
9 *OC*, III, p. 397.
10 Francisco García Lorca, *Federico y su mundo*, p. 93.
11 *OC*, III, p. 397.
12 Federico García Lorca, *Prosa inédita de juventud*, ed. Christopher Maurer (Madrid, 1994), pp. 465–6.
13 'Crepúsculo espiritual' (Spiritual Dusk), in Lorca, *Poesía inédita de juventud*, pp. 182–3.
14 'Los crepúsculos revelan' (Dusks Reveal), ibid., p. 444.
15 Ibid., p. 260.
16 Ibid., pp. 466–7 and 288–91.
17 See, for example, 'Mediodía' (Midday), ibid., pp. 397–400; 'Melodía de invierno' (Winter Melody), ibid., pp. 159–60; and 'Aria de primavera que es casi una elegía del mes de octubre' (Spring Aria That is Almost an Elegy for the Month of October), ibid., pp. 272–9.
18 Ibid., pp. 174–5.
19 Ibid., p. 90.
20 Ibid., p. 407.
21 Lorca, *Prosa inédita de juventud*, p. 237.
22 Gibson, *Federico García Lorca*, pp. 169–70. See, for example, the poem 'Bruma del corazón' (Heart Mist), in Lorca, *Poesía inédita de juventud*, pp. 105–6.
23 Lorca, *Prosa inédita de juventud*, pp. 59–165.
24 See, for example, the poem 'Oración' (Prayer), in Lorca, *Poesía inédita de juventud*, p. 307.
25 See, for example, the poem 'Romanzas con palabras' (*Romanzas* with Words), ibid., pp. 233–6.
26 Ibid., p. 237.
27 Lorca, *Prosa inédita de juventud*, p. 247.
28 Ibid., pp. 246–9.
29 See, for example, 'Los crepúsculos revelan' (Dusks Reveal), in Lorca, *Poesía inédita de juventud*, pp. 441–4.
30 Ibid., pp. 119–21, 379–81 and 393–6.
31 Lorca, *Prosa inédita de juventud*, pp. 159–65.
32 See Lorca, *Poesía inédita de juventud*, pp. 228–32, 288–91, 511–12 and 524–8.
33 For a perceptive reading of Lorca's lifelong relationship with religion and the Catholic Church, see Eric Southworth, 'Religion', in *A Companion to Federico García Lorca*, ed. Federico Bonaddio (Woodbridge, 2007), pp. 129–48.

34 Lorca, *Prosa inédita de juventud*, p. 89, and Lorca, *Poesía inédita de juventud*, pp. 414–18.

35 See the poem 'Un tema con variaciones pero sin solución' (A Theme with Variations but No Solution), in Lorca, *Poesía inédita de juventud*, pp. 107–10.

36 Lorca, *Prosa inédita de juventud*, pp. 309–48 and 416–25.

37 Francisco García Lorca, *Federico y su mundo*, pp. 106–13.

38 *OC*, III, p. 390.

39 See Lorca, *Poesía inédita de juventud*, p. 349 and *OC*, III, p. 386.

40 Lorca, *Prosa inédita de juventud*, p. 417.

41 *OC*, III, pp. 77–83 and 320.

42 Ibid., p. 410.

43 Ibid., p. 140.

44 Ibid., pp. 86–8.

45 Lorca, *Poesía inédita de juventud*, pp. 348–54.

46 See *OC*, III, p. 139.

47 Ibid., p. 683.

48 Ibid., pp. 139–40.

49 Ibid., pp. 83–6.

50 Ibid., pp. 319–33.

51 Ibid., pp. 132–6.

52 Ibid., pp. 83–4.

53 Ibid., pp. 135–6.

54 Ibid., pp. 33–57.

55 Ibid., p. 5.

56 See Pablo Valdivia, *La vereda indecisa. El viaje hacia la literatura de Federico García Lorca* (Granada, 2009).

57 *OC*, III, pp. 8–11.

58 Lorca, *Prosa inédita de juventud*, pp. 298–304.

59 Francisco García Lorca, *Federico y su mundo*, pp. 56–7.

3 Madrid: Cockroaches, *Cante Jondo* and Puppets, 1919–23

1 See José Mora Guarnido, *Federico García Lorca y su mundo. Testimonio para una biografía* (Buenos Aires, 1958), p. 117.

2 David Castillo and Marc Sardá, *Conversaciones con José 'Pepín' Bello* (Barcelona, 2007), p. 39. For a further insight into life at the Residencia, see the essays contained in Christopher Maurer et al., *Ola Pepín! Dalí, Lorca y Buñuel en la Residencia de Estudiantes* (Madrid, 2007).

3 Castillo and Sardá, *Conversaciones con José 'Pepín' Bello* , p. 44.

4 Ibid., p. 43.

5 Luis Buñuel, *Mi último suspiro* [1982] (Barcelona, 1987), p. 81.

6 Castillo and Sardá, *Conversaciones con José 'Pepín' Bello*, p. 44.

7 Buñuel, *Mi último suspiro*, p. 190.

8 Francisco García Lorca, *Federico y su mundo* (Madrid, 1981), p. 61; Carlos Morla Lynch, *En España con Federico García Lorca* [1957] (Seville, 2008), p. 62.

9 See, for example, Francisco García Lorca, *Federico y su mundo*, pp. 62–4 and Castillo and Sardá, *Conversaciones con José 'Pepín' Bello*, p. 45.

10 See Buñuel, *Mi último suspiro*, p. 77; Morla Lynch, *En España con Federico García Lorca*, p. 62; and Rafael Alberti, *La arboleda perdida. Libros I y II de Memorias* [1975] (Barcelona, 1981), p. 168.

11 Francisco García Lorca, *Federico y su mundo*, p. 64.

12 Buñuel, *Mi último suspiro*, p. 190; Guillén cited in Castillo and Sardá, *Conversaciones con José 'Pepín' Bello*, p. 42.

13 See Castillo and Sardá, *Conversaciones con José 'Pepín' Bello*, p. 43, and Aleixandre, García Carrillo and Llanos cited in Marta Osorio, ed., *Miedo, olvido y fantasía. Crónica de la investigación de Agustín Penón sobre Federico García Lorca, 1955–1956* [2000] (Granada, 2009), pp. 116–18, 247 and 279–84.

14 Castillo and Sardá, *Conversaciones con José 'Pepín' Bello*, p. 48.

15 See Rafael Martínez Nadal, *Cuatro lecciones sobre Federico García Lorca* (Madrid, 1980), p. 28.

16 Ibid., p. 57.

17 Buñuel, *Mi último suspiro*, p. 78.

18 Ibid., p. 80.

19 Salvador Dalí, *Vida secreta de Salvador Dalí* [1942, in English] (Girona, 1981), pp. 189–209.

20 Federico García Lorca, *Teatro inédito de juventud*, ed. Andrés Soria Olmedo (Madrid, 1994), pp. 131–221.

21 Osorio, ed., *Miedo, olvido y fantasía*, p. 73.

22 Ibid., pp. 138–40.

23 *OC*, I, pp. 9–14.

24 See María Francisca Vilches de Frutos, 'Directors of the Twentieth-century Spanish Stage', *Contemporary Theatre Review*, VII/3 (1998), pp. 1–9; and María M. Delgado, *Federico García Lorca* (Abingdon, 2008), pp. 39–43.

25 See *OC*, II, p. 1203. On the figure of La Argentinita and her artistic relationship with Lorca, see Jesús Ortega (coord.), *Querida comadre. Lorca y Argentinita en la danza española* (Granada, 2016).

26 Castillo and Sardá, *Conversaciones con José 'Pepín' Bello*, p. 31.

27 Morla Lynch, *En España con Federico García Lorca*, p. 65.

28 *OC*, II, p. 5. For an analysis of the *Libro de poemas*, especially of the collection's Andalusian qualities, see C. Brian Morris, *Son of Andalusia: The Lyrical Landscapes of Federico García Lorca* (Liverpool, 1997), pp. 145–81.

29 See 'Prólogo' (Prologue) and 'El macho cabrío' (The Billy Goat); in *OC*, I, pp. 86–9 and 148–50.

30 Ibid, pp. 21–3.

31 Ibid., p. 51.

32 Ibid., pp. 56–8.

33 Cited in Ian Gibson, *Federico García Lorca* (Barcelona, 2011), pp. 295–8.

34 Alberti, *La arboleda perdida*, p. 146.

35 Federico García Lorca, *Epistolario completo*, ed. Andrew A. Anderson and Christopher Maurer (Madrid, 1997), pp. 72–6.

36 Osorio, ed., *Miedo, olvido y fantasía*, p. 170.

37 For an excellent insight into the artistic relationship between Lorca and Falla, see Nelson R. Orringer, *Lorca in Tune with Falla: Literary and Musical Interludes* (Toronto, 2014).

38 *OC*, III, pp. 195–7.

39 Ibid., pp. 198–201.
40 Ibid., p. 198.
41 Ibid., p. 205.
42 Ibid., pp. 208–11.
43 Ibid., p. 201.
44 Ibid., pp. 215–16.
45 Ibid., pp. 205 and 208.
46 *OC*, I, pp. 155–63.
47 Ibid., pp. 177–86.
48 Lorca, *Epistolario completo*, p. 136.
49 See Andrés Soria Olmedo's 'Introducción' to Lorca, *Teatro inédito de juventud*, pp. 50–60.
50 Cited in Lorca, *Teatro inédito de juventud*, p. 51, n. 110.
51 *OC*, II, p. 39.
52 Lorca, *Epistolario completo*, p. 124.
53 *OC*, II, pp. 155 and 158.
54 Ibid., pp. 116 and 135.
55 Ibid., p. 159.
56 Lorca, *Epistolario completo*, pp. 137–8.
57 *OC*, III, p. 427. For a reproduction of the illustration from the *Codex Granatensis* that features the sun tree and moon tree, see Federico García Lorca, *Dibujos*, ed. Mario Hernández (Madrid, 1986), p. 92.
58 Francisco García Lorca, *Federico y su mundo*, pp. 84–102.
59 Miguel Caballero Pérez and Pilar Góngora, *La verdad sobre el asesinato de García Lorca. Historia de una familia* (Madrid, 2007), pp. 201–3.
60 Lorca, *Epistolario completo*, pp. 150 and 160–61.
61 Ibid., p. 143.
62 Ibid., p. 141.

4 Madrid, Granada and Cadaqués: Seeking Success, 1923–7

1 Federico García Lorca, *Epistolario completo*, ed. Andrew A. Anderson and Christopher Maurer (Madrid, 1997), pp. 177–9.
2 Salvador Dalí, *Vida secreta de Salvador Dalí* [1942] (Girona, 1981), pp. 171–2.
3 *OC*, I, pp. 731–9.
4 See Paul Chambers, 'The Trembling of the Moment: On the Haiku of Federico García Lorca', *Times Literary Supplement*, 6 October 2017, pp. 16–17.
5 *OC*, I, pp. 713 and 891.
6 Ibid., pp. 894 and 720.
7 Ibid., pp. 853 and 845.
8 Ibid., pp. 297–304.
9 Ibid., pp. 321–6.
10 Ian Gibson, *Federico García Lorca* (Barcelona, 2011), p. 387.
11 *OC*, I, p. 349.
12 Ibid., pp. 350–55.
13 Ibid., p. 381.
14 See Federico García Lorca, *Lola la comedianta*, ed. Piero Menarini (Madrid, 1981).
15 Ibid., pp. 123–5.

16 Ibid., pp. 115–25.
17 Federico García Lorca, *Epistolario completo*, pp. 179–80, n. 520.
18 Ibid., pp. 179–80, 206, 210–11, 239 and 250.
19 Gibson, *Federico García Lorca*, p. 350.
20 Lorca, *Lola la comedianta*, pp. 78–80.
21 Lorca, *Epistolario completo*, pp. 183 and 186.
22 Ibid., p. 208.
23 Ibid., pp. 208–9.
24 *OC*, II, p. 214.
25 Lorca, *Epistolario completo*, p. 254.
26 Ibid., p. 209.
27 *OC*, II, pp. 247–8.
28 Ibid., pp. 232–3.
29 Lorca, *Epistolario completo*, p. 208.
30 *OC*, II, pp. 242 and 261.
31 Ibid., p. 191.
32 Ibid., p. 202.
33 *OC*, I, p. 901; Lorca, *Epistolario completo*, pp. 196–7.
34 *OC*, I, pp. 889 and 901.
35 Ibid., pp. 915–21.
36 Lorca, *Epistolario completo*, pp. 293 and 299–300.
37 Ibid., p. 369.
38 Ibid., p. 301.
39 Ibid., pp. 220 and 346.
40 Ibid., pp. 229, 266 and 319.
41 Ibid., p. 293.
42 Dalí, *Vida secreta de Salvador Dalí*, pp. 188–9.
43 See Agustín Sánchez Vidal, *Buñuel, Lorca, Dalí: El enigma sin fin* [1988] (Barcelona, 1996), p. 126.
44 See Rafael Santos Torroella, *La miel es más dulce que la sangre. Las épocas lorquiana y freudiana de Salvador Dalí* (Barcelona, 1984), pp. 13–43 and 206–9; Ian Gibson, *The Shameful Life of Salvador Dalí* (London, 1997), p. 119; and Mary Ann Caws, *Salvador Dalí* (London, 2008), pp. 44–55.
45 Sánchez Vidal, *Buñuel, Lorca, Dalí*, pp. 126–8. See also Ian Gibson, *Lorca-Dalí. El amor que no pudo ser* (Barcelona, 1999), pp. 159–61.
46 Sánchez Vidal, *Buñuel, Lorca, Dalí*, pp. 99–100, and Dalí, *Vida secreta de Salvador Dalí*, p. 218.
47 Dalí, *Vida secreta de Salvador Dalí*, p. 189.
48 Lorca, *Epistolario completo*, pp. 283–4.
49 *OC*, II, pp. 277–80.
50 Ibid., pp. 299–302.
51 Gibson, *Federico García Lorca*, p. 459.
52 *OC*, I, pp. 953–7.
53 Dalí's letter is cited in Gibson, *Federico García Lorca*, pp. 456–7.
54 Lorca, *Epistolario completo*, p. 241.
55 Ibid., p. 355.
56 Two insightful readings of this play can be found in Reed Anderson, *Federico García Lorca* (London, 1984), pp. 57–63, and Sarah Wright, *The Trickster-function in the Theatre of García Lorca* (Woodbridge, 2000), pp. 39–61.

57 Lorca, *Epistolario completo*, p. 332.
58 Ibid., p. 384.
59 Ibid., p. 418.
60 Ibid., p. 488.
61 Dalí's letter is cited in Gibson, *Federico García Lorca*, pp. 489–90.
62 The photographs have been reproduced in *Federico García Lorca. Vida*, a special number of *Poesía. Revista ilustrada de información poética*, no. 43 (1998), p. 111.
63 Lorca, *Epistolario completo*, p. 496.
64 Many of these drawings are reproduced in Federico García Lorca, *Dibujos*, ed. Mario Hernández (Madrid, 1986), pp. 119–25.
65 See Lorca, *Dibujos*, pp. 151 and 153.
66 Lorca, *Epistolario completo*, p. 499.
67 Ibid., p. 500.
68 Ibid., pp. 507–8.
69 Ibid., p. 557.
70 Miguel de Unamuno, *Manual de quijotismo, Cómo se hace una novela, Epistolario Miguel de Unamuno / Jean Cassou*, ed. Bénédicte Vauthier (Salamanca, 2005), pp. 200–202.

5 Granada, Madrid, New York and Cuba: Success, Escape and Return, 1928–30

1 *OC*, III, p. 341.
2 Ibid., p. 342.
3 Ibid., p. 343.
4 Ibid., p. 342.
5 For a mythical reading of 'Romance de la guardia civil', see Herbert Ramsden, *Lorca's Romancero gitano: Eighteen commentaries* (Manchester, 1988), pp. 94–8.
6 *OC*, III, pp. 340 and 344.
7 *OC*, I, pp. 408–9.
8 *OC*, III, p. 340.
9 Ibid.
10 Ibid., p. 342.
11 Federico García Lorca, *Epistolario completo*, ed. Andrew A. Anderson and Christopher Maurer (Madrid, 1997), p. 293.
12 José Ortega y Gasset, *La deshumanización del arte* [1925], ed. Paulino Garagorri (Madrid, 1984), pp. 36–7.
13 *OC*, III, p. 230.
14 Ibid., pp. 229 and 235.
15 *OC*, I, pp. 393 and 408.
16 Ibid., pp. 399, 401 and 404.
17 Ibid., p. 423.
18 Ibid., pp. 436–7.
19 *OC*, III, p. 243.
20 *OC*, I, pp. 400–403.
21 Ibid., pp. 433–5.

22 *OC*, III, p. 340.

23 Ibid., p. 245.

24 See Lorca's talk 'Sketch de la nueva pintura' (Sketch of the New Painting); in *OC*, III, pp. 272–81 (p. 279).

25 *OC*, I, pp. 400–403.

26 Ibid., p. 401.

27 Baeza, cited in Ian Gibson, *Federico García Lorca* (Barcelona, 2011), p. 572.

28 Dalí's letter is reproduced in Gibson, *Federico García Lorca*, pp. 587–90.

29 For Buñuel's letters to Pepín, see Agustín Sánchez Vidal, *Buñuel, Lorca, Dalí: El enigma sin fin* [1988] (Barcelona, 1996), pp. 158–80.

30 On the making of *Un Chien andalou* (and Lorca's reaction to it), see Ian Gibson, *Luis Buñuel: La forja de un cineasta universal, 1900–1938* (Madrid, 2013), pp. 275–346 and Ian Gibson, *The Shameful Life of Salvador Dalí* (London, 1997), pp. 191–8. It is possible that Lorca's only film screenplay, *Viaje a la luna* (*Trip to the Moon*; in *OC*, II, pp. 1137–48), written in New York in late 1929, was at least in part a response to what he had heard about Dalí and Buñuel's film.

31 Lorca, *Epistolario completo*, p. 414.

32 *OC*, III, pp. 258–71.

33 Ibid., pp. 272–81.

34 Ibid., p. 267.

35 Ibid., p. 280.

36 Marta Osorio (ed.), *Miedo, olvido y fantasía. Crónica de la investigación de Agustín Penón sobre Federico García Lorca (1955–1956)* [2000] (Granada, 2009), pp. 239–53.

37 Aladrén's letters are reproduced in Roger Tinnell, 'Epistolario de Emilio Aladrén a Federico García Lorca', in Autores varios, *Federico García Lorca. Estudios sobre las literaturas hispánicas en honor a Christian De Paepe* (Leuven, 2003), pp. 219–29.

38 Lorca, *Epistolario completo*, pp. 572–91.

39 Ibid., p. 587.

40 Ibid., p. 577.

41 Ibid., p. 582.

42 *OC*, III, pp. 381–7.

43 Lorca, *Epistolario completo*, p. 587.

44 Ibid., pp. 576 and 582.

45 Ibid., p. 588.

46 *OC*, I, p. 961.

47 Ibid., p. 963.

48 Lorca, *Epistolario completo*, pp. 582 and 590.

49 See Gibson, *Federico García Lorca*, pp. 617–19.

50 Buñuel, cited in Sánchez Vidal, *Buñuel, Lorca, Dalí*, p. 198.

51 Lorca, *Epistolario completo*, pp. 635–6 and 670.

52 See Sofía Megwinoff's testimony of Lorca's stay in New York, reproduced in Christopher Maurer and Andrew A. Anderson, *Federico García Lorca en Nueva York y La Habana* (Barcelona, 2013), pp. 185–9 (p. 188).

53 Ibid., p. 189.
54 See, for example, Lorca's summer 1930 letter to Dalí, where he refers to the huge amount of 'amigos idiotas' (idiot friends) he has made in New York; in Lorca, *Epistolario completo*, p. 693.
55 See Dinitia Smith, 'Poetic Love Affair with New York', *New York Times*, www.nytimes.com, 4 July 2000.
56 See Leslie Stainton, *Lorca: A Dream of Life* (London, 1998), pp. 226–7, and Maurer and Anderson, *Federico García Lorca en Nueva York y La Habana*, pp. 265–6.
57 Lorca, *Epistolario completo*, p. 626.
58 Ibid., p. 637.
59 Ibid., pp. 616, 633, 637, 655 and 676.
60 Ibid., pp. 621 and 655.
61 Ibid., p. 648.
62 Ibid., pp. 647 and 673.
63 Ibid., p. 626.
64 Maurer and Anderson, *Federico García Lorca en Nueva York y La Habana*, p. 187.
65 Lorca, *Epistolario completo*, pp. 627–8 and 633–4.
66 Ibid., pp. 626–7.
67 See Lorca, *Dibujos*, p. 176.
68 Maurer and Anderson, *Federico García Lorca en Nueva York y La Habana*, p. 134.
69 Lorca, *Epistolario completo*, p. 624.
70 Ibid., p. 677.
71 Maurer and Anderson, *Federico García Lorca en Nueva York y La Habana*, p. 186.
72 Ibid., p. 133.
73 Stainton, *Lorca: A Dream of Life*, p. 245.
74 Rafael Martínez Nadal, *Cuatro lecciones sobre Federico García Lorca* (Madrid, 1980), p. 30.
75 *OC*, I, p. 448.
76 Ibid., pp. 1048–9.
77 Ibid., pp. 489–90, 495–6 and 498–9.
78 Maurer and Anderson, *Federico García Lorca en Nueva York y La Habana*, p. 142.
79 Ibid., pp. 140–41.
80 Ibid., p. 141.
81 *OC*, I, pp. 469–72 and 517–19.
82 Ibid., pp. 525–7.
83 Maurer and Anderson, *Federico García Lorca en Nueva York y La Habana*, p. 139.
84 Ibid., p. 208.
85 Ibid., p. 140.
86 Ibid., p. 139.
87 *OC*, I, pp. 459–63.
88 Maurer and Anderson, *Federico García Lorca en Nueva York y La Habana*, p. 147.
89 Lorca, *Epistolario completo*, p. 686.

90 Ibid., p. 681.
91 Maurer and Anderson, *Federico García Lorca en Nueva York y La Habana*, p. 147.
92 See Urbano Martínez Carmenate, *García Lorca y Cuba: todas las aguas* (La Habana, 2002), pp. 139–55.
93 Maurer and Anderson, *Federico García Lorca en Nueva York y La Habana*, p. 147.
94 *OC*, I, pp. 541–2.
95 Lorca, cited in Gibson, *Federico García Lorca*, p. 756.

6 Granada and Madrid: Revolution and Roots, 1930–33

1 See Vicenta Lorca and Federico García's letter of 25 May 1930; reproduced in Christopher Maurer and Andrew A. Anderson, *Federico García Lorca en Nueva York y La Habana* (Barcelona, 2013), pp. 126–7.
2 Adams and Brickell, cited in Maurer and Anderson, *Federico García Lorca en Nueva York y La Habana*, p. 332.
3 Ian Gibson, *Federico García Lorca* (Barcelona, 2011), p. 757.
4 See, for example, Federico García Lorca, *Epistolario completo*, ed. Andrew A. Anderson and Christopher Maurer (Madrid, 1997), p. 658.
5 See Urbano Martínez Carmenate, *García Lorca y Cuba: todas las aguas* (La Habana, 2002), pp. 164–5.
6 Lorca, *Epistolario completo*, pp. 678–80.
7 Ibid., p. 688.
8 *OC*, I, pp. 528–32.
9 Ibid., p. 531.
10 Ibid., pp. 529 and 531.
11 Ibid., p. 531.
12 For the story of how the manuscript reached his hands, see Rafael Martínez Nadal, *Lorca's The Public: A Study of his Unfinished Play 'El Público' and of Love and Death in the Work of Federico García Lorca* (London, 1974), pp. 11–17. Martínez Nadal finally published the manuscript in 1976: see Rafael Martínez Nadal, *Federico García Lorca. Autógrafos II: El público, edición facsimilar* (Oxford, 1976).
13 *OC*, II, p. 601.
14 Ibid., p. 604.
15 Ibid.
16 Ibid., p. 635.
17 Ibid., p. 632.
18 Ibid., pp. 628 and 637.
19 Ibid., pp. 650–54.
20 Ibid., p. 653.
21 Ibid., p. 657.
22 Ibid., p. 658.
23 Ibid., pp. 659–60.
24 Ibid., p. 638.
25 Federico García Lorca, *Prosa inédita de juventud*, ed. Christopher Maurer (Madrid, 1994), pp. 309–48 and 416–25.
26 *OC*, II, pp. 606–8. *Viaje a la luna* is reproduced in *OC*, I, pp. 1139–48.

27 *OC*, II, pp. 621–7 and 637–40. For insightful, and often contrasting, interpretations of these scenes, see Martínez Nadal, *Lorca's The Public*, pp. 27–103; Paul Binding, *Lorca: The Gay Imagination* (London, 1985), pp. 151–60; Paul Julian Smith, *The Theatre of García Lorca: Text, Performance, Psychoanalysis* (Cambridge, 1998), pp. 105–38; Chris Perriam, 'Gender and Sexuality', in *A Companion to Federico García Lorca*, ed. Federico Bonaddio (Woodbridge, 2007), pp. 149–69 (pp. 167–9); and Ian Gibson, *Lorca y el mundo gay* (Barcelona, 2010), pp. 284–93. Possibly the best introduction to Lorca as a gay writer is Ángel Sahuquillo, *Federico García Lorca and the Culture of Male Homosexuality* (Jefferson, NC, and London, 2007).

28 *OC*, II, pp. 640–47.

29 See Ian Gibson, *Lorca y el mundo gay*, pp. 291–3.

30 Marta Osorio, ed., *Miedo, olvido y fantasía. Crónica de la investigación de Agustín Penón sobre Federico García Lorca, 1955–1956* [2000] (Granada, 2009), p. 636.

31 Lorca, *Epistolario completo*, pp. 692–3.

32 See Lorca's letter to Rafael Martínez Nadal, reproduced ibid., p. 690.

33 Federico García Lorca, *Palabra de Lorca. Declaraciones y entrevistas completas*, ed. Rafael Inglada (Barcelona, 2017), pp. 37–42. None of these works (the last two of which would be amalgamated to form *Poeta en Nueva York*) would be published in Lorca's lifetime.

34 Lorca, *Epistolario completo*, p. 695.

35 See Gibson, *Federico García Lorca*, p. 764.

36 Lorca, *Epistolario completo*, pp. 698, 700, 702 and 704.

37 See Lorca's letters and telegrams reproduced ibid., pp. 699–702.

38 See ibid., pp. 696, 700 and 702–4.

39 Ibid., p. 706.

40 Lorca, *Palabra de Lorca*, pp. 42 and 44–5.

41 *OC*, II, p. 520.

42 *OC*, I, pp. 915–21.

43 *OC*, II, p. 557.

44 Ibid.

45 *OC*, III, pp. 420–21 and 431.

46 Ibid., p. 423.

47 Ibid., pp. 422–3.

48 Ibid., pp. 423 and 431–2.

49 Ibid., p. 431.

50 Letter from Miguel Pizarro to Federico García Lorca of 3 September 1931; reproduced in María Isabel Elizalde Frez, 'Miguel Pizarro y Zambrano, poeta y pensador del 27', PhD thesis, Universidad Autónoma de Madrid, 2014, pp. 135–6.

51 See Miguel Caballero Pérez, *Lorca en África. Crónica de un viaje al Protectorado español de Marruecos, 1931* (Granada, 2010).

52 Lorca, *Palabra de Lorca*, p. 243.

53 Ibid., pp. 68–70.

54 Lorca, *Epistolario completo*, pp. 742–3.

55 Lorca, *Palabra de Lorca*, p. 64.

56 Ibid., pp. 73 and 76–7. See also p. 138.

57 Carlos Morla Lynch, *En España con Federico García Lorca* [1957] (Seville, 2008), pp. 149 and 280–86.
58 Ibid., pp. 299–300.
59 Ibid., pp. 174–5.
60 Ibid., pp. 251–2.
61 Lorca, *Epistolario completo*, p. 718.
62 Ibid., pp. 744–9 and 753–9.
63 Ibid., pp. 755 and 758.
64 Ibid., p. 745.
65 Lorca, *Palabra de Lorca*, p. 59.
66 Francisco García Lorca, *Federico y su mundo* (Madrid, 1981), p. 19, and Isabel García Lorca, *Recuerdos míos* (Barcelona, 2002), p. 53.
67 On Lorca's father's landowning and commercial interests, see Miguel Caballero Pérez and Pilar Góngora, *Historia de una familia. La verdad sobre el asesinato de García Lorca* (Madrid, 2007), pp. 135–290.
68 *OC*, II, pp. 724–6.
69 Ibid., p. 796.
70 Ibid., p. 785.
71 See, for example, the poem 'Melodía de invierno' (Winter Melody); reproduced in Federico García Lorca, *Poesía inédita de juventud*, ed. Christian De Paepe (Madrid, 2008), pp. 159–60.
72 *OC*, II, pp. 777–9.
73 Ibid., pp. 776–7.
74 Ibid., p. 788.
75 Ibid., pp. 713–16, 722–3, 738–9, 744–54, 776–7 and 783–8.
76 Ibid., pp. 793–9.
77 Morla Lynch, *En España con Federico García Lorca*, pp. 327–8.
78 Lorca, *Palabra de Lorca*, pp. 129 and 135.

7 Argentina and Madrid: Triumph and Trepidation, 1933–6

1 See Federico García Lorca, *Epistolario completo*, ed. Andrew A. Anderson and Christopher Maurer (Madrid, 1997), pp. 772–84.
2 See 'Juego y teoría del duende' and 'Cómo canta una ciudad de noviembre a noviembre', in *OC*, III, pp. 306–33.
3 Federico García Lorca, *Palabra de Lorca. Declaraciones y entrevistas completas*, ed. Rafael Inglada (Barcelona, 2017), p. 160.
4 See Lorca, *Epistolario completo*, pp. 780–82 and 799.
5 Lorca, *Palabra de Lorca*, p. 156.
6 Pablo Neruda, *Confieso que he vivido* (Barcelona, 1980), pp. 132–3.
7 See Ian Gibson, *Federico García Lorca* (Barcelona, 2011), pp. 929–31.
8 Santiago Roncagliolo, *El amante uruguayo. Una historia real* (Alcalá la Real, 2012).
9 See, for example, Lorca, *Epistolario completo*, pp. 770 and 781.
10 Lorca tells his parents about this encounter in one of his first letters home: see ibid., p. 773.
11 The interviews with Lorca that appeared in the Argentine and Uruguayan press over these months have been reproduced in Lorca, *Palabra de Lorca*, pp. 147–305.

12 Ibid., pp. 157, 162–5, 174, 192, 211, 238 and 302.
13 See ibid., pp. 250–60.
14 Pablo Neruda, *Confieso que he vivido*, p. 128 and Richard Burgin, *Conversaciones con Jorge Luis Borges* (Madrid, 1974), pp. 112–14.
15 Lorca, *Palabra de Lorca*, p. 282.
16 Lorca, *Epistolario completo*, p. 794.
17 Lorca, *Palabra de Lorca*, pp. 287–94.
18 *OC*, II, pp. 675–97.
19 See Pablo L. Medina, 'Los títeres de Federico García Lorca en el Teatro Avenida de Buenos Aires, 25 de marzo de 1934', www.titeresante.es, 1 May 2017. I would like to thank Enrique Lanz, grandson of Hermenegildo Lanz and founder and director of the puppet company Títeres Etcétera, for sharing his insights into this process during a discussion held in Granada on 25 November 2014.
20 Lorca, *Epistolario completo*, pp. 774, 779, 784, 786, 788.
21 Ibid., p. 790.
22 Ibid., pp. 794 and 796.
23 Lorca, *Palabra de Lorca*, pp. 151 and 227.
24 Ibid., pp. 181–2.
25 Ibid., pp. 181–4, 199–200, 244 and 312.
26 See Carlos Morla Lynch, *En España con Federico García Lorca* [1957] (Seville, 2008), pp. 386–94 and Pablo Neruda, *Confieso que he vivido*, p. 134. For a description of Neruda's life in Madrid, see Adam Feinstein, *Pablo Neruda. A Passion for Life* (London, 2004), pp. 104–29 and Dominic Moran, *Pablo Neruda* (London, 2009), pp. 64–83.
27 Morla Lynch, *En España con Federico García Lorca*, pp. 346–7, 354 and 359.
28 Gibson, *Federico García Lorca*, p. 885.
29 Morla Lynch, *En España con Federico García Lorca*, p. 349.
30 *OC*, II, p. 880.
31 Lorca, *Palabra de Lorca*, p. 343.
32 Ibid., pp. 874 and 830–40.
33 Ibid., pp. 434–5.
34 *OC*, II, pp. 806, 810, 846–7, 859.
35 Ibid., p. 848.
36 *OC*, I, pp. 915–21 and *OC*, II, pp. 577 and 810.
37 Lorca, *Palabra de Lorca*, p. 343.
38 *OC*, II, pp. 844 and 853.
39 Ibid., pp. 818–21, 836–40, 859, 863–5 and 874.
40 Ibid., pp. 869–70.
41 Lorca, *Palabra de Lorca*, pp. 252, 394 and 416.
42 Lorca, *Epistolario completo*, p. 803.
43 See Gibson, *Federico García Lorca*, pp. 963–70.
44 Morla Lynch, *En España con Federico García Lorca*, pp. 407–10.
45 Lorca, *Epistolario completo*, pp. 803–5.
46 *OC*, I, pp. 549–58.
47 Ibid., pp. 553–5 and 557.
48 Ibid., p. 558.
49 See *OC*, II, pp. 816–21 and 873–6. For a summary of some of the reactions and reviews, see Gibson, *Federico García Lorca*, pp. 980–85.

50 The article is reproduced in Ian Gibson, *Lorca y el mundo gay* (Barcelona, 2010), pp. 339–40. Pura Maórtua de Ucelay is cited in Marta Osorio, ed., *Miedo, olvido y fantasía. Crónica de la investigación de Agustín Penón sobre Federico García Lorca, 1955–1956* [2000] (Granada, 2009), p. 634.

51 See Morla Lynch, *En España con Federico García Lorca*, pp. 446–7.

52 Lorca, *Palabra de Lorca*, pp. 315–16.

53 Ibid., pp. 133–4.

54 See Lorca, *Palabra de Lorca*, pp. 76, 138, 150 and 330, and Lorca, *Epistolario completo*, pp. 732–4.

55 Lorca, *Palabra de Lorca*, p. 339.

56 Ibid., pp. 339–40, 343 and 349.

57 See Luis Sáenz de la Calzada's description of one act of the play, reproduced in Gibson, *Federico García Lorca*, pp. 977–8, and Rafael Martínez Nadal, *Lorca's The Public: A Study of his Unfinished Play 'El Público' and of Love and Death in the Work of Federico García Lorca* (London, 1974), pp. 15–16.

58 Lorca, *Palabra de Lorca*, p. 349. See also p. 432.

59 Ibid., p. 336.

60 See Gibson, *Federico García Lorca*, pp. 874–8, 957–8 and 1019–21.

61 *OC*, I, pp. 559–67.

62 On the Arabic influences on the work, and for a commentary on each of its poems, see Andrew A. Anderson, *Lorca's Late Poetry: A Critical Study* (Leeds, 1990), pp. 16–152. See also Federico Bonaddio, *Federico García Lorca: The Poetics of Self-consciousness* (London, 2010), pp. 170–96.

63 *OC*, I, pp. 573 and 575.

64 Ibid., p. 589.

65 Ibid., pp. 576 and 590–91.

66 Ibid., pp. 577 and 564.

67 Ibid., pp. 573, 579–80, 583 and 585.

68 Ibid., p. 598.

69 Ibid., pp. 583 and 581.

70 Ibid., pp. 581 and 589.

71 Ibid., p. 594.

72 See Lorca, *Palabra de Lorca*, pp. 335–6, 349 and 521–2; and *OC*, II, pp. 907–10, 922–41 and 950–56.

73 Lorca, *Palabra de Lorca*, pp. 349, 432 and 439.

74 In a talk given in December 1935, Lorca wondered aloud about what would happen to rich children if they didn't have maids to put them in contact with the 'truth' and 'emotion' of the *pueblo*: see Lorca, *Palabra de Lorca*, p. 446.

75 Ibid., pp. 439 and 443–4.

76 See Gibson, *Federico García Lorca*, pp. 1017 and 1020.

77 Eric Hawkins, 'Listening to Lorca', radio programme first broadcast on BBC Radio 7 on 23 September 2008. See also his autobiography, *Listening to Lorca: A Journey into Language* (London, 1999).

78 Lorca's resignation letter can be found in Lorca, *Epistolario completo*, p. 820.

79 See, for example, Lorca, *Epistolario completo*, p. 557.

80 See, for example, Lorca, *Palabra de Lorca*, pp. 422, 426–7 and 432.

81 Ibid., p. 426.

82 Ibid., pp. 407–13.

83 Ibid., pp. 431–6.

84 See Gibson, *Federico García Lorca*, pp. 1041–2.
85 Lorca, *Palabra de Lorca*, pp. 563–72.
86 Ibid., p. 447.
87 Ibid., p. 573.
88 The photograph is reproduced in Lorca, *Palabra de Lorca*, p. 477.
89 *OC*, II, 1069–75.
90 Ibid., pp. 1092–3.
91 Lorca, *Palabra de Lorca*, p. 460.
92 *OC*, II, pp. 1080–84.
93 See Gibson, *Federico García Lorca*, pp. 970–71. On Lorca's possible friendship with José Antonio, see ibid., pp. 1075–6.
94 See Morla Lynch, *En España con Federico García Lorca*, pp. 346, 369, 372 and 445–6.
95 See Gibson, *Federico García Lorca*, pp. 1086 and 1103.
96 See, for example, Lorca, *Palabra de Lorca*, p. 428.
97 The interview with Bagaría is reproduced in Lorca, *Palabra de Lorca*, pp. 464–70, and Lorca's letter to Salazar in Lorca, *Epistolario completo*, pp. 823–4.
98 *OC*, II, pp. 1099–1133. Agustín Penón met Aurelia in 1955 and provided a vivid description of her: see Osorio, ed., *Miedo, olvido y fantasia*, pp. 501–4.
99 *OC*, II, p. 984.
100 For a description of the real people on whom Lorca based his characters, see Isabel García Lorca, *Recuerdos míos* (Barcelona, 2002), pp. 70–73.
101 *OC*, II, p. 973.
102 Ibid., pp. 1012–13.
103 Ibid., pp. 1038–9.
104 Ibid., pp. 979 and 1066.
105 David Castillo and Marc Sardá, *Conversaciones con José 'Pepín' Bello* (Barcelona, 2007), p. 35; Morla Lynch, *En España con Federico García Lorca*, pp. 530–34.
106 Morla Lynch, *En España con Federico García Lorca*, pp. 534–8.
107 José Caballero's and Santiago Ontañón's testimonies are taken from the programme *La Clave*, shown on Televisión Española (TVE) on 21 June 1980. See also Osorio, ed., *Miedo, olvido y fantasía*, p. 621.
108 Castillo and Sardá, *Conversaciones con José 'Pepín' Bello*, p. 158; Lorca, *Palabra de Lorca*, pp. 583–90.
109 See Amelia Castilla and Luis Magán's article entitled 'Las lágrimas de Lorca a su último amor', www.elpais.com, 13 May 2012. Pura Maórtua de Ucelay mentioned Juan Ramírez de Lucas to Agustín Penón in the 1950s: see Osorio, ed., *Miedo, olvido y fantasía*, p. 640.

8 Granada: Refuge and Death, July–August 1936

1 See Gerald Brenan, *The Face of Spain* [1950] (London, 1988), pp. 126–50; Jean-Louis Schonberg, *Federico García Lorca. L'homme – l'oeuvre* (Paris, 1956), pp. 101–22; Claude Couffon, *Granada y García Lorca* [1962] (Buenos Aires, 1967); Ian Gibson, *The Assassination of Federico García Lorca* [1973] (London, 1983); José Luis Vila-San-Juan, *García Lorca, asesinado: toda la verdad* (Barcelona, 1975); Miguel Caballero Pérez and Pilar Góngora,

Historia de una familia. La verdad sobre el asesinato de García Lorca (Madrid, 2007); Gabriel Pozo, *Lorca, el último paseo. Claves para entender el asesinato del poeta* (Granada, 2009); Miguel Caballero Pérez, *Las trece últimas horas en la vida de García Lorca* (Madrid, 2011).

2 See Marta Osorio, ed., *Miedo, olvido y fantasía. Crónica de la investigación de Agustín Penón sobre Federico García Lorca, 1955–1956* [2000] (Granada, 2009); Gibson, *The Assassination of Federico García Lorca*; Eduardo Molina Fajardo, *Los últimos días de García Lorca* (Granada, 2011).

3 This letter, which has still not been published in full, only came to light in 2012: see the articles by Amelia Castilla and Luis Magán entitled '"Querido Juan, es preciso que vuelvas a reír . . ." and 'La última carta de García Lorca' that appeared in the Madrid newspaper *El País* on 10 and 12 May 2012.

4 Osorio, ed., *Miedo, olvido y fantasía*, pp. 273, 313 and 615–16.

5 See Caballero Pérez and Góngora, *Historia de una familia*, pp. 232–5, and Caballero Pérez, *Las trece últimas horas en la vida de García Lorca*, p. 18.

6 Lorca, *Palabra de Lorca*, p. 585.

7 Osorio, ed., *Miedo, olvido y fantasía*, p. 194.

8 Ibid., pp. 194, 211 and 311.

9 Isabel García Lorca describes the Roldán family as being the richest family in Asquerosa, very right-wing and, despite their close family ties, quite hostile to her father. See Isabel García Lorca, *Recuerdos míos* (Barcelona, 2002), p. 76.

10 Caballero Pérez, *Las trece últimas horas en la vida de García Lorca*, p. 76. See also Caballero Pérez and Góngora, *Historia de una familia*, pp. 232–5 and 244.

11 See Ian Gibson, *Federico García Lorca* [1985] (Barcelona, 2011), pp. 1115–6.

12 For Luis Rosales' account of this meeting, see Osorio, ed., *Miedo, olvido y fantasia*, pp. 643–5.

13 Ibid., p. 435.

14 Ibid., p. 646.

15 The recording of Ian Gibson's 1966 interview with Luis Rosales was used as part of Emilio Ruiz Barrachina's documentary *Luis Rosales, así he vivido yo* (Icrania Producciones, 2010).

16 See, for example, Joaquín Soler Serrano's interview with Luis Rosales for the television programme *A fondo*, shown on Televisión Española (TVE) on 23 October 1977.

17 David Castillo and Marc Sardá, *Conversaciones con José 'Pepín' Bello* (Barcelona, 2007), pp. 156–7.

18 Osorio, ed., *Miedo, olvido y fantasia*, p. 638.

19 Rosales spoke to Joaquín Soler Serrano about this matter during his interview for the TVE television programme *A fondo* (see n. 16).

20 See in particular *OC*, I, pp. 942, 943 and 946.

21 Ibid., p. 948.

22 Both Miguel and Luis Rosales place the time of the visit between 4 and 5 p.m.: see Osorio, ed., *Miedo, olvido y fantasia*, pp. 87 and 647.

23 Ibid., pp. 648–50.

24 See Luis Rosales's interview for the TVE television programme *A fondo* (see n. 16). On Ruiz Alonso's career, see Ian Gibson, *El hombre que detuvo a García Lorca. Ramón Ruiz Alonso y la muerte del poeta* (Madrid, 2007), and Caballero Pérez, *Las trece últimas horas en la vida de García Lorca*, pp. 85–100.

25 This report was first published on 22 April 2015 on the website of the
    Spanish radio station Cadena SER: Javier Torres, 'La versión franquista del
    asesinato de Federico García Lorca', www.cadenaser.com, 22 April 2015.
26 See Caballero Pérez, *Las trece últimas horas en la vida de García Lorca*,
    pp. 85–100 and 105–12.
27 Ibid., p. 161.
28 Ibid., pp. 168–70.
29 Gerald Brenan, *The Face of Spain*, p. 144.
30 Caballero Pérez, *Las trece últimas horas en la vida de García Lorca*,
    pp. 180–89.

SELECT BIBLIOGRAPHY

First Editions of Lorca's Prose and Poetry in Spanish

Impresiones y paisajes (Granada, 1918)
Libro de poemas (Madrid, 1921)
Oda a Salvador Dalí (Madrid, 1926)
Canciones (Málaga, 1927)
Romancero gitano (Madrid, 1928)
Oda al Santísimo Sacramento (Madrid, 1928/1974)
Poema del cante jondo (Madrid, 1931)
Llanto por Ignacio Sánchez Mejías (Madrid, 1935)
Primeras canciones (Madrid, 1935)
Seis poemas galegos (Santiago de Compostela, 1935)
Poeta en Nueva York, ed. José Bergamín (Mexico City, 1940)
Diván del Tamarit, ed. Francisco García Lorca and Ángel del Río (New York, 1940)
Suites, ed. André Belamich (Barcelona, 1983)
Sonetos del amor oscuro, ed. Miguel García-Posada (Madrid, 1984)
Prosa inédita de juventud, ed. Christopher Maurer (Madrid, 1994)
Poesía inédita de juventud, ed. Christian De Paepe (Madrid, 2008)

Premieres of Lorca's Plays

El maleficio de la mariposa (Teatro Eslava, Madrid, 22 March 1920)
La niña que riega la albahaca y el príncipe preguntón (Lorca family home, Granada, 5 January 1923)
Mariana Pineda (Teatro Goya, Barcelona, 24 June 1927)
La zapatera prodigiosa (Teatro Español, Madrid, 24 December 1930)
Bodas de sangre (Teatro Beatriz, Madrid, 8 March 1933)
Amor de Don Perlimplín con Belisa en su jardín (Teatro Español, Madrid, 5 April 1933)
Retablillo de Don Cristóbal (Teatro Avenida, Buenos Aires, 25 March 1934)
Yerma (Teatro Español, Madrid, 29 December 1934)
Doña Rosita la soltera (Teatro Principal Palace, Barcelona, 12 December 1935)
Tragicomedia de Don Cristóbal y la Señá Rosita (Teatro de la Zarzuela, Madrid, 10 September 1937)
La casa de Bernarda Alba (Teatro Avenida, Buenos Aires, 8 March 1945)
Así que pasen cinco años (Teatro Zócalo, Mexico City, 1 July 1969)
El público (Teatro Fossati, Milan, 10 December 1986)

First Editions of Lorca's Incomplete Plays or Librettos

Comedia sin título, ed. Marie Laffranque (Bordeaux, 1976)
Lola la comedianta, ed. Piero Menarini (Madrid, 1981)
Los sueños de mi prima Aurelia, ed. Marie Laffranque (Granada, 1986)
Teatro inédito de juventud, ed. Andrés Soria Olmedo (Madrid, 1994)

Other Works by Lorca

Obras completas, ed. Arturo del Hoyo, 3 vols (Madrid, 1986)
Dibujos, ed. Mario Hernández (Madrid, 1986)
Epistolario completo, ed. Andrew A. Anderson and Christopher Maurer (Madrid, 1997)
Palabra de Lorca. Declaraciones y entrevistas completas, ed. Rafael Inglada (Barcelona, 2017)

Works by Lorca in English (Selection)

Blood Wedding, trans. David Johnston (Sevenoaks, 1988)
Poet in New York, trans. Greg Simon and Steven F. White (London, 1990)
The Shoemaker's Wonderful Wife, The Love of Don Perlimplín, The Puppet Play of Don Cristóbal, The Butterfly's Evil Spell, When Five Years Pass, trans. Gwynne Edwards (London, 1990)
Deep Song and Other Prose, trans. Christopher Maurer [1980] (London, 1991)
Mariana Pineda, The Public, Play Without a Title, trans. Gwynne Edwards and Henry Livings (London, 1994)
Blood Wedding, trans. Ted Hughes (London, 1996)
Four Major Plays (Blood Wedding, Yerma, The House of Bernarda Alba, Doña Rosita the Spinster), trans. John Edmunds (Oxford, 1997)
A Season in Granada: Uncollected Poems and Prose, trans. Christopher Maurer (London, 1998)
Book of Poems (Selection), trans. Stanley Appelbaum (New York, 2004)
Poem of the Deep Song, trans. Ralph Angel (Louisville, KY, 2006)
The Tamarit Poems, trans. Michael Smith (Dublin, 2007)
The House of Bernarda Alba, trans. Michael Jones and Salvador Ortiz-Carboneres (Oxford, 2009)
Lament for the Death of a Bullfighter and Other Poems, trans. A. L. Lloyd (London, 2009)
Six Major Plays (Blood Wedding, Doña Rosita, The House of Bernarda Alba, The Public, The Shoemaker's Prodigious Wife, Yerma), trans. Caridad Svich (Southgate, CA, 2009)
Gypsy Ballads, trans. Jane Durán and Gloria García Lorca (London, 2011)
Lorca's Yerma, trans. Anthony Weigh (London, 2011)
Sonnets of Dark Love: The Tamarit Divan, trans. Jane Durán and Gloria García Lorca (London, 2011)
Three Plays (Blood Wedding, Yerma, The House of Bernarda Alba), trans. Jo Clifford (London, 2017)

Anthologies

Selected Poems, various translators, ed. Christopher Maurer (London, 2001)
Collected Poems of Lorca, various translators, ed. Christopher Maurer (New
    York, 2002)
Selected Poems with Parallel Spanish Text, trans. Martin Sorrell (Oxford, 2009)
Poet in Spain: Federico García Lorca, trans. Sarah Arvio (New York, 2017)

Critical Works on Lorca

Biographical Works

Alberti, Rafael, *La arboleda perdida. Libros I y II de Memorias* [1975] (Barcelona,
    1981)
Auclair, Marcelle, *Enfances et mort de García Lorca* (Paris, 1968)
Barea, Arturo, *Lorca: The Poet and his People* (London, 1944)
Brenan, Gerald, *The Face of Spain* [1950] (London, 1988)
Buñuel, Luis, *Mi último suspiro* [1982] (Barcelona, 1987)
Burgin, Richard, *Conversaciones con Jorge Luis Borges* (Madrid, 1974)
Caballero Pérez, Miguel, *Lorca en África. Crónica de un viaje al Protectorado
    español de Marruecos, 1931* (Granada, 2010)
—, *Las trece últimas horas en la vida de García Lorca* (Madrid, 2011)
Caballero Pérez, Miguel, and Pilar Góngora, *Historia de una familia. La verdad
    sobre el asesinato de García Lorca* (Madrid, 2007)
Castilla, Amelia, and Luis Magán, '"Querido Juan, es preciso que vuelvas
    a reír . . .", *El País* (Madrid), 10 May 2012
—, 'La última carta de García Lorca', *El País* (Madrid), 12 May 2012
—, 'Las lágrimas de Lorca a su último amor', *El País* (Madrid), 13 May 2012
Castillo, David, and Marc Sardá, *Conversaciones con José 'Pepín' Bello* (Barcelona,
    2007)
Caws, Mary Ann, *Salvador Dalí* (London, 2008)
Correa Ramos, Amelina, '*Mater et magistra*: Reconstrucción de la trayectoria
    profesional de Vicenta Lorca, con la aportación de algunos documentos
    inéditos', *Analecta Malacitana*, XXXVI/1–2 (2013), pp. 135–60
Couffon, Claude, *Granada y García Lorca* [1962, in French] (Buenos Aires,
    1967)
Dalí, Salvador, *Vida secreta de Salvador Dalí* [1942, in English] (Girona, 1981)
Elizalde Frez, María Isabel, 'Miguel Pizarro y Zambrano, poeta y pensador del
    27', PhD thesis, Universidad Autónoma de Madrid, 2014
Feinstein, Adam, *Pablo Neruda: A Passion for Life* (London, 2004)
García Lorca, Francisco, *Federico y su mundo* (Madrid, 1981)
García Lorca, Isabel, *Recuerdos míos* (Barcelona, 2002)
Gibson, Ian, *The Assassination of Federico García Lorca* [1973] (London, 1983)
—, *Federico García Lorca: A Life* (London, 1989)
—, *Lorca's Granada: A Practical Guide* (London, 1992)
—, *The Shameful Life of Salvador Dalí* (London, 1997)
—, *Lorca-Dalí. El amor que no pudo ser* (Barcelona, 1999)
—, *El hombre que detuvo a García Lorca. Ramón Ruiz Alonso y la muerte del
    poeta* (Madrid, 2007)
—, *Lorca y el mundo gay* (Barcelona, 2010)

—, *La fosa de Lorca: Crónica de un despropósito* (Alcalá la Real, 2010)
—, *Federico García Lorca* [1985] (Barcelona, 2011)
—, *Luis Buñuel. La forja de un cineasta universal, 1900–1938* (Madrid, 2013)
Hawkins, Eric, *Listening to Lorca: A Journey into Language* (London, 1999)
Johnston, David, *Federico García Lorca* (Bath, 1998)
Martínez Carmenate, Urbano, *García Lorca y Cuba: todas las aguas* (Havana, 2002)
Martínez Nadal, Rafael, *Cuatro lecciones sobre Federico García Lorca* (Madrid, 1980)
Maurer, Christopher et al., *Ola Pepín! Dalí, Lorca y Buñuel en la Residencia de Estudiantes* (Madrid, 2007)
Maurer, Christopher, and Andrew A. Anderson, *Federico García Lorca en Nueva York y La Habana* (Barcelona, 2013)
Molina Fajardo, Eduardo, *Los últimos días de García Lorca* (Granada, 2011)
Mora Guarnido, José, *Federico García Lorca y su mundo. Testimonio para una biografía* (Buenos Aires, 1958)
Moran, Dominic, *Pablo Neruda* (London, 2009)
Morla Lynch, Carlos, *En España con Federico García Lorca* [1957] (Seville, 2008)
Neruda, Pablo, *Confieso que he vivido* [1974] (Barcelona, 1980)
Ortega, Jesús, ed., *Querida comadre. Lorca y Argentinita en la danza española* (Granada, 2016)
Osorio, Marta, ed., *Miedo, olvido y fantasía. Crónica de la investigación de Agustín Penón sobre Federico García Lorca (1955–1956)* [2000] (Granada, 2009)
Pozo, Gabriel, *Lorca, el último paseo. Claves para entender el asesinato del poeta* (Granada, 2009)
Roncagliolo, Santiago, *El amante uruguayo. Una historia real* (Alcalá la Real, 2012)
Sánchez Vidal, Agustín, *Buñuel, Lorca, Dalí: El enigma sin fin* [1988] (Barcelona, 1996)
Schonberg, Jean-Louis, *Federico García Lorca. L'homme – l'oeuvre* (Paris, 1956)
Smith, Dinitia, 'Poetic Love Affair with New York', *New York Times*, 4 July 2000
Stainton, Leslie, *Lorca: A Dream of Life* (London, 1998)
Tinnell, Roger, 'Epistolario de Emilio Aladrén a Federico García Lorca', in Nicole Delbecque et al., *Federico García Lorca et cetera. Estudios sobre las literaturas hispánicas en honor a Christian De Paepe* (Leuven, 2003), pp. 219–29
Umbral, Francisco, *Lorca, poeta maldito* (Madrid, 1975)
Vila-San-Juan, José Luis, *García Lorca, asesinado: toda la verdad* (Barcelona, 1975)

Other

Anderson, Andrew A., *Lorca's Late Poetry: A Critical Study* (Leeds, 1990)
Anderson, Reed, *Federico García Lorca* (London, 1984)
Binding, Paul, *Lorca: The Gay Imagination* (London, 1985)
Bonaddio, Federico, ed., *A Companion to Federico García Lorca* (Woodbridge, 2007)
Bonaddio, Federico, *Federico García Lorca: The Poetics of Self-consciousness* (London, 2010)
Federico García Lorca. Vida, a special number of *Poesía. Revista ilustrada de información poética*, XLIII (1998)
Chambers, Paul, 'The Trembling of the Moment: On the Haiku of Federico García Lorca', *Times Literary Supplement*, 6 October 2017, pp. 16–17

Delgado, María M., *Federico García Lorca* (Abingdon, 2008)

Edwards, Gwynne, *The Theatre Beneath the Sand* [1980] (London and New York, 1987)

Martín, Eutimio, *Federico García Lorca. Heterodoxo y mártir. Análisis y proyección de la obra juvenil inédita* (Madrid, 1986)

Martínez Nadal, Rafael, *Lorca's The Public: A Study of his Unfinished Play 'El Público' and of Love and Death in the Work of Federico García Lorca* (London, 1974)

—, *Federico García Lorca. Autógrafos II: El público, edición facsimilar* (Oxford, 1976)

Medina, Pablo L., 'Los títeres de Federico García Lorca en el Teatro Avenida de Buenos Aires, 25 de marzo de 1934', *Titeresante. Revista de títeres, sombras y marionetas* (1 May 2017)

Morris, C. Brian, *Son of Andalusia: The Lyrical Landscapes of Federico García Lorca* (Liverpool, 1997)

Orringer, Nelson R., *Lorca in Tune with Falla: Literary and Musical Interludes* (Toronto, 2014)

Ortega y Gasset, José, *La deshumanización del arte* [1925], ed. Paulino Garagorri (Madrid, 1984)

Ramsden, Herbert, *Lorca's Romancero gitano. Eighteen commentaries* (Manchester, 1988)

Ruiz Barrachina, Emilio, dir., *Luis Rosales, así he vivido yo* (Icrania Producciones, 2010)

Sahuquillo, Ángel, *Federico García Lorca and the Culture of Male Homosexuality* (Jefferson, NC, and London, 2007)

Santos Torroella, Rafael, *La miel es más dulce que la sangre. Las épocas lorquiana y freudiana de Salvador Dalí* (Barcelona, 1984)

Smith, Paul Julian, *The Theatre of García Lorca: Text, Performance, Psychoanalysis* (Cambridge, 1998)

Stone, Rob, *The Flamenco Tradition in the Works of Federico García Lorca and Carlos Saura* (Lewiston, NY, 2004)

Unamuno, Miguel de, *Manual de quijotismo, Cómo se hace una novela, Epistolario Miguel de Unamuno / Jean Cassou*, ed. Bénédicte Vauthier (Salamanca, 2005)

Valdivia, Pablo, *La vereda indecisa. El viaje hacia la literatura de Federico García Lorca* (Granada, 2009)

Vilches de Frutos, María Francisca, 'Directors of the Twentieth-century Spanish Stage', *Contemporary Theatre Review*, XII/3 (1998), pp. 1–23

Wright, Sarah, *The Trickster-function in the Theatre of García Lorca* (Woodbridge, 2000)

ACKNOWLEDGEMENTS

I would like to thank my colleagues and friends in Spanish, Portuguese and Latin American Studies at the University of Nottingham, especially Jean Andrews, Simon Breden, Tony Kapcia, Rocío Martínez Espada, Adam Sharman and Álvaro Vidal Bouzón, as well as José Luis Mora and Tomás Albaladejo of the Universidad Autónoma, and Lilí Belzunce, María Jesús Jurico, Alicia Martínez Jurico, Blanca Martínez Urdangarín and Jesús Sarasa for their unflagging support during the preparation of this book. I would like to acknowledge the help and assistance of the following archives where I carried out research for the book: the Fundación Federico García Lorca, its President Laura García Lorca de los Ríos, and its staff (while the main Lorca archive was based at the Residencia de Estudiantes in Madrid) Rosa Illán and Sonia González García; the Centro Federico García Lorca in Granada and Javier Álvarez, Marisa Bautista, Carmen Casares, Rocío Liñán and Jesús Ortega; the Archivo Manuel de Falla in Granada and its Director Elena García de Paredes de Falla and archivist Dácil González Mesa; and the Centro de Estudios Lorquianos in Fuente Vaqueros and its archivist Inmaculada Hernández Baena. I am also grateful for the kind attention of José Rodríguez Montero at the Museo Casa Natal Federico García Lorca in Fuente Vaqueros, of Eduardo Ruiz Baena at the Casa Museo Federico García Lorca in Valderrubio, and of Juan José García Martínez at the Casa Museo Federico García Lorca at the Huerta de San Vicente in Granada. Thanks too to Enrique Lanz, founder and director of the puppet company Etcétera, for his insights into the life and work of his grandfather Hermenegildo Lanz. I am immensely grateful to four friends who have acted as wonderful guides during my research stays in Granada: Miguel Caballero, Antonio Carvajal, Pedro Cerezo Galán and Amelina Correa. Special thanks to Graham Robb and Eric Southworth for their invaluable comments on the manuscript and to Michael Leaman at Reaktion Books for his support and patience throughout the project. Most importantly, I could not have written this biography without the love and inspiration of María José Martínez Jurico. This book is for her and for Alba.

PHOTO
ACKNOWLEDGEMENTS

The author and publishers wish to express their thanks to the below sources of illustrative material and/or permission to reproduce it:

Photos courtesy Laura García Lorca de los Ríos, President of the Fundación Federico García Lorca, © Fundación Federico García Lorca: pp. 6, 12, 15, 18, 19, 20, 23, 27, 30, 34, 38, 44, 56, 59, 68, 74, 81, 82, 85, 101, 102, 103, 120, 126, 153, 155, 157, 165, 166, 171, 174, 176, 178, 183, 187, 192, 195, 196, 203; photo courtesy The New York Public Library, © Fundación Federico García Lorca: p. 124; private collection: p. 49; photos courtesy Residencia de Estudiantes, Madrid, © Fundación Federico García Lorca: pp. 106, 129.

INDEX

Page numbers in *italics* indicate illustrations